Capital Transport

LONDON
TRAMWAYS

JOHN REED

First published 1997

ISBN 1 85414 179 1

Published by
Capital Transport Publishing
38 Long Elmes
Harrow Weald
Middlesex

Tram Terminus, Hampton Court.

CONTENTS

High Road, Streatham Hill, S.W.

Woolwich Common, (Looking North)

INTRODUCTION AND ACKNOWLEDGMENTS

Trams are the friend of anyone who cares about the environment. Their ability to move large numbers of people economically, while confining the small amount of pollution necessary for their existence to their power source, makes them an essential ingredient of modern times.

Until fairly recently any talk of trams in London, and indeed the rest of the country, has been in the past tense. For between 1935 and 1952 the capital's vast tramway network was systematically closed down in favour of its successor the trolleybus, now itself extinct in Britain, and the diesel bus. The story was much the same in the rest of the country.

This book traces the development of the tram in London from its beginnings to the last night of services in July 1952. It is a story of enterprise, experimentation, innovation, unification and finally, in a fast moving world awash with fossil fuels, annihilation.

Today, over forty years after the celebrations to mark the end of London's trams, a new generation of British tram, looking very Continental but still in essence a light rail vehicle, is here. Already it is familiar to travellers in London's Docklands and in the cities of Manchester and Sheffield, and will soon be seen once again on the streets of Croydon, where its forebears once enjoyed such a long and happy association. After that who knows?

My grateful thanks go to John Gillham for compiling the material on horse trams, painstakingly checking the text of the other chapters and providing many useful pieces of information, to John Gent for the loan of many early illustrations; to John Barrie, Ken Glazier, D. W. K. Jones, Frank Mussett, John Price and John Wills, who also commented on the text; to Sheila Taylor at the LT Museum, Dave Jones and John H. Meredith, for help with photographs; to Dr Andrew Gilks who provided some useful information, and finally Graham Tonks, who did a splendid job copying some rare and delicate prints.

London, March 1997   JOHN REED

MAKING TRACKS

London in the middle of the nineteenth century was undergoing change in a way which today would be unimaginable. Whole areas were being dragged from the decay and muddle of centuries past and graced with wide thoroughfares and majestic buildings. New railways were making the capital accessible from great distances and a transport network within the metropolis was taking shape.

By 1860 horse-drawn omnibuses had been providing regular transport in and around London for 30 years. The design of the vehicle, which had at the beginning been little more than a large stagecoach, was gradually being perfected and by 1850, the year when top decks first appeared, there were over 1,200 omnibuses licensed in London. Although omnibuses served most corners of the Metropolis their favours were not within the pockets of many inhabitants because fares were expensive. What was needed was a form of transport capable of carrying more people at less cost.

Like the omnibus, which was a French idea, the tram had its origins overseas, this time across the Atlantic in New York. Such was the fervour surrounding railway building in mid-nineteenth century America that any broadening of the basic concept was bound to cause excitement.

It was a New York engineer called John Stephenson who took the idea a stage further; instead of making people go to the railway he brought the railway to them. In 1832 he opened the world's first street railway, in New York, connecting the main city with Harlem. His street cars seated 30, and by 1834 his line stretched four miles, offering customers a 15-minute interval service. One of his passengers was a Frenchman, Alphonse Loubat, who returned to Paris full of plans to start up a tramway there. He persuaded the authorities to let him build a line between Place de la Concorde and Passy. The line duly opened in 1833, and was eventually incorporated into the Parisian transport system.

It was in Paris in 1856 that a company was formed to operate horse buses in London. The Compagnie Generale des Omnibuses de Londres, soon anglicised to London General Omnibus Company, quickly saw the potential of trams also. It formed the London Omnibus Tramways Company (LOTC) and announced proposals in 1857 for a route from Notting Hill Gate to Bank via Bayswater Road and Grand Junction Road (Sussex Gardens) through the wealthy backwaters behind Edgware Road, joining up with George Shillibeer's pioneer bus route of 1829, along Marylebone and Euston Roads to Angel, then down City Road to Moorgate and Bank. There was also to be a branch from King's Cross via Farringdon Road to Ludgate Circus.

When the Company deposited the London Tramways Bill in Parliament it encountered immediate hostility from the residential districts on its route. The Bill was defeated at its second reading and the LOTC was wound up soon afterwards. It was revived in 1860, but was finally dissolved two years later.

The reason for its brief revival was the arrival in London of a bombastic American tramway promoter called George Francis Train. By the late 1850s street cars had found their way into the thoroughfares of many American cities, and Train had been active in their progression, especially in Philadelphia. Seeing a potential market in Europe, he crossed the Atlantic and sought and obtained permission to build a line from Birkenhead Ferry to Woodside Park. It opened in August 1860. Birkenhead thus has the distinction of pioneering public tramway services in Britain.

Flush with his success Train turned his eyes towards London. Undaunted by the cool reception given to the LOTC's attempts to open a street railway he announced his own proposals for a loop line from Baker Street to Wigmore Street, Cavendish Square, Regent Street, Oxford Street, Portman Square, Gloucester Place and Finchley Road. This was an odd choice because it sliced through the very areas where those likely to voice fierce opposition were to be found; the rich, whose travel requirements in the metropolis were ably catered for by their own carriages. Train also planned to build three short lengths of route as an experiment to prove the practicability of his ideas. His 'loop' line went the same way as the LOTC proposals, but to his great delight the Turnpike Commission granted permission for his three experimental routes. These were:

Marble Arch - Porchester Terrace
Westminster Abbey - Victoria Street
Westminster Bridge - Kennington Gate

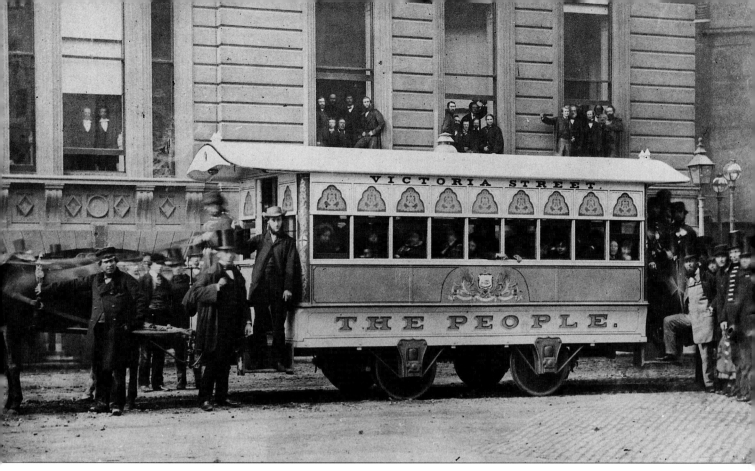

The first to open was the Bayswater Road line, which was launched on 23rd March 1861. The occasion was witnessed by several notables of the day, including Charles Dickens, William Thackeray and the artist George Cruickshank. The Marble Arch Street Railway, as it was called, had got off to a very auspicious start.

Just over three weeks later, on 15th April, Train's second line opened. This one ran from Pimlico to Victoria along Victoria Street, and it was called the Victoria Street Tramway.

Train's third and final line, The Surrey Side Street Railway, opened four months later on 15th August 1861. It ran from Westminster Bridge to Kennington, and brought the trams within the reach of a much larger and less well-heeled populace than hitherto.

London's first horse trams were based on designs already proven in America. An often published drawing showing two cars on Train's Bayswater Road route at Marble Arch depicts one with an upper deck, complete with covered awning for the passengers. This was fantasy. The three cars which began London tram history on the Marble Arch Tramway were single-deckers. They seated 24 with 12 more being allowed to ride on the platforms. There were platforms at each end because trams couldn't be turned unless a turntable was provided. The driver holding the reins stood behind a metal panel called a dash plate, fixed to the platform. The elliptical roofed cars were built by Prentiss of Birkenhead.

Train's next car, the only one required to operate the Victoria Street Tramway came, it is believed, from the Oldbury Railway Carriage and Wagon Company and carried 48 passengers. It was in a blue and white livery with 'Victoria Street' painted on one side. As if to suggest that Train was getting his market about right the legend, 'The People' was painted on the other. This was very apt because in the only known photograph taken of any of London's original trams the car is seen packed to the gunwales with excited folk.

The cars on Train's Surrey Side Street Railway were probably similar to the Victoria Street tram. It is worth noting though that Train had used two double-deck tramcars, along with two single-deckers, on his original Birkenhead route in 1860. Had events moved in his favour larger cars may have found their way onto his London routes; but it was not to be. The intervening four months between the Victoria Street and the Surrey Side had brought a severe setback for Train and his idea, despite the promoter making a valiant attempt to give his future schemes the stamp of authority.

One of the problems lay in the type of track Train insisted on using. He favoured the step-rail, an L-shaped rail set partly in the road surface with the topmost section protruding above. In some cities in the United States the step-rail had been used to good effect, acting as a guide rail to other horse drawn traffic which welcomed it as a way of assisting their passage along the generally poor quality road surfaces. In Britain all the protruding step-rail did was antagonise other road users, particularly the wealthy in their carriages. A grooved rail set into the road surface was available, and had been favoured by the LOTC in its 1857 proposals. In an attempt to deflect criticism of his step-rail, Train experimented with a flange rail and flange wheel tramcar which could be adapted to run on an ordinary road. But it was all to no avail. The problems caused to other road users by the protruding step-rail led to the legality of tramways being questioned in the courts. The judiciary ruled against Train, who received a heavy fine. Worse still he was ordered to dismantle his street railways beginning, after a six month period from commencement, with the Bayswater Road route which ceased to run during October 1861. The Victoria Street dropped off its last passenger in March 1862.

At the same time as his first trams were taking to the streets and beginning to make many enemies, Train was attempting to get tramways on a firm legal footing. He promoted a Parliamentary Bill aimed at allowing anyone to build a tramway in Britain, providing the local highway authority gave the proposed scheme full approval. His Bill was defeated in April 1861, despite having influential support.

Facing page **This is how an artist viewed the new concept of railed, street transport in the early 1870s, with this impression of a horse car at Kennington. Two horses were needed to draw the ornately decorated vehicle which weighed over two tons. The conductor holds on to a rather basic 'staircase' to the top deck which was normally the preserve of manual workers and artisans. Social conventions decreed that the lady in the foreground would have travelled on the bench seats in the lower saloon.**
LT Museum 8404131

Above **This first known photograph of a horse tram in London depicts the single deck car which operated on G.F.Train's Victoria Street line. Maybe the promoter himself is somewhere among the throng? The two horses seem to be restless as the driver has had to pull quickly on the reins. On the driver's left is a metal column which was attached to a chain operated wheel brake. Contemporary reports suggest that this Starbuck designed vehicle was adorned in bright colours with gold and purple lettering.**
LT Museum H8731

The opening of the 'Surrey Side' came at the end of a sad and sorry period for Train, the line went the same way as his other two, the rails coming up in June 1862. Train, obviously embittered by London's cool reception to the tramcar, left the capital and eventually returned to the United States, taking with him James Clifton Robinson, a young Birkenhead man who shared Train's unquenchable enthusiasm for building tramways.

If Train's misfortunes in Britain can have a happy ending, it is that history does not regard him simply as a pompous businessman but, more kindly, as the originator of the tramcar concept in this country. His two mistakes were the type of rails he favoured and his choice of routes. The latter was partly redeemed by the 'Surrey Side' which had brought the tram, which moved twice as many people as an ordinary omnibus but for half the cost, to a large and welcoming market. It was obvious by 1862 that steel wheels rotating along steel rails formed the basis for the rapid and safe movement of large numbers of people; the railways had proved that. A two-horse tramcar could give up to 50 passengers a smooth, comfortable ride. Trams easily outshone an ordinary horse drawn omnibus in every respect. They sat lower to the ground, so it was easier to get on and off. They had better braking, an omnibus relying heavily on the driver's skill and equine co-operation, and the fares were cheaper because the ratio of staff to passenger numbers was lower.

But the omnibus had won the first round of the battle, and for the next few years consolidated its supreme position by continuing to serve London's growing residential, industrial and commercial traffic unhindered. The initial excitement surrounding trams subsided after Train's departure. It had a brief revival in December 1865, courtesy of the newly formed Metropolitan Tramway Company, which immediately sought to promote a Parliamentary Bill for a tramway using grooved track flush to the road surface. Within a year their Bill joined the list of earlier unsuccessful attempts to give tramways some legal clout.

So to trace the next and more positive stage of the story, it is back to Liverpool. In 1868 Parliament approved a Bill for a tramway to run between Walton and Dingle. The inaugural line opened on 1st November 1869, the first to be built under Act of Parliament. This spurred on tramway promoters in London, and in 1869 three separate companies deposited Bills in Parliament. The Companies concerned and the routes they proposed were:

The Metropolitan Street Tramway (Kennington Church, via Kennington Road to Brixton, with a branch from Kennington Road to Clapham Road, the two branch ends being linked by a third branch).

The North Metropolitan Tramways Company (Whitechapel to Bow Church).

The Pimlico, Peckham and Greenwich Street Tramway (New Cross to Brixton Hill).

All three Bills went before the same Commons Committee, and despite opposition from several quarters, including the LGOC, the Bills were passed The

Metropolitan Board of Works, which had been established by the Metropolis Management Act 1855 to oversee London's local government, had argued that some experimentation with trams was essential, and the lines were approved on that basis. However the 1855 Act had also reconstituted the powerful parish vestries as elected bodies. As the Metropolitan Board of Works was not directly elected it was not able always to discharge its responsibilities in the way it wished. The vestries still held sway and in the event had some say in how London's tram services developed. Nevertheless, as far as the first routes were concerned all was signed and sealed. The tram had come to London.

More forceful legislation was on the way, but on 2nd May 1870 the Metropolitan Street Tramway opened the first London tram service backed by Act of Parliament, between Kennington Church and Brixton. A week later the first North Metropolitan trams ran along Whitechapel Road to Bow Church. Lagging behind by several months, the Pimlico and Greenwich Tramway finally opened its line from New Cross to Blackheath Hill on 13th December 1870.

The tramway companies were financed by private money, just like the omnibuses which were still expanding services to cater for new markets. Investors were paid a dividend if the operation showed a profit. They were not to be disappointed. In its first six months the North Metropolitan was able to

pay its shareholders a handsome 12% dividend; the other two were healthily in the black as well. Nevertheless, this did not prevent the Metropolitan Street and the Pimlico, Peckham and Greenwich merging to form the London Tramways Company. In 1871 a fourth company, the London Street Tramway Company, was formed with the aim of developing a tramway network in north west London.

With things going so well, it was considered essential to bring in some form of statute book legislation in a general Act of Parliament to ensure future stability and control. John Bright, who had championed tramways a decade previously, and who between 1868-70 was President of the Board of Trade, proposed in a Parliamentary Bill that a certificate from the Board of Trade would be all that was required before a tramway could be built once this proposed Tramway Act had become law. Certificates would be granted after a fixed period during which anyone could object to the proposals. If no objections were raised the tramway could proceed. This had attractive possibilities for the tramway promoters since they might be able to extend their routes into lucrative central London. As things stood they could only watch in despair as their legions of passengers hurried off the trams and onto omnibuses to get to destinations in the City and West End.

Another feature of the Bill was a clause giving local authorities the option to

Evelyn Street, Deptford, with an LCC horse car plodding past the Black Horse public house. The line along Evelyn Street was not electrified until June 1911. Commercial View

It is worth noting that in 1896 another piece of legislation, The Light Railways Act, was passed by Parliament. This short circuited some of the more contentious features of the 1870 Act, including the requirement to get parliamentary approval through Provision Orders for tramway schemes. A body called the Light Railway Commissioners, working under the auspices of the Board of Trade, was created to process applications. Powers granted under the Light Railways Act stood for the same period as under the Tramways Act, usually for three years, but sometimes for two. The more favourable clauses in the Light Railways Act tempted many of the Councils then planning tramways to seek powers under that legislation rather than the Tramways Act, although such applications were usually rejected in large towns. It came too late to be of much use to the pioneer companies, which by the turn of the century were in the process of being acquired by the local authorities in whose areas they lay, but many companies in smaller towns made good use of it.

The Tramways Act helped shape the future of Britain's tramway systems for the next half century. It had mixed implications for the tramway companies, but as the 1870s progressed there was little doubt that the population at large was making full use of the cheap, frequent and comfortable service trams provided. Figures published show just how popular trams quickly became. The North Metropolitan is reported to have carried one million passengers on its Whitechapel Road service in the first six months it was running.

Street transport in Victorian London was almost exclusively horse drawn, and tramways, like omnibuses, were as horse-intensive as they were labour intensive. A horse could work little more than four hours each day, so to keep a tram on the road for the entire day a company would need ten horses for each of its trams. A large company would require several hundred animals to run a network of services. In 1880 the North Metropolitan owned 223 tramcars and over 2094 horses. In those days a strong and mature horse, and those used to pull trams were usually about five years old, could cost between £25 and £30 (equivalent to between £1400 and £1650 at today's prices) so a considerable sum of money was tied up in the motive power. Most companies wisely retained the services of a vet to ensure the continuing health of their assets. A tram depot had to provide full stabling facilities, often on two or more levels, which would include feeding, watering, grooming and a smithy. A useful sideline was the sale of the constant and plentiful supply of manure.

By contrast, the humans who sought employment on the horse trams were not so well looked after. Conditions were appalling. Low pay, long hours, and very little time off were the rewards for working on the trams. And how could conditions be expected to change while men queued for work and the Trade Union Movement was still in its infancy? No real improvement came until the gradual takeover of the independent tramways by the London County Council from 1896.

purchase, at a fair price, tramways which ran within their boundaries. This would be after a period of 21 years, or any subsequent seven years. The clause was later modified to allow local authorities to purchase the tramway at book value, without the need to pay the owner a goodwill sum on top. This was in exchange for a reduction in the power local authorities had to veto tramway proposals. A public inquiry would sit in judgement to consider proposed routes, and if it ruled in favour then local authorities could do little to prevent the line being built. This would have made the onward grind of the tramcar into central London inevitable, but it was not to be.

The Bill received rough treatment in the Commons and eventually had to be redrafted into what was to become the Tramways Act 1870, the most important piece of British tramway legislation hitherto, and one which affected the whole industry from promoters to passengers. Briefly the Act stated that anyone wishing to open a tramway could apply for a Provisional Order, which required the consent of the Board of Trade and the respective local authorities. The Orders then had to be ratified by Act of Parliament and could be petitioned against by objectors. Alternatively a tramway promoter could, and frequently did, promote his own Bill and obtain his own local Tramway Act, with roughly the same concessions and the same restrictions. Local authorities which exercised their right to acquire tramway routes in their areas (irrespective of whether sanctioned by Provisional Order and subsequent Confirmation Act, by direct local Tramway Act, or who built lines themselves) could lease the route to an operator, usually a company but in later years sometimes another adjacent municipality, for a further seven or 21 years.

The 1870 Act also set down rigid guidelines for the laying and maintenance of track, which was to have a gauge as specified in the subsequent Confirmation Act or Local Act, or, if not so specified, was to be of four feet eight and a half inches and be set flush to the road surface. Most tramways in the London area adopted the 4 foot 8½ inches standard. Some of the conditions, like the one which required tram operators to pay to maintain the road surface eighteen inches either side of the track, which became worn by the constant clop of horse hoofs, were regarded as unfair at the time, and even more so when it was not rescinded with the advent of electric power. Tracks could not be laid less than 9 foot 6 inches from the kerb if one third or more of the property owners along that particular stretch of road objected. This was one of the contributory factors to the eventual downfall of the tram because in most cases the companies laid the track in the middle of the roadway. The of this, half a century later, was the annoying delay caused to other road users when trams stopped to pick up and set down their passengers.

THE HORSE TRAM ERA

Top A view of Stratford Broadway, looking north-east, in about 1899, showing St John's Church (1834), the Memorial to Samuel Gurney (a prominent banker), and six North Metropolitan tramcars. On the left is the tramway route towards Leyton, in the centre is the one along Romford Road to the Princess Alice Inn, and on the right, through a narrow alley just beyond the Swan Hotel, is a large North Met tram depot. This picture shows where it all started. The very first Act of Parliament for any tramway in the London area was passed on 12th July 1869, even before the famous 1870 Act. It authorised a tramway from Whitechapel to a point "at or near the Gurney Memorial Fountain, three chains west of the west end of Stratford Churchyard", and another Act of 10th August 1870 authorised extensions from "a point 2½ chains west of the Gurney Memorial Fountain" to Leytonstone and the Princess Alice. The junction thus created is visible at the bottom of this picture.

Above North Metropolitan knifeboard car No. 270 in Union Road, Leytonstone, in about 1890, outside the West Ham Union workhouse. The car is brand new, having just been built in the NMT workshops off to the left of the picture, and is here posed prior to delivery to its operating depot.

A garden-seat car of the Lea Bridge Leyton & Walthamstow Tramway Company at the Bakers Arms Junction, looking north-east in 1905. The car is loading in Lea Bridge Road ready for its journey to Clapton. The Bakers Arms Hotel is on the left, and the junction for the branch along Leyton High Street can be seen on the right.

The principal manufacturers of early tram-cars were John Stephenson & Co of New York (who supplied most of the very early cars used in Britain), the Starbuck Car and Wagon Co Ltd of Birkenhead (which later became G.F. Milnes & Co Ltd), the Metropolitan Railway Carriage & Wagon Co Ltd, of Saltley, Birmingham (which eventually became a part of Metro-Cammell), the Falcon Engine and Car Works of Henry Hughes at Loughborough (which later became Brush), the Ashbury Railway Carriage and Iron Co Ltd of Manchester, and the Lancaster Railway Carriage and Wagon Co Ltd, of Lancaster. The North Metropolitan Tramways Company, which was by far the largest of the sixteen London horse-tram operators, eventually built its own cars at its works in Union Road (now Langthorne Road), Leytonstone, where in due course the London County Council also built some of its own electric trams.

The horse trams used by the earliest companies differed little from Train's origi-nals. A typical car built in 1870 by John Stephenson for the North Metropolitan was 24 feet long and 6ft 6ins wide, and could carry 46 seated passengers, 22 in the lower saloon and 24 on top, and needed two horses to pull it. The side panelling was divided into two sections, the upper being the waist panel and the lower, the 'rocker' panel. The lower saloon had longitudinal bench seating on each side, and was reached through a sliding door at each end, creating a totally enclosed compart-ment while the car was in motion. In the earliest cars the upper deck was reached by an iron ladder, moved to either end as required, but this was very soon replaced by a fixed curved staircase with an outer protec-tive panel called a stringer, at each end.

The seating on top was provided by a centrally-placed bench, running the length of the deck, where people sat back-to-back facing outwards. This seat was known as a knife-board, so christened because people thought it looked like a felt-covered knife-cleaning board commonly used in those days. Later the so-called decency boards were fixed to the sides of the upper deck to make lady passengers feel more protected. These boards also made good advertisement hoardings, whilst on a few cars either commercial adver-tisements or route and destination details were displayed along the staircase stringers. In the mid-1880s experiments were made with transverse reversible seats on the upper deck so that passengers could face the way they were going. These were called garden seats, and by the end of the horse-tram era were a standard feature of almost all cars, except of course the very few single-deckers used on certain routes.

A look at the respective fleets of the horse-tram companies operating around London in the late nineteenth century would find many similar vehicles, all in eye-catching liveries proudly displaying the Company name and details of the route on which they worked, just like the horse omnibuses did. Almost all the trams seated 46, 20 on longitudinal seats downstairs plus 26 on transverse seats upstairs. Only a small number (including the knifeboard survivors) seated fewer. The only cars larger than these seated 52 (22 down-stairs and 30 up), and they ran on the Poplar to Aldgate service of the North Metropolitan. The single-deckers (latterly London Southern and Croydon only) seated 18 or 20; these were pulled by only one horse, all others by two. There were a few oddities, thus one of the London Southern routes passed beneath a

low railway bridge, so the top decks of the cars were fitted with end canopies to ensure the safety of passengers reaching the top of the stairs. Later this company developed a low-bridge car which sat on smaller wheels thereby reducing its height.

The routes were not numbered, but the trams were painted in differing liveries which distinguished them as operating on partic-ular services. The various companies had different methods of displaying the route destinations and intermediate points. Some painted these along the main side panels or above the windows, but others used detach-able boards along the waist rail or above the windows. Some painted the place names on the main end panels of the upper deck, while others used this space for a commercial advertisement and had a much smaller detachable board immediately above or below it. Some painted the two termini on the curved lower deck dash panel in front of the driver, but this was partly hidden behind the horses. Fleet numbers also were usually displayed on the dash panel, and sometimes also on the main side panels. Some companies had a small destination board at the bottom of the end window of the main saloon. Only very few horse trams displayed their route or termini (or any advertisement) along the staircase stringer panel, which was sur-prising because almost all horse omnibuses used this location to display their route in large prominent lettering.

The legacy of the horse tram in the design of the first generation of electric cars was plain for all to see, except that the latter were usually larger, but this did not become apparent until other forms of mechanical propulsion had been tried out and assessed; and usually rejected.

THE NORTH METROPOLITAN TRAMWAYS COMPANY

The NMT was not only by far the largest, it was also probably the most commercially progressive of all London's horse tram operators. It was one of the first three companies to obtain an Act of Parliament authorising a tramway in London. This was on 12th July 1869, even before the famous and very restrictive Tramways Act of 1870 had been passed, hence the routes authorised on that day were free of the harsh conditions imposed by the 1870 Act, notably the powers given to the local municipalities for compulsory purchase of the tramways 21 years after the date of the passing of each individual Act, or after every subsequent seven years, at almost scrap-iron prices and with no allowance for goodwill or past or future profits.

The 1869 North Metropolitan Tramways Act did, however, allow for a voluntary sale to the local municipality after 21 years, but upon terms of paying the full value of the tramway and all other property, and with an allowance for goodwill. It authorised 3½ miles of tramway from Whitechapel Church along Mile End Road and Bow Road to Stratford Broadway. The main Tramways Act of 1870 was passed on 9th August and twelve individual Tramway Acts were then passed on 10th August 1870. Seven of these concerned provincial cities and five were in the London area, including one for the North Metropolitan Tramways.

The NMT Act of 1870 allowed 28 years before compulsory purchase, not the 21 which became standard for almost all subsequent tramway Acts everywhere. It authorised a main trunk route Archway Tavern – Holloway Road – Upper Street – Angel, Islington – City Road – Moorgate Street – Lothbury; also five shorter sections: Liverpool Road from Holloway Road to the Angel; Finsbury Park Station – Seven Sisters Road – Nags Head – Park Road; Whitechapel High Street to Aldgate Minories; Stratford Broadway along Romford Road to the Princess Alice; and Stratford Broadway along Leytonstone Road to Harrow Green with a branch along Union Road. The tramway from Whitechapel Church as far as Bow Bridge was opened to traffic on 9th May 1870, thus missing by only seven days the honour of being the first tramway in the London area (except G.F. Train's). The short stretch into Aldgate and also Bow to Stratford, were both opened at the end of 1871.

The NMT obtained another Act on 31st July 1871, which authorised Shoreditch Church – Kingsland Road – Stamford Hill; City Road – Bridport Place – Mildmay Park – Green Lanes – Manor House; Islington Green – Essex Road – Balls Pond Road – Dalston; Goswell Road – Old Street – Shoreditch – Hackney Road – Cambridge Heath; Mile End – Cambridge Heath Road – Mare Street – Clapton Road – Stamford Hill; Limehouse – Burdett Road – Grove Road – Old Ford Road; Aldgate – Commercial Road – East India Dock Gates; and Angel – Goswell Road – Aldersgate. Almost all these 1870-71 routes were opened to traffic in 1871-73, except Green Lanes and Upper Clapton Road which opened in 1874-75 and Aldgate to the Minorities and Finsbury Place to Lothbury which never were built. George Richardson became Chairman of the company in 1871 and remained thus until it was wound up in 1912. He was a leading figure in the British tramway industry and also held directorships with a number of Continental tramway companies.

Another NMT Act in 1877 authorised Shoreditch Church to Bishopsgate; Canonbury Road and New North Road; Dalston to Hackney; and Grove Road to Cassland Road. All four were built and opened in 1878-79. An Act of 1880 authorised a tramway along Leytonstone High Road from Harrow Green to the Green Man, and this was opened on 12th August 1881. The 1884 NMT Act authorised Great Eastern Street, also West India Dock Road, also Stratford Broadway – Romford Road – Manor Park, and also Canning Town – Barking Road – Greengate (which was always physically isolated from the rest of the North Met). These four were opened between 1885 and 1888. An 1885 Act authorised Clerkenwell Road, which was opened in September of that year.

An Act of 1887 authorised a tramway along Theobalds Road, also part of Grays Inn Road south of this (another company built the northern part, see later), and along Commercial Street from Shoreditch to Whitechapel, and these three sections were all opened in 1887-88. All the 1885-88 lines, also the doubling of the single track in 1888 in Goswell Road, were made with a much heavier rail section than previously. Finally an 1888 Act authorised Leman Street, Whitechapel, which was opened at the end of 1890 and brought the total North Met route mileage up to 43.32, exclusive of the North London company, which was taken over by the North Met in 1892 (see later).

Until 1878 the North Met hired all its horses, of which by now over 2000 were needed every day, from the London General Omnibus Co Ltd, but from 1898 onwards it owned them itself, building many new blocks of stables for them. Each tramcar needed ten or eleven horses each day, in five shifts of two horses each working only about three hours, with one spare. Looking after all these horses was an enormous task in itself quite apart from building and repairing the trams and operating them. By 1891, when they took over the North London company (see later), the North Met had 376 of its own trams and over 3500 horses. At first, its trams were bought in many small batches, mainly from Stephenson, Hughes and Starbuck. From 1885 onwards the NMT built tramcars in its Union Road Works, about 500 for itself, plus more than 100 for other operators.

The North Met was a pioneer of mechanical and electrical traction, and tried six systems, all in Essex. A Merryweather steam loco, towing an ordinary double-deck car, ran for a few weeks in 1877 between Stratford and Leytonstone. The track on this route was of much heavier construction, to carry the extra weight, and it was not felt that locos could run elsewhere at that time. At the end of 1880 the NMT made arrangements with the Beaumont Compressed-Air Locomotive Co Ltd of Col F.E.B. Beaumont to work the Leytonstone route, so an engine pulling two cars ran from Stratford depot to the Green Man (2¼ miles) for one month towards the end of 1881. It was reasonably successful, but not perfect, so it was then proposed to try a combined engine and car. During March 1882 a Faure accumulator car was tested along Union Road, Leytonstone; this was an ordinary horse car with a number of batteries placed under the seats, and an electric motor. Mr Jarman experimented with his battery-electric car on the NMT at Canning Town in 1883. Later, six electric locomotives were built for the Elieson Electric Light & Power Co, each towing one passenger car on the Romford Road route from July 1886 to July 1888. Arrangements were made early in 1888 with the Electric Power & Traction Company for working cars with Immisch electric motors on the isolated Barking Road line; six such cars had been built by the start of 1889, of which three ran from June 1889. By July 1892 all six were working, but not for long. An Act of 1890 authorised full mains electrification, but this was not carried out.

The London County Council was created, as from 21st March 1889, as successor to the previous Metropolitan Board of Works, and soon gave notice that it intended compulsorily to purchase, under the 21-year powers in Section 43 of the 1870 main Tramways Act, all the nine North Met routes (almost 19 miles) authorised in the 1871 NMT Act, which would become purchasable on 31st July 1892. The NMT naturally protested strongly, on the grounds that its surviving sections, newer but disconnected, would be useless on their own. But the LCC was adamant, and so a bitter battle resulted which dragged on for four years. The NMT took its case to the High Court, but lost, and appealed, and lost again. The LCC still insisted on the compulsory purchase of all the 1871 routes plus eleven depots, but finally agreed to lease them all back again to the North Met for operation for 14 years. The sale also now included the original 1869-70 routes and those from the 1877-87 Acts, except those in the County of Essex. This took effect from 24th June 1896 although not finally confirmed until 14th October 1897. Finally the LCC terminated the lease of all these routes on 1st April 1906, and took over direct operation itself, gradually electrifying most of them in 1907-14. At this takeover the NMT had 533 trams and 5571 horses.

Meanwhile the three municipalities in Essex also decided to exercise their powers of compulsory purchase, so on 1st July 1903 West Ham Corporation took over the lines from Bow Bridge via Stratford Broadway to Forest Gate and to Leytonstone Road, also Canning Town to Plaistow. Leyton Urban District Council took over the rest of the route in Leytonstone Road, to the Green Man, on 25th June 1906, and finally East Ham Corporation purchased Forest Gate to Manor Park on 24th April 1908. The North Metropolitan Tramways Company was finally wound up on 21st February 1912 after 42 glorious years, for most of which it was one of the most important in Britain.

A North Metropolitan Tramways garden-seat car outside the enormous Bishopsgate Goods Station of the Great Eastern Railway, on the Stamford Hill - Dalston - Shoreditch - Aldgate - London Docks route, later electric route 47.

A view looking south-west in Camden Road at the Brecknock Road cross-roads going off to the right, showing trams of the London Street Tramways Company on the Nags Head to Euston Road service, passing. The horse bus is probably owned by the Camden Town Association on a service from Victoria terminating here.

LONDON STREET TRAMWAYS COMPANY (LST)

The LST was less than one-third the size of the North Met, with a maximum of 13½ route miles, and it occupied the territory immediately to the west of the NMT. Its promoters had optimistically prepared a scheme for 53 route miles, most of which was deleted from the Parliamentary Bill, so that when the Company was incorporated by Act of 10th August 1870 (one of the twelve that were held back until the next day after the big main Act) only 4½ route miles were actually sanctioned. These were from the Holloway Road via Camden Road and Camden Town High Street to the south end of Hampstead Road, also from Kentish Town Station (Midland Railway) via Kentish Town Road, College Terrace, Great College Street, St Pancras Road, and Pentonville Road to King's Cross Station, Metropolitan Railway (which in those days was further east than it now is). These were opened in 1871-72.

An Act of 1874 authorised a route from Kentish Town Station along Junction Road to just beyond the Archway Tavern. The Act was passed on 7th August, but the line had opened in April/May 1874 under a Provisional Order. An LST Act of 1877 authorised Caledonian Road from a junction with the LST at King's Cross to a junction with the North Met in Holloway Road. This was opened in 1878, except that the NMT refused to allow the junction to be inserted. Discussions for a possible leasing of the LST to the NMT dragged on during 1876-78 but came to nothing, although the NMT did obtain powers in its Act of 1880 to do this.

The LST Act of 1879 authorised a tramway from Kentish Town Road along Prince of Wales Road and Malden Road to Southampton Road, which was opened in 1880. Proposals in 1880 for extensions in Bayswater, Marylebone, Islington, and Holborn were strongly opposed, and later rejected; only the line along Pentonville Road from King's Cross to the Angel, Islington survived, authorised by Act of 1882 and opened in 1883.

The LST Act of 1885 was larger, and authorised the tramway from Southampton Road along Fleet Road to South End Green, Hampstead, also from Kentish Town Road to Camden Town, along King's Cross Road and Farringdon Road from Pentonville Road to Clerkenwell Road, and several doublings of existing single track. All these were opened in 1886. An 1887 Act authorised Highgate Road from Kentish Town to Swains Lane, also from Camden Town via Chalk Farm Road and Ferdinand Street to Malden Road, also along Grays Inn Road from King's Cross to Theobalds Road, and also along Crowndale Road. All these except Crowndale Road were built and opened in 1887 or 1889.

Soon after the LCC was created in 1889 it decided to compulsorily purchase the 4⅓ miles of the LST from its 1870 Act, under the 21-year rule. The LST had not been lucky enough to get 28 years into its Act like the North Met. Naturally the LST protested strongly, as did the tramway industry as a whole, and even some individual members of the Council. Again there was the problem of splitting up one complete network and leaving the company with various disjointed parts which would be useless by themselves. The LST demanded the appointment of an Arbitrator, and with the approval of the Board of Trade an Inquiry was held in June-July 1892. It eventually decided that the LCC should pay far less compensation than the LST demanded, and should take 68 cars and 649 horses. The LST then took the matter to the Divisional Court, and won, but the LCC went to the High Court of Appeal. After a long and bitter hearing, the LCC won, so the LST finally took its case to the House of Lords in June 1874, but lost.

The final Award allowed the LCC to buy the LST tramways, depots, horses, cars, and equipment, but offer them back to the LST to operate on lease. The lease was finally handed over on 1st August 1895. An LST Act of 1888 had authorised it to build 1¾ miles of tramway from Archway Tavern along Archway Road as far as Manor Farm House, but with the proviso that the line could not be

built until the Archway itself, which was the boundary between the Counties of London and Middlesex, had been rebuilt and the road widened. The LST would have to pay £3000 towards the cost of rebuilding the Archway. With the threat of losing its London lines, the LST obtained an Act in 1895 to allow it to abandon this route and its obligation towards rebuilding the Archway. This Act also authorised the LST to accept a lease of any tramway which might be acquired or constructed by the LCC.

Meanwhile the LCC was worried that, although it hoped eventually to own all the various tramways in London, it had no legal powers to operate any of them. So it obtained an Act in 1896 authorising it to operate any tramway it might acquire, or to lease it to any company. Not until 27th May 1897 was it finally decided that the LCC must purchase all the 1870/73/74 LST tramways and depots, and then lease them all back, not to the LST but to the North Met instead. This lease was to run until 24th June 1910, and the North Met was required to purchase all the LST cars, horses, harness, tools, and stores etc. The LST routes from its 1877/79/82/84/85/87 Acts were also now to be operated by the North Met on a lease for 14 years starting on 24th June 1896, but for the time being they would still be owned by the LST. Also the LST now surrendered to the NMT the lease of the original 4⅓ miles from the 1870 Act, which LST had been operating during 1895-97 while owned by the LCC. At five places where LST and NMT routes were adjacent to each other the LCC inserted connecting curves in about 1897-99, and several new through services were started.

The LST was the first tramway in London, or almost anywhere else, to suffer the consequences of its 21st anniversary. Hence the whole tramway industry was deeply worried and sympathetic to its confiscation battle, and so most London, and even some provincial, companies contributed to the LST's legal costs, but to no avail so far as preventing the transfer of powers. The LCC terminated the lease of the LST routes to the NMT, as from

1st April 1906, four years before it was due to expire, because the LCC was anxious to start electrification north of the Thames, having nearly completed it south of the river. Thereafter the LCC operated all the routes itself, electrifying them all in the next few years. The LST was wound up soon after.

Another great figure throughout 25–30 years of the Victorian tramway industry was J. Barber Glenn, who shows how closely some of the various companies were linked with each other. Glenn was for all this time the secretary of the London Street, London Southern, Provincial (Cardiff, Portsmouth, and Gosport), Belfast, Southampton, Edinburgh Northern, Lea Bridge, and Rouen (France) Tramway Companies, and all of these shared the same Head Office.

The earliest LST tramcars were very similar to those of all the (very few) other companies then operating, and probably built by either Starbuck or MRCW. The fleet eventually grew to a maximum of 139 cars by 1897, with seven operating depots. Everybody agreed by now that horses were too expensive for tramway work, which was very arduous for them, as many survived only about 4½ years. The search was on for a mechanical or electrical alternative.

The LST contribution to this development was its use of the Mekarski compressed-air car, which was invented in 1872 by M. Louis Mekarski in Paris. It gradually evolved into a conventional double-deck tramcar with a stronger underframe, two of its four wheels being driven by a two-cylinder engine which was powered by compressed air at the enormous pressure of nearly 1000 lb/sq in to get sufficient power. Further design developments eventually brought this down to only 450. The compressed air was stored in tanks under the tram's bodywork and passed through a tank of boiling water immediately before use. The system required a stationary compressor or pumping engine at the terminus of the route to re-charge the car's tank at the start of each journey.

A contract was signed in 1883 between the London Street Tramways and a new British Mekarski Improved Air Engine Co Ltd to work the entire service on the Caledonian Road from King's Cross to Holloway Road, just two miles. Eight of these Auto-Mobile cars were required and after three months of experimental testing the first one was officially inaugurated on 16th May 1883 with great ceremony, easily tackling the gradient of 1-in-27 on part of the route. The pumping plant with two 20-hp steam engines to supply the compressed air, was installed in the LST depot in Warlters Road near the Holloway terminus, the air being pumped to a stand-pipe in the top of Camden Road. At the inaugural luncheon the Mekarski Chairman said his system would soon work a revolution in tramways by completely superseding horses, and would be of the utmost value in working the Channel Tunnel when that was opened. Mekarski cars continued to run on Caledonian Road for, it seems, at least a further five years, though it seems with only six cars and not eight. The second Mekarski company was wound up in July 1891.

After 1891 the North London Tramways Company steam trams were withdrawn and replaced by horse cars, and at the same time this company was taken over by the North Metropolitan. Here we see one on the Finsbury Park to Edmonton service at the junction of Tottenham High Road (in the foreground) and Seven Sisters Road (in the centre).

The NORTH LONDON SUBURBAN TRAMWAYS CO LTD (NLST)

The NSLT was formed in 1878 and obtained powers in 1879 to build a tramway from Stamford Hill via Tottenham, Edmonton, and Waltham Cross to Turners Hill, 9¼ miles. However the line was built only as far as Ponders End, 5½ miles, and opened in four sections in 1881. Eventually 116 horses and 20 one-horse single-deck cars which had single-ended Eades reversible bodywork which rotated 180° around the underframe at termini were used. A few of these were later fitted with upper-deck seating, which turned out to be too heavy both for the underframe and the horses.

The NORTH LONDON TRAMWAYS COMPANY (NLT)

The NLT was incorporated by Act of 1882 to dissolve and re-incorporate the limited-stock NLST as a statutory undertaking and also to build new tramways from Seven Sisters Corner to Finsbury Park Station (for access to the West End) and from Manor House to Wood Green (for access to the then-new Alexandra Palace), a total of 4½ miles. The lines were opened in 1885 and at the end of 1887 respectively. As early as 1882 the Company Chairman said he had no doubt that some day or other the clever people who were always inventing something would bring forward a scheme by which cars may be drawn by air or electricity. Indeed the NLT horses and small cars did not last long, and by an Act of 1883 all the routes were operated by steam; the Ponders End line from 1st April 1885, and the other two from their first opening. Steam tramways were quite common in the Midlands and the North of England, but this was the only company in the London area to use them. There were 14

(later 15) Merryweather steam locomotives and 20 double-deck eight-wheel knifeboard-seat Falcon trailer cars, later augmented by ten Dick Kerr steam locos and a further seven Falcon bogie trailers, this time with garden seats. Main car depots were at Edmonton and Wood Green, with a small one in Seven Sisters Road. An 1887 Bill for a Tottenham – West Green – Wood Green route was later withdrawn.

The locos proved too heavy for the NLT track, which soon deteriorated, causing derailments, and there were complaints of noise and smoke; also the locos proved expensive to maintain and repair. Sadly the company got into financial difficulties, and went into voluntary liquidation in 1890. One proposed outside purchase fell through, but then on 1st August 1891 it was purchased by the North Met, whose routes already met the NLT's at three places, all on or near the London–Middlesex County boundary, namely Stamford Hill, Manor House, and Finsbury Park Station. All steam operations ceased on 31st July 1891, as the locos and cars were not included in the purchase and the NMT immediately on takeover went back to using horse traction. The Middlesex County Council (MCC), or alternatively the several local urban councils, did not compulsorily purchase the ex-NLT routes, as the 21 years from 1879 had not yet been reached. Instead, the North Met continued to own and operate them until they were taken over in 1901 (by agreement with the MCC) by an associated Metropolitan Tramways and Omnibus Co Ltd (formed in 1894). At about the same time the MTO was purchased by the British Electric Traction Co Ltd, who changed its name to the Metropolitan Electric Tramways Limited and in due course electrified all the NLT routes.

METROPOLITAN STREET TRAMWAYS COMPANY (MST)

The MST after various proposals in 1865 and 1867, promoted a Bill in 1869 for tramways along the whole of Kennington Road and Brixton Road to Stockwell Road; from Kennington Park along Clapham Road to Stockwell Road; along Stockwell Road from Clapham Road to Brixton Road; along Westminster Bridge Road, Borough Road, Southwark Bridge Road, New Kent Road, Old Kent Road, Park Street, and Hill Street to Peckham High Street; a loop around Stangate, Crozier Street, and Hercules Buildings back to Kennington Road; along York Road, Stamford Street, Southwark Street, and Southwark Bridge Road to the Elephant & Castle; along Great Suffolk Street and Gravel Lane; and also along Upper Kennington Lane, Vauxhall Cross, Nine Elms Lane, Battersea Park, Queens Road (North), Prince of Wales Road, and back to Lower Wandsworth Road.

This Act was passed on 12th July 1869, one of the three Acts before the principal 1870 Act. It incorporated the Company, but authorised only the first three tramways listed above, with the addition of routes along Upper Kennington Lane to Wandsworth Road; and also along Kennington Park Road. All the others were deleted. The MST obtained another Act in 1870, one of the twelve on the first day after the main Act. This authorised routes along Westminster Bridge Road from Stangate to Kennington Road; along Clapham Road and Clapham High Street from Stockwell to Park Road; along Brixton Road from Gresham Road, via Brixton Rise, Water Lane, and Effra Road back to Brixton Road; and along Cold Harbour Lane to Barrington Road.

The section from The Horns, Kennington, to Gresham Road, Brixton, 1⅓ miles, was opened on 2nd May 1870. It was, apart from Train's original lines, the very first tramway anywhere in the London area. It was extended at both ends on 5th October, to Westminster Bridge Road and to Acre Lane, and then on 22nd October to the foot of Westminster Bridge. Then in 1871 it was extended to The Plough, Clapham, to Water Lane, and to St Georges Circus. All the MST trams were knifeboard double-deckers, but of several different designs, from at least four manufacturers, Stephenson, Starbuck, the MRCW, and a firm in Denmark.

PIMLICO, PECKHAM AND GREENWICH STREET TRAMWAYS COMPANY

The PPGST was incorporated by the third of the three Acts on 12th July 1869, which authorised a tramway from Vauxhall Station via Harleyford Road, Kennington Oval (both sides), Camberwell New Road, Church Street, High Street Peckham, Queens Road, New Cross Road, Deptford Broadway, and Blackheath Road to South Street, 5¼ miles, all single track with loops. Another Act, one of the twelve on 10th August 1870, authorised tramways in Victoria Street, Artillery Row, Horseferry Road, Lambeth Road, and St Georges Road to Elephant & Castle; also Victoria Station, Vauxhall Bridge Road, Vauxhall Bridge, and Upper Kennington Lane; Elephant, London Road, Blackfriars

Road, to Blackfriars Bridge; St Georges Circus, Westminster Bridge Road, to Belvedere Road; Elephant via Walworth Road to Camberwell Green; also via New Kent Road and Old Kent Road to New Cross Gate; from Deptford Broadway via Greenwich High Road, Greenwich, Trafalgar Road, Woolwich Road, Church Street, and Powis Street or Beresford Street, to Beresford Square; and also along South Street, Greenwich.

The first section to be built and opened was from New Cross to Blackheath at the end of 1870, and to Greenwich early in 1871. The main line from New Cross via Old Kent Road, Elephant, and St Georges Circus to Westminster Bridge opened gradually in five sections in 1871, and made a junction with the Kennington line of the MST. The Walworth Road route opened later in 1871, then the Camberwell to New Cross section, and finally Camberwell to Vauxhall in 1872. The isolated Vauxhall Bridge Road route to Victoria Station opened in 1873, but officialdom never allowed horse trams to run over Vauxhall Bridge, and the authorised Horseferry Road/Lambeth Bridge route, and the line from Greenwich to Woolwich, were never built. To get "through" passengers across Vauxhall Bridge the company worked a short shuttle service with horse omnibuses. The PPGST tramcars were of the conventional knifeboard design, but quite comfortable, with velvet cushions, velvet curtains and even a carpet on the floor.

LONDON TRAMWAYS COMPANY LIMITED (LTC)

The LTC was registered on 14th December 1870, and by Act of 28th July 1873 was authorised to purchase the whole of the share capital of both the MST and the PPGST; to amalgamate them and to inherit all their powers and responsibilities. By another Act eight days later the MST was authorised to build a tramway along Kennington Park Road, Newington Butts (which had until then been too narrow for trams), Newington Causeway, and Borough High Street to St Georges Church. The PPGST was authorised to continue this route from St Georges Church along Great Dover Street to the Bricklayers Arms, the two totalling exactly two miles. Both opened on 11th January 1875. The combined company now became the second-largest in the London area with, eventually, 24.37 miles of route, 17 car depots, a main overhaul works just off the Walworth Road, and head offices at Camberwell behind one of the depots.

There was a lot of criticism in 1877-79 as to how the LTC was and was not conducting its affairs, both financially and in respect of maintenance of the track. Certain people registered a new company with the aim of taking over the LTC, but this failed, though it did cause the Chairman and the Secretary to be ousted, and much of the track to be relaid during 1880-81. Another company proposed in 1882 to build a tramway from Clapham

The London Tramways Co Ltd was the second-largest (after the North Met) of the 16 tramway companies in London. This car, built by Stephenson in 1885, is standing at the Greenwich terminus of the route via Old Kent Road and Elephant & Castle to the south side of Westminster Bridge, later electric route 38.

Facing Page Top **The entrance to Telford Avenue Depot, Streatham Hill, of the London Tramways Company. On the slope leading out to the main road we see one of the tractors or dummies which hauled passenger cars on the cable-operated tramway from here to Kennington (Handforth Road) until 1899. The cars, such as the one this tractor is pulling and the two others in the picture, worked through to Westminster Bridge or Blackfriars Bridge, changing at Kennington from tractor haulage to horse, as shown by the destination board of this car which reads 'Streatham Hill & Westminster'). This picture was taken during 1892-95. The cable route was later extended from Streatham Hill to Streatham Library. Three more tractors are visible in this picture at the far end of the depot and on the extreme right. Movement of cars inside the depot was by a traverser.**

Facing Page Centre **The passenger cars working on the London Tramways Co Ltd cable tramway from Streatham Library to Kennington Church were themselves fitted in 1898-99 with cable gripping mechanism on their end platforms, and the separate tractor cars were then eliminated. Operation was taken over by the London County Council early in 1899, as seen here, but this did not last long and the route was electrified in 1903, cable working having lasted only eleven years.**

Avenue, the terminus of the route. Separate gripper cars or tractors were used, of which there were 30 at first and later 42. These hauled ordinary double-deck passenger cars from Streatham to Kennington Church, where they were detached and replaced by horses which took the same tram onwards to Westminster or Blackfriars. Installing the conduit slot and all its numerous pulleys on nearly three miles of street, all double track, with a cable over 5½ miles long, was a mammoth task, and took until the end of 1892, the whole line from Kennington to Telford Avenue then opening on 7th December, with a one-year only licence to operate. The licence had to be renewed each year of operation. All through 1893 there were complaints of excessive noise from the cable on the pulley wheels. This was later reduced by putting beechwood linings in the grooves of the pulleys.

An LTC Act of 1894 authorised a half-mile extension of the cable tramway from Telford Avenue along Streatham High Road to the Tate Library, Pinfold Road. Dick Kerr installed this, with a separate cable, and an enormous pit in the roadway outside the depot by which the gripper cars changed from the one cable to the other. The extension was opened at the end of 1895, and was later given a three-year licence. In 1898-99 the passenger cars on this route were fitted with gripping equipment on their end platforms, thus eliminating the need for separate tractors, which had to be removed from or added to each through car in a change pit in the road at Kennington. On 15th May 1903 the horse tramways from Kennington to Westminster and Blackfriars were electrified, so the through service had to cease, all passengers changing cars at the Kennington change pit. Then the cable tramway from Kennington to Streatham was itself closed on 5th April 1904 to allow electrification, using the conduit system, with which it was re-opened in three stages in May and June 1904. It seems a great pity that this magnificent cable system had to be scrapped after only 11½ years.

The LTC tramways authorised in 1871 became compulsorily purchasable by the London County Council in 1892. The LCC tried to negotiate for them, but lost its chance, so tried again in 1894 for the two miles from the 1873 Act (Newington Butts and Great Dover Street). The LTC naturally protested, so the Board of Trade appointed an Arbitrator. His valuation was much too low to satisfy the LTC, which then went to law. The Judge upheld the Arbitrator's decision, allowing the LCC to purchase the whole of the LTC undertaking, which the Council did on 1st January 1899. The sale included the cable tramway and all the former MST and PPGST systems. The LCC also took over direct operation itself, and did not lease the tramways back to the former owners as it did north of the Thames. Meanwhile the LTC had built up a large fleet of horse omnibuses which worked beyond the tram termini across the river by way of Blackfriars, Waterloo, Westminster, and Vauxhall Bridges. Finally all the ex-LTC horse-tram routes were replaced by LCC electric trams in 1903-04.

Common to Balham. This failed, but it did provoke the LTC to obtain an Act in 1888 for an extension from Clapham High Street to Tooting Bec, just over two miles, which opened in 1888. This Bill also sought authority for trams to cross Westminster Bridge, but this was strongly opposed and rejected. Another Act of 1889 authorised a half-mile extension from Tooting Bec to Totterdown Street, which opened at the end of 1890. This 1889 Act also authorised an extension up Brixton Hill from Water Lane to Telford Avenue, just one mile. It was soon realised that the gradient here was too steep for horses to climb except very slowly, and that some sort of mechanical traction was needed. Steam, compressed-air, and battery-electric had been used elsewhere in London (see pages 29–30), but Andrew Hallidie had an innovative and successful new system in San Francisco which had now also been adopted on Highgate Hill and in Edinburgh.

This was the cable tramway, whereby an endless steel cable many miles long, supported on pulley wheels and driven by a huge stationary steam engine in the car depot, ran in a conduit slot in the middle of the track between the running rails and below the road surface. A device underneath either the tramcar itself or a separate locomotive hauling it poked through the slot and gripped the moving cable and thus was pulled along by it. The grip was released when the car needed to stop.

The LTC now decided to adopt this system, as modified by Dick Kerr & Co Ltd of Edinburgh, and in 1890 obtained an Act valid for seven years authorising it from Water Lane to Telford Avenue and on the existing horse tramway from Kennington Park (St Marks Church, Handforth Road) to Water Lane, almost a further two miles. The car depot, power station, boiler house, and two haulage engines were built at Telford

SOUTH LONDON TRAMWAYS COMPANY (SLT)

The SLT was incorporated by Act of 1879, and occupied the long thin strip of territory south of and parallel to the River Thames out to Wandsworth, intermixed in the Lambeth and Southwark area with the routes of the London Tramways Company. The South-West Metropolitan Tramways Company gained powers here in 1879 but did not use them. The SLT Bill of 1879 sought operating powers for York Road and Battersea Park Road from Plough Lane to Vauxhall Cross, and also along Wandsworth Road from Westbury Street to Vauxhall. The London and South Western Railway objected strongly because it had three level crossings with seven tracks, used by 200 wagons every day, crossing Nine Elms Lane into its Nine Elms Goods Depot. After much debate the House of Lords rejected this part of the SLT tramway and the whole of the other one, so the 1879 Act sanctioned only Plough Lane to a point just before the level crossings. This was opened on 7th January 1881, with one-horse single-deck cars at first, very soon replaced by 28 double-deckers requiring 108 horses.

An SLT Act of 1880 authorised lines from Alma Road, Wandsworth, along St Johns Hill, Lavender Hill, and Wandsworth Road to Westbury Street; also along Queens Road from Chelsea Bridge to Wandsworth Road; along North Street, Wandsworth (now Fairfield Street) and York Road to Plough Lane; and along Falcon Lane from St Johns Hill to York Road; and also along Bridge Road to Battersea Bridge. The SLT tried to extend to Putney and Roehampton but permission was refused. Its 1881 Act authorised lines from Vauxhall along Albert Embankment to Stangate, also along Lambeth Road, St Georges Circus, Borough Road and Southwark Bridge Road to Southwark Bridge, with a branch along Southwark Street to the Hop Exchange just before Borough High Street.

A separate City of London and Metropolitan Tramways Co Ltd was authorised by its Act of 1881 to build from St Georges Circus along Waterloo Road, and also along St Georges Road from Lambeth Road to the Elephant & Castle, but these powers were taken over by the SLT in its Act of 1882, which also now authorised (at last) lines in Nine Elms Lane over the level crossings to Vauxhall; Wandsworth Road from Westbury Street to Vauxhall; along the eastern end of Prince of Wales Road, and also along Lancaster Street. All these 1880/81/82 routes were built, and opened in 1881-83, except the one to Battersea Bridge, which did not manifest until electric days.

All were single track with passing loops, and three different types of rail section were used. The system was now at its maximum of 13½ route miles, eventually requiring 95 cars and 750 horses. Many additional passing loops were added in 1883-84 and 1886-87, which usually involved the Company in the expense of having to set back the pavement. Chain horses (extras hitched temporarily in front of the regular two) were needed on St Johns Hill and Lavender Hill. The Waterloo Road line was not used by its owners after the first few months, and was leased to the LTC in 1881 and to the LCC in 1899, and then sold to the LCC in 1900. At the end of 1884 the SLT acquired the London Tramways Omnibus Company, with 13 buses and 92 horses in Walworth. It also ran its own buses from Battersea to South Kensington from 1884, and over London Bridge to the City from 1893. Special low-height trams were used under the low railway bridge in York Road.

In February 1885 a battery-electric tramcar invented by Anthony Reckenzaun was run for a time in Queens Road Battersea. It was a 46-seat eight-wheel car with a 9-hp motor on each bogie, and driven by worm gearing, probably the first such anywhere. Many sections of track were doubled in 1896-99, eventually about two-thirds of the total. The Albert Embankment had a one-year Extension of Time by Act of 1883, but all the 1879/80/81/82/83 tramways became compulsorily purchasable by the LCC in 1900-04 respectively. The SLT objected, as the price offered was far too low, so the case went to arbitration. The judgement refused to allow the network to be split up, and said the LCC must buy all or nothing. Therefore the whole system was purchased by the LCC on 21st November 1902, part of it before its compulsory date. By then the Company had carried about 20 million passengers in each of nearly 20 years, working six through services with 40 or 46-seat cars painted in six different colours, from depots at Wandsworth, Battersea, Clapham Junction, and Borough Road, and a main overhaul works in Queens Road. Its horse-bus services, with 24 buses in 1899, just lapsed, and were not taken over by the LCC or anybody else. All the tram routes were electrified in four stages in the autumn of 1906 and four more stages in the autumn of 1909.

Left **Two knifeboard cars at the Wandsworth terminus in North Street (now Fairfield Street) of the South London Tramways Company, by the Two Brewers Hotel. The end destination board reads 'Wandsworth & Borough, via North St, Battersea Park Rd, Nine Elms, Vauxhall, & Obelisk' whilst above the side windows it reads 'Wandsworth via Battersea Park Rd, Nine Elms, Vauxhall, & Obelisk to London Bridge'. The terminus was actually in Southwark Street, nearly half a mile from London Bridge or the railway station of that name, whilst the Obelisk was at the crossroads of Lambeth Road and St Georges Road.** London Transport Museum U27830

Below **The complicated junction at Vauxhall Cross, looking north. In the foreground is South Lambeth Road with a car of the London Southern Tramways Company on a service from Vauxhall to Brixton Road. Off to the lower left and also in the centre right are the through tracks of the South London Tramways Company from Wandsworth Road onto the Albert Embankment. The LST tracks made a junction with the SLT tracks but through services were never worked except for five months in 1888-89. Under the bridge to the right are the terminating tracks of the London Tramways Company in Harleyford Road for Camberwell and New Cross. In the upper left is the road leading to Vauxhall Bridge and Victoria. The LTC tried hard several times to get permission to lay a tramway here, but it was never granted, so LTC ran a horse-bus service instead. The railway on the viaduct to the right is the LSWR main line from Waterloo.** R. B. Parr Collection

Bottom **The terminus, looking north, of the London Southern Tramways Company at West Norwood. Immediately behind the camera is St Luke's Church and the junction of Knights Hill and Norwood High Street. The car on the left has just arrived and the one on the right is ready to depart. Both are the new design introduced in 1895 with garden seats, smaller wheels, and a much lower floor level on both decks, so as to pass under a low railway bridge without the need for special passenger protection fitted to the original 1883 knifeboard Falcon-built cars. Destination boards of both cars say 'Vauxhall & Norwood', with, on the left, 'via Stockwell, Brixton and Loughboro', and on the right, 'via Brixton, Loughboro and Herne Hill'.**

LONDON SOUTHERN TRAMWAYS COMPANY (SLT)

The LST was incorporated by Act of 18th August 1882 with power to build tramways from Vauxhall Cross via South Lambeth Road, Stockwell (Swan), Stockwell Road, Brixton, and Gresham Road; along the full length of Cold Harbour Lane from Brixton High Road to Camberwell Green; from Loughborough Junction via Hinton Road, Milkwood Road, Herne Hill, and Norwood Road to West Norwood at the corner of Park Road (now Robson Road), a total of 5⅔ miles. The South Lambeth Road line was not to be laid until the road was widened between Wheatsheaf Lane and Wilcox Road. All routes were to be paved (mostly with granite setts), at the Company's expense, to three feet outside the rails instead of the eighteen inches usual everywhere else.

An Act of 1884 gave an Extension of Time for South Lambeth Road, where the delay in the widening was holding things up, and authorised junctions with the LTC at Camberwell Green and with the SLT at Vauxhall Cross, with permission for through running, but in fact through services never were operated, except by LST over the SLT to Stangate for five months in the winter of 1888-89. All the routes were constructed, opening from The Swan to Camberwell 7th December 1883, Hinton Road to Herne Hill 30th May 1884, to West Norwood 4th June 1885, and to Vauxhall 21st August 1887. The main depot was in Stockwell Road, with a smaller one almost at the Norwood terminus. The original cars were standard 46-seat knifeboard type from Falcon, but there was a low bridge in Hinton Road under the London Chatham & Dover Railway just south of Loughborough Junction Station, so the trams had to be fitted with a protective canopy above the top of the stairs. From 1895 the cars were drastically rebuilt, with smaller wheels, a much lower floor both downstairs and up, and garden seats. The maximum fleet size reached was 33.

All the routes became compulsorily purchasable by the LCC in 1903, but the Council decided not to take them for the time being, as it intended to electrify only Vauxhall to Brixton on its normal conduit system; Brixton to Camberwell and Norwood to be by the overhead trolley wire system which was not yet ready. The LST optimistically promoted a Bill in 1906 for permission to electrify all its routes itself using the overhead system, and operate for a further 21 years. This was supported by the local Lambeth Council, but opposed by the LCC and defeated. After arbitration it was agreed that the LCC should purchase the whole of the LST, and this was done on 20th December 1906. Brixton to Vauxhall was electrified on 4th April 1908, using conduit, Camberwell to Brixton (Gresham Road) was electrified on 21st November 1908, using the overhead system (the LCC's third after Hammersmith to Harlesden and Woolwich to Abbey Wood); and Loughborough Junction to Norwood on 30th May 1909 by overhead. The western end of Cold Harbour Lane was abandoned and never electrified, and has never even had a motor-bus service except briefly in the summer of 1911.

PECKHAM AND EAST DULWICH TRAMWAYS COMPANY (PEDT)

The Peckham and East Dulwich was incorporated by Act of 10th August 1882 to build a tramway from Peckham High Street via Rye Lane, Peckham Rye, East Dulwich Road, Crystal Palace Road, and a tiny part of Lordship Lane to The Plough at Barry Road, almost two miles. A part of it, along Peckham Rye, East Dulwich Road, and a part of Crystal Palace Road was built in 1883 but not opened. An Act of 1883 authorised tramways from Nunhead Station along the quiet local residential Cemetery, Hollydale, Evelina, Kimberley, Kirkwood, Brayard, Atwell, Choumert, Bellenden, Maxted, Nutbrook, Adys, and Ondine Roads to Champion Hill Road, a distance of 2½ miles. An Act of 1885 gave an Extension of Time for some 1882 and all 1883 tramways, also new routes along Hollydale Road from Evelina Road to join the existing LTC in Queens Road, also from East Dulwich Road along Nunhead Lane to Evelina Road, and also along Oglander Road from Maxted Road to Grove Vale. In 1885 Hollydale Road, Brayard Road, Chounert Road, Maxted Road and Adys Road were built but not opened until a few years later.

LONDON CAMBERWELL AND DULWICH TRAMWAYS COMPANY (LCDT)

The LCDT was by Act of 1887 the new name for the Peckham and East Dulwich. This Act also authorised the abandonment of Rye Lane, much of the 1883 Act, and almost all the 1885 Act, also an Extension of Time for the rest. In 1888 the track was laid in Crystal Palace Road and Lordship Lane. Despite several sections having now been built none were yet opened and the Company had no cars. At long last in 1896 three route-miles were opened, using 40-seat single-deck open toast-rack cars and one-man fare-box operation with no tickets. The junction with the LTC was not made, and operations ceased again in 1900. The local Council, the LCC and the Board of Trade all tried to get the Company to re-start, but it never did. The whole thing had been a huge waste of money which achieved almost nothing. Eventually after it had lain derelict for a further five years the LCC purchased it, and immediately abandoned the whole lot except the lines in East Dulwich Road and the tiny bit of Lordship Lane, which it rebuilt for conduit working and reopened in 1907 and 1906 respectively. The LCDT and its predecessor appear to have spent money laying track in streets with little potential and then found there was insufficient money left for trams.

Above Right **The London Camberwell and Dulwich Tramways Company had two short routes in the Peckham and Dulwich area, but traversing quiet residential roads with very little traffic potential. It is difficult to see why they were ever built. Although mostly completed in 1888 they were not opened until 1896, and they were closed again in 1900, lying derelict until purchased in 1905 by the LCC, which immediately abandoned them. Only single-deck toastrack cars were used; this one is standing at Peckham Rye terminus and its roof board reads: Kings Arms, Peckham Rye, Goose Green & Silvester Road.**

Right **Having acquired the nickname 'The Ha'penny Bumper', the LDGT service along Rotherhithe New Road is seen in latter days, after LCC takeover.**

SOUTHWARK AND DEPTFORD TRAMWAYS COMPANY (SDT)

The SDT was incorporated by Act of 3rd July 1879, with powers to build tramways from the Bricklayers Arms, with a junction both ways to the LTC in Old and New Kent Roads, then along Bermondsey New Road (now Tower Bridge Road), Grange Road, Spa Road, Jamaica Road, Union Road, Lower Road, and Evelyn Street to the Noahs Ark at the corner of Deptford High Street; also along Grange Road, Blue Anchor Road (now Southwark Park Road), Raymouth Road, and Rotherhithe New Road to join Lower Road, a total of 4¾ miles, all single track with 27 passing loops. All these were built, and opened in four stages in 1880-81, and worked with both double and single-deck cars from MRCW. An Act of 1881 authorised extensions from Jamaica Road along Dockhead and Tooley Street as far as Bermondsey Street, and along the rest of Rotherhithe New Road to St James Road near the canal bridge, totalling 1½ miles single track with nine passing loops. Both were opened on 17th December 1882. An Act of 1889 authorised a tramway along the whole of St James Road, but this was never built.

LONDON DEPTFORD AND GREENWICH TRAMWAYS COMPANY (LDGT)

This was the new name to which the SDT was changed by Act of 1893. The Company wanted to extend from Deptford to Greenwich, and ran its own horse buses there. It offered to contribute to the cost of a new road and bridge over Deptford Creek. However, its application for tramway powers was deleted from its 1889 and 1893 Bills, and the whole of its 1887 and 1891 Bills were rejected, all because the Board of Works had still not obtained powers to build the bridge and the road over it. The LDGT continued to press for its powers for many years, but the Greenwich route had to wait until LCC operation and the electric era.

Meanwhile the threat of compulsory purchase in 1900 of the 1879 routes by the LCC prevented further progress, and from 1900 onwards the LCC gave frequent reminders of its intentions. The LDGT of course objected strongly, and there were the usual legal battles. The Company managed to hold out for four more years, but inevitably the LCC won and purchased all the routes on 7th July 1904, abandoning most of them by 1915, only Tooley Street to Deptford being electrified.

SOUTH EASTERN METROPOLITAN TRAMWAYS COMPANY (SEMT)

A company was incorporated by Act of 14th July 1884 to build a tramway from London Street, Greenwich, along South Street, Lewisham Road, Lewisham High Street, and Rushey Green to the Black Horse Inn at Catford at the junction with Catford Road, a route of just 2½ miles. Construction was not started, and no application was made for an Extension of Time, so the powers lapsed two years after the passing of the Act, as was normal in all such cases. A new company, entitled South Eastern Metropolitan Tramways, obtained another Act in 1888 for an identical route. This was not constructed until the summer of 1890, and completed just a few days before its own two years would have elapsed, but no rolling stock was available until the grand opening ceremony on 11th October 1890. Ten standard 46-seat garden-seat cars were built for the SEMT by the North Metropolitan at Union Road, Leytonstone, and all the horses were hired from Thomas Tilling Limited, the local bus operator. The depot was at the Catford terminus. The route was entirely single track with loops, and no extensions were ever made.

Compulsory purchase would not be due until 1909, hence in 1900 the Company obtained an Act authorising it to electrify its route on the conduit system, but this work was not carried out, and instead the Company voluntarily sold out to the LCC from 1st April 1902, being wound up six months later after an active life of only 14 years. The LCC replaced most of the SEMT trams by others which it had acquired in 1899 from the LTC, but it continued hiring horses from Tilling. The horse cars on the Catford to Lewisham section were replaced in 1906 by new electric cars on a long route from London via New Cross and Loampit Vale, the latter never having had horse trams. The horse cars between Lewisham and Greenwich were replaced by electric cars in 1908.

The Rushey Green, Catford, terminus of the South Eastern Metropolitan Tramways Company, looking north outside the 'Black Horse and Harrow' Hotel. The SEMT depot is just off the picture to the right. Car No. 338 is not a genuine SEMT one, but an ex-London Tramways Company car which the London County Council brought here in 1902 after purchasing the SEMT company. On the left is a standard LCC electric car No. 290 going to 'Westminster via Walworth Road' (also Lewisham and New Cross). This service started on 10th June 1906, but the horse trams from Rushey Green to Greenwich continued to run over the electrified tracks via Lewisham for the time being, so this photo was taken in the summer of 1906.

A view dated 26th February 1898 at the junction of Lewisham High Street and Lewis Grove. A well-loaded 46-seat car of the type built for the SEMT proceeds southbound on its route from Greenwich to Catford. It almost has the road to itself. Capital Transport Collection

The 3ft 6ins tracks of the Woolwich & South East London Tramways Company from Plumstead met the 4ft 8½ins tracks of the London Tramways Company from Westminster and Blackfriars end-on in Trafalgar Road, East Greenwich. After both companies had been purchased by the LCC, and to allow for gauge-conversion work from narrow to standard, the meeting point was moved from Trafalgar Road to Rainton Road, Charlton, in three stages in 1905/09. The other end of the WSELT route was also by now closed for conversion, which is why this photo of the narrow-gauge ex-WSELT car repainted in LCC livery and taken at Rainton Road between July 1909 and August 1910 carried a destination board reading 'Rainton Road & Beresford Street, Change cars for Plumstead & Abbey Wood'.

WOOLWICH AND SOUTH EAST LONDON TRAMWAYS CO LTD (WSELT)

This company started life in 1879 as the Woolwich & Plumstead Tramways Company (WPT), and by Act of 26th August 1880 gained powers to build a tramway from Hare Street, Woolwich, via Powis Street, Beresford Square, and Plumstead Road to Plumstead Church, just over 1½ miles. The track gauge was 3ft 6ins, the only horse (or electric) tramway in the London area that was not 4ft 8½ ins. The WPT was very quickly purchased by the WSELT, which took over its powers, and started construction at once, finishing the line by April 1881, although it was not opened until 4th June because the cars had not yet been delivered. These were double-deckers, but shorter and smaller than normal, with only 32 seats. In horse days there were many different forms of tramway permanent-way rails and foundations, but Woolwich to Plumstead was especially unusual in having longitudinal inverted steel troughing set in concrete with no transverse sleepers or tie-bars.

An Act of 1881 authorised a tramway along Beresford Street, Woolwich High Street, Church Street, Albion Road, Lower Road, and Trafalgar Road, a total of 2¾ miles, finishing in Old Woolwich Road, Greenwich, end-on to the existing LTC tracks. All of this was built in the early summer of 1882, but it

was not opened until 21st November. The rails were supported on more conventional chairs and baseplates. As this route ran via Beresford Street it rather left the parallel Powis Street line isolated and surplus. Permission to extend it westwards to rejoin the Greenwich route was refused in 1883, so it was not normally used much afterwards. The depot was built in Cage Lane, Plumstead, later renamed Lakedale Road. Woolwich Arsenal, with its main entrance located in Beresford Square, employed a huge workforce and so to get them home to their midday meal and back again quickly the tramway ran special non-stop Express 'Dinner' cars to Plumstead and back, intermediate passengers boarding and alighting in motion. Most of the route was single track with loops, but two stretches in Woolwich High Street and Church Street were double tracks placed too close together for cars to pass, so they were protected by signal lamps and frequent crossovers. These were widened to conventional double track in 1893, and over the years many passing loops were altered and others added. More cars were purchased, to bring the fleet up to a maximum of 32, all double-deckers.

Compulsory purchase by the LCC became due in 1901 for Plumstead and in 1902 for Greenwich. The Company demanded twice as much money as the LCC was willing to pay, so

there was another legal battle with arbitration, but inevitably the Company had to surrender and the LCC took over on 1st June 1905. On electrification the LCC needed to change from 3ft 6in to standard 4ft 8½ins gauge track. Its own electrification from London reached the end-on Greenwich terminus in Trafalgar Road on 17th January 1904. The line from there as far as Tunnel Avenue was closed in two stages near the end of 1905, and reopened with conduit working on 10th June 1906, followed in 1909 by the short section to Rainton Road where the LCC established its main overhaul works. Meanwhile Beresford Square to Plumstead had closed in several stages in 1907-08, preventing access to the depot, so a temporary depot, or open yard, was established at Tunnel Avenue. The horse tramway from Rainton Road to Church Lane closed on 22nd August 1910, and to Chapel Street on 1st September. A short shuttle service of narrow-gauge horse cars then worked from Chapel Street to Nile Street (Free Ferry) and, the Tunnel Avenue yard having now closed and Lakedale Road re-opened, the cars were carried to and from the depot on a standard-gauge wagon. Finally this last little bit of horse tramway closed on 23rd November 1913, and re-opened for electric traction on 5th April 1914. A conduit to overhead change pit was built at Nile Street.

CROYDON TRAMWAYS COMPANY (CTC)

The CTC was incorporated by Act of 8th August 1878, with powers to build tramways along Brighton Road from the Red Deer to the Green Dragon; along North End and London Road to Thornton Heath Pond; along Oakfield Road, part of Whitehorse Road, Northcote Road, and Selhurst Road as far as Princes Road, and along St James Road from Oakfield Road to Milton Road. The first part, along London Road, was opened on 9th October 1879 and all the rest in four parts in 1879-80. Five single-deck Starbuck cars were bought at first, and there were no double-deckers until 1883. An Act of 1880 authorised extensions along Brigstock Road, Thornton Heath High Street, and the rest of Whitehorse Road; also from North End along George Street, Cherry Orchard Road, and Lower Addiscombe Road as far as Clyde Road; these were opened in 1881-82. The depot was at Thornton Heath Pond, but the St James Road branch was soon abandoned.

NORWOOD DISTRICT TRAMWAYS COMPANY (NDT)

The NDT was incorporated by Act of 24th July 1882, with powers to build tramways from Thornton Heath High Street along Whitehorse Lane and Clifton Road; from Princes Road along Selhurst Road, South Norwood High Street, and Penge Road to the Croydon-Penge Boundary; and from Clyde Road along Lower Addiscombe Road, Spring Lane, Woodside, and Portland Road to South Norwood High Street. Work started on these, but did not get very far.

CROYDON AND NORWOOD TRAMWAYS COMPANY (CNT)

This company was incorporated by Act of 2nd August 1883, to dissolve and amalgamate the separate Croydon and Norwood companies and all their property, with 7½ miles now in operation in Croydon and powers for 4½ miles in Norwood. This Act also gave powers to build extensions along Brighton Road from the Red Deer to Godstone Road, Purley, and along Windmill Road, and for 16 new passing loops on older routes. It also gave powers to use steam or other mechanical traction on all routes. The routes to South Norwood, both via Selhurst Road and via Addiscombe and Woodside, also probably the Clifton Road link, were all opened on 15th December 1883, but Penge Road, Windmill Road, and from Red Deer to Purley were never built as horse tramways.

It was decided that the Addiscombe – Woodside – South Norwood service, also Clifton Road and most of Whitehorse Road, did not attract as many passengers as had been hoped, and although routes in Croydon itself were doing well, these three were abandoned in 1887-89. An Act of 1889 sanctioned this, and also the liquidation of the CNT Company, which was re-incorporated as the CROYDON TRAMWAYS COMPANY (CTC). In 1891 the Electric Traction Syndicate Limited operated an open-top knifeboard self-propelled car, with storage batteries under the seats, on the Jarman system, on London Road, followed in early 1892 by a similar but slightly larger garden-seated car. The Connelly Oil Motor Tractor, which had already run on the Southwark & Deptford Tramway, was tried at Croydon at the end of 1891, running at first with light oil as a fuel. It was then converted to run on gas for six months in 1893. It was used on London Road. The Luhrig self-propelled tramcar, powered by coal-gas as a fuel, was tested at Croydon in 1893, and an improved version of the Luhrig was tested for several months in 1894 on the London Road and Brigstock Road route.

The Brighton Road had always been separated from London Road and the other routes, isolated by the narrow Croydon High Street. In 1893-94 Croydon Corporation widened the High Street, and obtained powers to build a tramway along it, thus uniting the two routes. This was opened on 6th June 1897, owned by the Corporation and leased to the CTC, who now worked a through service from the Red Deer to Thornton Heath High Street. Meanwhile 21-year compulsory purchase was looming, in this case by Croydon Corporation, and it appears to have taken place on 22nd January 1900 without much controversy, including 18 cars and 175 horses, a large depot at Thornton Heath and a small one in Brighton Road. Instead of then operating the horse tramways themselves or leasing them back to the owning company the Corporation leased them to the British Electric Traction Co Ltd. The Red Deer to Thornton Heath Pond horse trams, after various interruptions during electric conversion, finally ceased running on 25th September 1901, with new electric cars taking over the next day. The Addiscombe horse service ceased on 3rd January 1902, Brigstock Road on 9th January, and Selhurst on 23rd January.

LEA BRIDGE, LEYTON AND WALTHAM-STOW TRAMWAYS COMPANY (LBLW)

The LBLW was incorporated by Act of 11th August 1881, to build a 3½ mile tramway from Clapton Road, at a point six feet from the North Met tramway, via Lea Bridge Road, Leyton Bakers Arms, Whipps Cross, Forest Road, and Woodford Road to the Rising Sun Inn, using single track with loops. It was to be known then as the Epping Forest Tramways. The 6000 acres of Epping Forest was due to be handed over by H.M. The Queen to the City of London Corporation on 6th May 1882, for use by the public for ever, and the LBLW expected to carry well over two million people per annum from the vast population of north

A Lea Bridge, Leyton & Walthamstow garden-seat car.

and east London to enjoy the Forest. The first 200 yards of road from Clapton Road to Cornthwaite Road were very narrow, and the Act stipulated that the Company must buy and demolish the houses here and widen the road at its own expense, which it could not afford to do. So the tramway as built started at the west entrance to the waterworks. It was opened from there to Whipps Cross, Wood Street, on 12th May 1883 and in due course had ten cars, mostly single-deck. The powers to build the rest of the system expired.

That gap at Clapton contributed to a significant loss of passengers and hence revenue. All the original directors were replaced in 1883, and only £30,000 of the authorised £65,000 share capital had been issued. The LBLW got another Act on 7th August 1884 reviving powers for the half-mile from Clapton to the Waterworks, but they did not have enough money to pay the Contractor who had built the line, so he pressed for a Winding-Up Order. All trams ceased running towards the end of 1884, and a liquidator was appointed in February 1885.

A new Company with the same name, but with yet a third set of directors, was formed on 19th October 1888. It obtained an Act on 12th August 1889 reviving the powers for all of the 1881 route and granting an extension from the Bakers Arms along Leyton High Road to Trelawn Road, almost as far as Leyton GER Station, a distance of 1½ miles, using either mechanical or electrical power. The original route was quickly re-opened, then the extension to the Rising Sun was built and opened in 1889. The route to Leyton Station opened in 1890, with that to Cornthwaite Road following in 1892, but the 200-yard gap to the NMT was never closed, as Hackney Council would not yield in its demand for road widening. All cars from now on were double-deckers, both 40-seat knifeboard and 46-seat garden-seat type. The depot was just west of the Bakers Arms junction, and passenger numbers rose by nearly a million each year, increasing from 600,000 in 1890 to 8,400,000 in 1898.

Compulsory purchase powers would be by the LCC as far as the River Lea in 1910, by Leyton Council from the Lea to Whipps Cross in 1902, from Whipps Cross to the Rising Sun by Walthamstow Council in 1905, and from Bakers Arms to Leyton Station by Leyton Council in 1910. Walthamstow did not want to buy their part, so Leyton UDC bought it and operated from the River Lea right through to the Rising Sun, as well as the Leyton Station branch, from 1st November 1905. The section west of the River Lea Bridge (and County Boundary) was purchased by the LCC in 1905 and leased by them to Leyton UDC until 1911 so as to maintain a through service. The LBLW built up a large network of horse-bus services in the surrounding territory, and when compulsory purchase of the tramways was drawing near they created a separate company for these, which thus escaped municipalisation and continued to thrive. Horse-tram operation ceased on 30th November 1906 on all the lines in Leyton and to the Rising Sun, and on 9th December 1908 on the LCC section, all then being replaced by Leyton UDC electric cars.

The Harlesden terminus of the Harrow Road & Paddington Tramways Company, at Manor Park Road, near the subsequent famous Jubilee Clock, looking east. The oval board on the upper deck of the Falcon-built car reads 'Lock Bridge and Harlesden', Lock Bridge being about a quarter of a mile west of Paddington Green.

HARROW ROAD AND PADDINGTON TRAMWAYS COMPANY (HRP)

The HRP was incorporated by an Act of 25th June 1886 to build a tramway from the Royal Oak at Harlesden Green (now High Street) at Manor Park Road, along Harrow Road to the Lock Hospital Bridge at Amberley Road (2½ miles) with a branch along Chippenham Road and Cambridge Road to Cambridge Gardens, Kilburn (¾ mile) both single track with loops. Both routes were opened on 7th July 1888, but the Chippenham branch was built only as far as Carlton Vale, Prince of Wales. An Act of 1891 authorised a further 1¼ miles along Harrow Road to Edgware Road, and also a quarter of a mile along Walterton Road, but these two lines were not built, despite both getting Extensions of Time in 1893 and 1894. The Chippenham Road route was too short to be useful (the original intention had been to continue through to Maida Vale, but this was not authorised), so it was not used much after 1891, but survived until 1912. Earlier cars

were Milnes knifeboard double-deckers and later ones were by Falcon with garden seats, a total of 21, the depot being at Harlesden near the junction with Scrubs Lane.

An Act of 1903 authorised the HRP to electrify its main route (but not Chippenham Road) and lease it to the Metropolitan Electric Tramways Limited. In 1904 the Company was purchased by the MET but retained as a separate subsidiary, and on 16th August 1906 it was completely absorbed by the MET, with all its routes and cars and horses. The horse tramway closed on 26th August 1906, and the horses and cars were sold by auction on 6th September. The line re-opened with MET electric trams on 22nd December. The section from Lock Bridge to Kensal Green was in the County of London, so was compulsorily purchased by the LCC on 18th October 1909 and immediately leased back to the MET. The part beyond here was bought by the Middlesex County Council and also leased back to the MET.

SOUTHALL, EALING AND SHEPHERDS BUSH TRAM RAILWAY CO LTD (SESB)

This company was formed on 12th May 1870, and the same year applied for powers to build tramways from Uxbridge Road (West London Railway Station) via Acton, Ealing and Hanwell to Southall High Street at North Road, a total of seven miles. However powers were not granted until 7th July 1873, delayed by red tape arising out of the Tramways Act of 1870. The line was built as far as Askew Crescent (one mile) and opened with two cars on 1st June 1874 despite being refused permission from the Board of Trade. The contractors (Reid Bros) who built it had not yet been paid, which led to a Winding-Up Order and the appointment of a liquidator. Trams ceased running on 23rd February 1875. An auction sale was arranged, but no buyer could be found, so Reid Bros then offered to buy it, and complete the route to Southall. They applied for an Extension of Time, but this was not granted. The trams

By 1886 the West Metropolitan had 243 horses and 35 trams and six omnibuses. The main depot was in Chiswick High Road, with a small one at Richmond terminus, and also a small one in Uxbridge Road, Shepherds Bush, which was moved to Goldhawk Road in 1892. A car on its Kew Bridge to Hammersmith service is seen with the old Kew Bridge in the background. This was replaced by a new and wider bridge in 1903.

resumed running as far as Askew Crescent on 21st September 1875. The line was now leased to C.C. Cramp (who in later years became also a director of the Harrow Road & Paddington and Chairman of the Rossendale Valley Tramway in Lancashire), but the powers beyond Askew Crescent expired.

The Shepherds Bush and Priory Road Acton Tramway Order (SBPRA) was granted to Reid Bros on 24th July 1876, with powers to continue the SESB line to just beyond Priory Road (Acton Lane today), a distance of one mile. Beyond there lay Acton High Street, thought to be too narrow for trams. Reids purchased the original line early in 1878 and opened their new extension on 18th February, creating one through route, soon worked with four cars.

The SESB company was dissolved in 1883. Reids deposited plans in 1880 for an extension from Acton to Ealing Broadway (two miles) which was refused. A route from Shepherds Bush – Goldhawk Road – Youngs

Corner – Chiswick to Kew Bridge (2½ miles) was authorised, but only as far as Youngs Corner, by an Act of 11th August 1881. However, this was not proceeded with by Reids, as they sold their interest to Charles Phillips in November 1880.

WEST METROPOLITAN TRAMWAYS CO LTD (WMT)

The WMT was registered on 14th November 1878, and published plans for tramways from Shepherds Bush to Youngs Corner and from Hammersmith Broadway – Chiswick – Kew Bridge. There were also plans for several routes in the Camden Town and Paddington areas, and one to Barnes. All this proved too much to take on, and the company was wound up a year later. A new company with the same name was formed on 12th August 1881, which purchased the SESB and the SBPRA as a going concern. It also bought the powers from Phillips for the Goldhawk Road route then being built and opened it with single-deck

Falcon cars on 18th March 1882. The WMT then applied for powers for a 5¼ mile route from Hammersmith – Chiswick – Kew Bridge – Richmond Station (LSWR). All this was granted by Act of 10th August 1882, except the section across the (then) narrow and steep Kew Bridge, which left the Richmond route isolated.

This Act also included a new WMT Company, statutory and not Limited. Construction soon started, and the route from Youngs Corner to the north side of Kew Bridge was opened on 16th December 1882. The route from the south side of Kew Bridge to Richmond (150 yards short of the station) opened on 17th April 1883, and the one from Youngs Corner to Hammersmith on 14th July. This included a one-way loop via Studland Road, Glenthorne Road, and Beadon Road, returning via King Street. This brought the WMT up to its maximum of 8¾ route miles. All the company's trams were now double-deck.

Early in 1888 the Lineff Electric Traction & Lighting Syndicate Limited produced its electric conduit tramcar, inspired by the conduit tramway at Blackpool, and possibly the first electric car powered from an outside source in the London area. The WMT laid 200 yards of conduit track in the yard alongside its Chiswick depot, on which the Lineff car ran. The open conduit had a slot at the top through which poked an arm fixed to the underneath of the car, and a fixed conductor rail along its bottom. Electricity from an external dynamo was conveyed along this, and up into the car, a magnet under the car lifting the rail to make contact. The car was a small open 20-seater, with a 4-hp 220-volt motor. The trials were successful, and the WMT enthusiastically announced that the design would save 50% on the cost of horse working, and would soon be introduced over the whole of their lines, increasing the average speed from 4½ to 6½ mph and needing only 19 cars instead of 28 to keep the same headway.

However, Hammersmith Council objected to the open conduit slot, so in June 1890 Lineff converted the car to surface-contact collection. Overhead wires or other intrusions were also prohibited. So the slot in the road was eliminated, whilst keeping the conduit, and to convey current to the cars a strip of flexible hoop iron lay loose on the bottom. Above it, but not in contact with it, was an ordinary rail, with a top surface flush with the road and no groove in it or anything to be objected to. When the car came over any given part of the track the magnet lifted up a small piece of the flexible conductor, which was briefly brought into contact with both the electrical conductor and the surface magnetic rail and opened the way for current to pass to the motor and drive the car. As soon as the car had passed, the flexible conductor dropped down to its original position. The surface rail was in short lengths, each insulated, so only the one below the car was charged at any one time. Discussions took place with Lineff about electrifying the whole of the Acton route, but later in 1890 they ended, and the car was converted back to being just an ordinary horse-drawn open-bench car for summer use on the Richmond route.

In August 1889 Acton Council demanded that the 13-year-old single-track route be reconstructed and doubled. This and the doubling of lines in Chiswick and Hammersmith was sanctioned in the 1889 WMT Act, which also sought powers for new routes from Acton to Hanwell and Shepherds Bush to Westbourne Park, plus the building of many 1883 or 1884 routes that had been rejected, but all of these were now rejected again. The relaying and doubling was not completed until 1893 in Chiswick and 1895 in Acton. The 1889 Act also postponed compulsory purchase of the Hammersmith lines by the LCC for 14 years (until 1903) or any subsequent seven years. By 1893 financial problems were looming, many shareholders were dissatisfied with the Chairman and Directors, and a receiver was brought in. The Receiver appointed by the High Court was George White, Chairman of Bristol Tramways and the WMT subsequently became part of the Imperial Tramways group.

BRENTFORD AND ISLEWORTH TRAMWAYS COMPANY

This company was incorporated by an Act of 11th August 1879, with powers to build a 1¼ mile tramway from Brentford End Schools (just west of the GWR Station) to Isleworth (Gumley House, in the town centre). Kew Bridge to Brentford, also Isleworth – St Margarets – Richmond Bridge, had been in the Bill but were rejected. Another Act in 1880 authorised a route from Busch Corner to Hounslow Heath (The Hussar, Barrack Road), also from Hounslow along the Bath Road to Barrack Lane (Martindale Road today), and from Isleworth via London Road to Twickenham, Holly Road, a total of 5½ miles in all. From Brentford Station to Isleworth town centre was complete and ready for use by the end of 1881, and Busch Corner to just beyond Isleworth LSWR Station a few months later. But they were never used, and just left lying idle. A third Act, in 1883, authorised a tramway from Brentford Canal Bridge, via The Butts, and a new road by-passing to the north of Brentford, partly along the site of what later became the Great West Road, joining the WMT in Chiswick High Road. But the last little bit of this was rejected, which spoilt the whole thing, so none of it was built, and the powers lapsed. A new Brentford & District Tramways Company was incorporated by Act of 1885 to acquire the still-existing trackwork. The Directors included G.F. Fry from the 1879 company and C.C. Cramp from the SESB and WMT. Tramways authorised totalled 6¼ miles from Kew Bridge, (junction with WMT) via Brentford High Street, Hounslow High Street, and Staines Road to The Hussar; also Busch Corner to Isleworth (North Street); and along the Bath Road to Barrack Lane. But despite a 3-year Extension of Time in 1887 they could not raise enough capital. The lines were not finished, and an 1890 Act sanctioned abandonment.

LONDON UNITED TRAMWAYS (LUT)

The LUT was the new Company registered on 19th July 1894 by the Imperial Group, of Bristol, to take over all the WMT routes, the depots at Chiswick, Richmond, and Shepherds Bush, and 33 trams, which included some from Milnes almost brand new. Ten more new cars were built at Chiswick depot soon afterwards. Many of the senior staff were sacked by the new owners and replaced in the LUT by Bristol people, including James Clifton Robinson, a protégé of George Francis Train. The permanent way on all routes was improved, Chiswick was enlarged to provide a new overhaul depot, workshop and offices, and many trams were repaired or totally rebuilt here. An Act of 1895 authorised a half-mile extension along Acton High Street to just beyond Gunnersbury Lane, which was opened on 31st August 1895. By 1897 there were 49 trams and 359 horses.

The new LUT was anxious to electrify all routes using overhead wires, but the LCC rejected this for the Hammersmith area, so horse trams had to continue running until permission was granted for electric cars to start on 4th April 1901 on all routes except Kew to Richmond. A new car depot was built at the new Acton Hill terminus, and opened in March 1896, so subsequently Goldhawk Road depot was closed. Kew to Richmond horse trams ran until 19th April 1912, when they ceased due to competition from the LGOC motor-bus route 27 which had started four months previously.

The Richmond terminus of the horse tramway from Kew Bridge on, presumably, its abandonment day, which was 19th April 1912. The line had opened on 17th April 1883, but the car in this picture was a newer one which had been displaced from the Hammersmith and Shepherd's Bush routes when these were electrified in 1901. The car depot on the left, after many changes of function, still exists today.

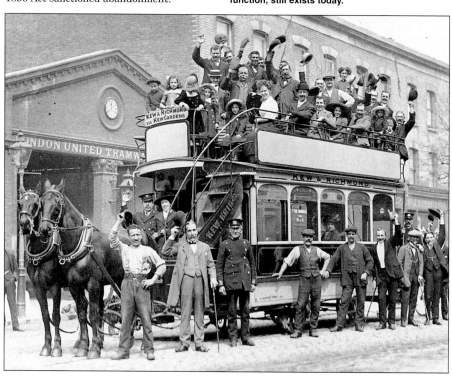

STEAM, AIR, BATTERY & CABLE

The 1870 Tramways Act had provisions for prospective tramway operators to stipulate whether they intended to use animal or mechanical power to operate their lines. 'Animal' usually meant horse, but not always. The North Metropolitan in fact tried mule power, without much success. A look at some of the methods being tried during the horse tram era will give an idea of how things were developing as the electric age approached.

STEAM and AIR

Steam traction had become a favourite method for 'horseless' movement. The railways prospered and expanded because of steam, ships were being propelled by steam, and there were even some tentative experiments with steam buses. Tramways readily lent themselves to the concept, and by the mid-nineteenth century steam street cars were already popular in the United States. In Great Britain steam was used extensively with some success in the provinces, but in London its success was very muted. Several tramway operators tried out a steam tram at some or other time. A Grantham machine was tried out by London Tramways Company in 1873. This was an all-in-one car, with one of the two axles being powered by two steam-producing boilers in the centre of the 54-seater double-deck car. A Merryweather steam locomotive, hauling a North Metropolitan horse car, operated between Stratford and Harrow Green (Leytonstone) in 1877. Croydon & Norwood tried out Hohenzollern fireless locomotives around 1884. London's most enduring dalliance with steam came in 1885 with the North London Tramways which, until going into liquidation in 1891, operated its entire service from Finsbury Park to Wood Green and Edmonton with 15 Merryweather and 10 Dick Kerr steam locomotives hauling 27 Falcon trailers.

The first known operation of compressed air to power a tram was in 1881 when a locomotive invented by a Colonel Beaumont and powered by compressed air was tried out between Stratford and Leytonstone. The operation required the installation of a compressor at the Stratford depot, and an 83 yard long pipe from there to a water hydrant in Stratford Broadway. This was to feed water to the reservoir in the engine. The operation of the loco was a reasonable success despite the 15 minutes taken to refuel. This resulted in cars stepping-back, the car hauled to the Stratford terminus refuelling point by the Beaumont vehicle making the return trip behind a horse, while the Beaumont locomotive took over the next tram. The cost of the compressor was such that at least four locomotives had to be worked to make it viable, a factor which probably decided the North Met not to proceed any further with the idea.

A North London Tramways Company Merryweather steam loco hauling an eight-wheel Falcon trailer car in 1885 on the Finsbury Park to Edmonton service, which in electric days became route 79. Note that steam trailer cars always had the bogies underneath the end platforms, whereas this was never the case with electric cars, which always had them under the main saloon, to give a much shorter wheelbase.

A view of similar vehicles towards the end of their six-year operation by North London Tramways. The passenger entrances were on the corner, rather than the side, of the end platforms, presumably to avoid the steps fouling the bogies.

BATTERY

In March 1882, as the North Metropolitan's experimentation with compressed air came to a close the Company accepted an offer from Michael Radcliffe Ward to demonstrate a battery-driven tram at the Union Road works. The batteries, weighing 1½ tons, were fitted inside a standard horse car which, although noisy, moved successfully under its own power. A year later, on 10th March 1883, another battery car was tried out, this time on the West Metropolitan system. It was a double-decker designed by Anthony Reckenzaun and it was powered by fifty cells, all placed beneath the seats on the lower deck. On its trial run it reached a speed of 6mph. Experiments continued. In 1885 a Jarman Battery Car ran between Clapham and Blackfriars, but for the most extensive use of battery power we go back to the North Metropolitan, where in October 1886 the Electric Locomotive Power Company made trial runs with a tram hauled by a battery loco between Stratford and Manor Park. A service using two of them began in 1887 but was fraught with problems caused mainly by the accumulators becoming quickly exhausted. Once this was overcome, and two more locomotives were added to the fleet, the service ran more successfully.

In 1889 the General Electric Power & Traction Company offered its new battery tram to the North Met for trial. The car was self-contained with the batteries placed under the platforms, so the problem of vapour getting into the passenger saloon, which had dogged earlier experiments, did not arise. The North Met subsequently built six cars to the same design at Union Road, and once terms had been agreed with General Electric a full service began on 14th June 1889 between Canning Town and Plaistow. It was the failure to agree new terms with General Electric which brought about the end of this most successful of mechanical services on 27th July 1892. About this time other battery experiments on Croydon Tramways, not a success because of acid spillage from the batteries, and between Clapham and Tooting, came to an end.

Centre Following his early experiments Mr Jarman persuaded the Croydon Tramways Company to convert an existing horse tram to the accumulator method of electrical traction. The standard eight-window knifeboard body was remounted inside Thornton Heath depot onto a new stronger underframe, which had to be higher off the ground so as to leave space for the traction motor under the floor. For several nights it was secretly tested up and down North End, and then in December 1891 it entered public service along the main London Road between Thornton Heath Depot and North End (Crown Hill).

Right At the end of 1891 the Electric Tramcar Syndicate Ltd, which had been formed to develop Mr Jarman's system, similarly mounted a standard seven-window horse car with garden seats on top, onto a stronger underframe higher off the ground. This worked with battery-electric propulsion in public service from January to March of 1892 on the main Thornton Heath Depot to Crown Hill route, but acid from the batteries under the seats gave off sulphuric-acid fumes, and also had a nasty habit of spilling onto the floor or burning the boots or clothing of passengers.

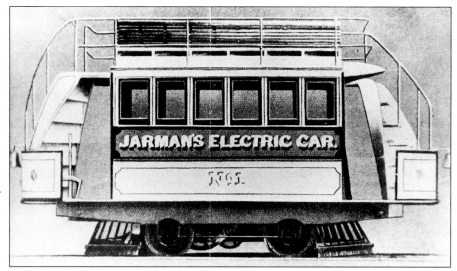

In 1891 a Mr Jarman experimented at Croydon with a battery-electric tramcar, which is thought to be this one, a small double-deck car with six windows per side downstairs and knifeboard seats on top.

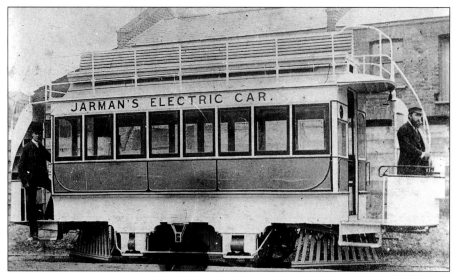

CABLE

Cable traction was used in many places worldwide, its most famous user being San Francisco where the cable cars are still in use today. Cable's first application in London was on the 1 in 11 gradient between Archway Tavern and the top of Highgate Hill, opened in May 1884. This was too steep for horse trams, and so cable – driven by two 25hp steam engines – was seen as the ideal solution. The cable ran in conduit just below ground level between 3ft 6ins gauge tracks. The line was built by the Patent Cable Tramways Corporation Ltd and operated by the Steep Grade Tramways and Works Company Ltd. The general manager of both companies was James Clifton Robinson, who by now had worked with tramways for 22 years in a number of cities.

This was the first cable tramway anywhere in Europe, so its progress was watched very closely. After the official inspection by the Board of Trade on 21st May 1884, there was a grand opening by the Lord Mayor of London on 29th May. It opened to the public the day after. The line, it was claimed, then carried 50,000 passengers in its first eight days. But the novelty wore off and the line failed to attract the number of regular passengers it needed. Two years after starting its service, both companies were in the hands of a Receiver, and the SGTW was wound up.

A new Highgate and Hampstead Cable Tramways Company took over in 1889, which was sold and re-sold before it too failed in 1892. The line was then sold to another new company, the Highgate Hill Tramways Ltd, who were not in charge for long before a nasty accident occurred. One car ran away down the hill on 5th December 1892 and collided with a stationary tractor and trailer standing at the terminus, pushing them off the track and 200 yards along Holloway Road. The Board of Trade ordered the line to be closed and it stayed closed for four years. Another new Highgate Hill Tramways Company Ltd was formed in 1893 but it failed to get permission to re-open the line.

The LCC offered to buy it in April 1896, but Hornsey Council prevented this. Another new company was formed in May, and then yet another which bought it on 14th August 1896, and at last it was re-opened to passengers on 19th April 1897, but with a licence for only three months, later renewed. It was closed again for a period in 1906, re-opened, and finally closed for the last time on 23rd August 1909, the whole undertaking being purchased on the 24th by the LCC, who re-opened it as a standard-gauge electric conduit tramway on 25th March 1910. There had been at least four other runaway accidents, caused by brakes not being applied properly.

GAS and OIL

A Connelly oil engined locomotive undertook experiments in Croydon in 1893. It later moved over to the London, Deptford & Greenwich. This earliest of oil powered vehicles which could also run on gas was replaced at Croydon by a Luhrig gas engined tramcar. Neither of these innovative systems caught the imagination, but they serve to add to the variety of traction methods tried out before the universal adoption of electric power.

Above **One of the two dummy gripper cars, Nos 5 and 6, of the Highgate Hill Tramway, pulling a four-wheeled open-top knifeboard-seat trailer car. Passengers were carried on the open-sided dummy on crossbench toastrack-type seating, or on longitudinal seats inside the saloon trailers.**

Below **One of the eight-wheel bogie double-deck cars descending Highgate Hill, just about half-way down, at the start of the double-track section. (The upper half was single track with loops). Note the drinking trough on the left, for horses pulling other vehicles up the hill.**

Bottom **Near the bottom of Highgate Hill we see one of the self-contained bogie cars, with a mechanic attending to some defect in the cable conduit. On the left, on the corner of Salisbury Road and enclosed in a protective iron cage with an elaborate ornamental lamp on top, is the famous Whittington Stone, a memorial to the legend of Dick Whittington and his cat.**

ELECTRICITY TAKES OVER

The first electric tramcars were little more than larger versions of the horse cars which had preceded them. They were open-top with the upper deck seating arranged to the garden seat pattern. Before long some were being built, or fitted retrospectively, with covered tops or fully enclosed top decks. This proved to be the first important design change for the electric tram, although not all cars were to benefit from it.

In London there were two basic types of electric tram, the bogie car, which sat on two four-wheel trucks, each truck usually having two large and two small wheels, and the single truck, or four wheel, car. Bogie cars were intended for busy, high frequency routes, while the four-wheelers inhabited the lesser used services.

Further concessions to comfort were made as time passed, but once a tram had been ordered and delivered its owner justifiably expected to get 20 or more years of life out of it. Many cars achieved this life span and more, but few reached the end of their days looking as they did when new. The add-ons and substitutions, like covered tops, and 'direct' staircases, as well as cushion seating and better lighting, did much to improve the fighting power of the tram in the face of stiff competition from the buses, whose design went through a metamorphosis between 1915 and 1930. The life of a bus rarely exceeded 12 years in those days, so bus operators could take advantage of any design advancements. In fact the development of the tram was very muted compared with that of the bus. The reason lies in that most of Britain's electric tramway systems were built before 1910, and the tramcar building boom of the early 1900s was soon over. Once the new fleets were in situ

tramcar manufacturers could expect no sizeable orders for some time. Indeed replacement of the tramcar, by buses or trolleybuses, began in some parts of the country as early as 1914. There was little impetus for the companies involved in building trams to sustain a continuing programme of development. They just kept on supplying spare parts, and marketing what was basically the same product year after year. This is the reason why, in 1930, at least two London area systems were still buying trams built to designs whose basic fundamentals were 20 years old. True, better motors and trucks were available in later years, but these had been produced mainly as replacements for life expired units or for British and foreign buyers.

Only at the very end of the 1920s were plans for new generations of tramcar rolling off the drawing boards. At the same time high capacity, fully enclosed, faster and even more comfortable buses were beginning to crisscross London, unhampered by road works and unrestricted by track and wire.

The electric tramcar functioned on a simple principle. The current running through the overhead wires was picked up by the trolleyhead on top of the trolley pole, and passed by cable through the car to the motors attached to the truck or bogies, depending on the type of car. A controller, mounted on the platform at each end of the tram, and operated by the driver, gave 'instructions' to the motor to start, stop and regulate the speed. The LCC's cars worked the same way except the current was picked up from a conduit set in the road between the running rails.

The use of the conduit current collection method placed a heavy financial burden on the LCC as conduit was far more expensive than

the overhead system favoured almost universally outside London. The conduit method consisted of two conductor rails, positive and negative, running inside a trough, or conduit, set in the roadway. A conductor shoe, or plough, fitted under the trams ran along the conductor rails transmitting the electric current to the car motors.

If a tram was working on a route which switched at some point from the conduit system to overhead power collection, the plough was ejected and power then supplied through the trolley poles. Latterly most LCC cars were fitted with trolley poles as well as plough carriers. Special staffed 'pits' were laid at the points where conduit changed to overhead, and the plough ejection or slotting-in process was carried out with the minimum of delay. The conduit system served the LCC well, despite being costly to install and maintain.

The LCC tried other road-based current collection methods. In 1908 experiments were carried out along Whitechapel Road and Bow Road with a stud contact system which was cheaper than conduit. An underground cable was laid in the roadway and connected to the studs on the road surface. A device like a ski was fitted under the trams. This picked up current from the studs which became 'live' as the ski made contact and died once the tram had passed. The system was prone to mishap; occasionally the studs didn't become live when required and, even worse, didn't always 'die' once the tram had passed overhead. On more than one occasion horses making contact with the still-live studs were electrocuted. Horse trams had to return to the Whitechapel Road on 18th July 1908 while the studs were removed and conventional conduit installed.

Facing Page **Electric tramways were the new wonder of the age and here by the Wellington in Wood Green High Road MET bogie cars 35 and 210 (from types B and C respectively) are still the centre of attraction. The two horse buses lined up on the left look distinctly archaic by comparison. It should be noted that trams unlike their omnibus competitors were always bound by fixed stopping places and a stop sign can be seen in the centre of the picture.**

Above **In this classic scene from the Edwardian era LCC A class car 90 rolls along in state past the Balham Conservatoire of Music. Notice the conduit equipped tramway which looked neater than a conventional overhead wire installation. Other road users employ either human or animal traction. Balham Station in the distance is a reminder that the new electric tramways caused a drastic drop in passengers as they poached trade from the suburban, steam railways.**

A side-slot system was tried out in the Kingsland Road, where the offside running rail also took on the role of the conduit track. Again this method was not too successful and was eventually replaced by normal conduit.

The total route mileage of the LCC system was 167 miles, of this 43 miles were powered by overhead lines. The LCC eventually came to use the overhead line system on new and later suburban route extensions more and more, especially in south east London, because it was cheaper. The overhead system as adopted by the LCC and the other tramways around London consisted of copper wire suspended about 20 feet above ground. Support was provided by steel poles placed at regular intervals on each side of the road. In early days these poles were quite elaborate affairs involving some intricate ironwork. Span wires

were strung between the poles and the overhead connected to the spans by means of insulator units. Current reached the overhead from section boxes placed every half mile which fed power to the wires through cables fixed to the outside of the poles. Return current travelled through the running rails.

With out exception the council and company owned systems around London, opted for the overhead line collection method to power their trams, and the top-deck mast supporting the trolley pole was a feature of all cars until the advent of the covered top around 1903.

Electricity to power the trams came from a variety of sources. In the days before nationalisation most local authorities maintained their own electricity supply installations, and these were used to power their trams as well as supply the local population with electricity. In 1899 the British Electric Traction Group, which in later years controlled the MET, formed a company called the North Metropolitan Electrical Power Distribution Co Ltd. It secured powers to supply a large area of north Middlesex, south east Hertfordshire, and west Essex, which it eventually did by purchasing power in bulk from a large power station in Brimsdown which was owned by the North Metropolitan Electric Power Supply Company. The power station was built by Brush and jointly equipped with BTH. The MET's trams were powered by electricity purchased direct from the NMEPSC.

The BET's interest in the SMET was also bound up with power generation. It acquired a registered company called the County of Surrey Electrical Power Distribution Co Ltd, changing the name, in 1904, to the South

Metropolitan Electric Tramways and Lighting Co Ltd. A power station was built in Sutton and eventually supplied power to the locality; and to the SMET except in the Croydon area, where the supply came from the Corporation, and in Penge, where it came from the Beckenham UDC.

The LCC built its own generating station at Greenwich, and the first section was opened in 1906. Before that LCC trams took their power from temporary generating stations supplied by the County of London Electric Supply Co. The power station, which initially contained four 3,500KW generators which delivered 6,600 volts, fed current to substations across the LCC system. The equipment at Greenwich was upgraded several times during the LCC tenure.

Power for the LUT trams came from the company's own power station at Chiswick, the complex also housing a tram depot, the company offices and main overhead works. Later the LUT were able to use the supply generated by the Underground Group at its Lots Road power station in Chelsea.

The story of the electric tramcar in London falls into three distinct camps; The London County Council, the local council systems, and finally the companies which eventually became part of the Underground Group. Rather than take the story of the London tramcar's development chronologically, it is easier to look at each camp separately, starting with the London County Council, which although not the first to run electric cars, quickly developed a standard car which became the yardstick by which tram design and efficiency would be judged for a quarter of a century.

The date is Friday 15th May 1903. White painted class A car 86 conveys the Prince and Princess of Wales on the ceremonial opening of the LCC electric tramways. On the top deck the future King George V raises his hat to the crowds of onlookers. In spite of showery weather the occasion was a great success, and on arrival at Tooting the royal party went on to inspect new houses on the Totterdown Fields Estate. Significantly the electrification of the tramway and the provision of new council housing on the tram route became part of the transport philosophy of the LCC.

THE LONDON COUNTY COUNCIL

By 1889 the Metropolitan Board of Works had been in existence for 34 years and had spent much of that time under severe criticism for being ineffectual, mainly because it was an indirectly elected body. Much power still rested with the forty local vestries and district boards, so in many respects London was without effective central government. All was put right with the setting up of the London County Council in 1888. The LCC was incorporated as the authority for the County of London created for it to administer. The County stretched from Hammersmith in the west to Bow Bridge in the east. From the north it embraced Hampstead and Hackney, with Wandsworth, Grove Park, Streatham and Abbey Wood making up its boundaries south of the river. An area of 117 square miles was covered in which lived 3 million people. Following its creation areas like Hackney and Shepherd's Bush ceased to be in Middlesex, Woolwich and Peckham were no longer in Kent, and the people of Lambeth and Battersea no longer lived in Surrey.

The London County Council, which eventually had under its wing 28 Metropolitan Boroughs, was from the outset a very radical authority anxious to implement social reform. The first administration of 1889 was dominated by the Progressive Party (Liberals). The elections of 1895 produced an equal share of councillors from the Progressives and Moderates (Conservatives), but the Progressives returned with a majority in 1898.

The LCC seized the first opportunity to become involved in tramways, an opportunity which, under the terms of the 1870 Tramways Act, presented itself in 1891, when the four and a quarter miles of London Street Tramway from Kentish Town and Nags Head to Euston Road and King's Cross could be legally acquired. It took some time for the LCC to realise its ambition, because the London Street held out for the £604,090 it believed its assets were worth. Arbitration reassessed the value at one tenth of that and

the House of Lords ruled in the LCC's favour. On 1st March 1895 the LCC became the Legal owner of its first piece of London tramway, but it had no organisational force and no legal power to operate its own services. It promptly entered into an agreement with London Street and leased back the line to the company which operated it on the Council's behalf paying rent and a proportion of the revenue for the privilege. The lack of legal powers was due to the London Street Tramways having been constituted prior to the 1870 Act and therefore not bound to its compulsory purchase terms.

Naturally the LCC wanted to run its own trams, so it got a Bill through Parliament enabling it to do just that. This was the London County Tramways Act (1896), and it became law at a time when the LCC had acquired all the London Street and the remaining North Metropolitan tracks which lay within its boundaries. However the Council was still not ready to become a fully fledged tramway operator and leased all these lines back to the North Metropolitan for a period of 14 years. The LCC was well aware of the appalling conditions endured by those who worked for the tramway companies and under the terms of the lease, it set down firm and fair conditions for staff employment including wages and hours worked. It also decided the fares to be charged.

On 1st January 1899 the London County Council went a stage further and actually ran a tram service by itself. This was over the 48 miles of track formerly owned by the London Tramways Company which, apart from a short stretch from Victoria to Vauxhall Bridge, were concentrated in south London. The newer of these lines were compulsory purchased, but the older (1870) routes were acquired either voluntarily or under some degree of pressure.

Gradually the LCC exercised its legal powers and took over and worked the services from the remaining horse tram companies within the County of London.

These were:

South London Tramways
22nd November 1902
South East Metropolitan Tramways
1st April 1902
London Deptford and Greenwich
7th July 1904
London Camberwell and Dulwich
15th August 1904
Woolwich & South East London
1st June 1905
North Metropolitan/London Street
1st April 1906 (on surrender of lease)
London Southern
2nd October 1906
Lea Bridge, Leyton & Walthamstow
(section within London boundary)
30th July 1908
Highgate Hill Tramways
24th August 1909

The LCC also acquired the Peckham & East Dulwich in August 1904 but immediately closed most of it, retaining only the two short sections essential for its large-scale electrification programme.

The first electrified LCC tram route, from Westminster Bridge to Tooting via Clapham, was ready in the spring of 1903, and on Friday 15th May the Prince and Princess of Wales (later King George V and Queen Mary) rode the entire route from Westminster to Tooting where they visited a new LCC housing estate, seeing at first hand the LCC's vision of the social nature of the tramcar – cheap council transportation to subsidised council housing. The LCC did not have the power to influence the location of jobs for its citizens, but it could house them in suitable locations and transport them to their places of work cheaply and efficiently by tram.

For almost the next 30 years, the LCC continued to expand its services and electrify lines. The massive electrification programme required over 1,800 electric tramcars, the last arriving in 1931 to work on new routes in south east London and replace cars from the early years of LCC electrification.

Naturally such a large fleet of trams merited a significant number of depots to house it, and the LCC operated 23 at some time or other. Very few of the horse car depots could be usefully converted to electric working, so new ones had to be built. The depots in the north area were at Bow, Hackney, Hampstead, Holloway, Kingsway Subway (closed 1908), Poplar and Stamford Hill. South of the river were Abbey Wood, Brixton Hill, Camberwell, Clapham, Hammersmith (situated north of the Thames but including in the LCC southern area for administrative purposes), New Cross, Norwood, Peckham (Rye Lane), Streatham (Telford Avenue) and Wandsworth. Many of these depots later housed trolleybuses and motor buses, and some survive today.

A few horse car depots were used for a time. The principal ones were Greenwich (Hoskins Street) which closed in 1905, two in Old Kent Road at Bowles Road and Leo Street, which also closed in 1905, and Plumstead which shut in 1913. The LCC also used the former horse car depot in Marius Road, Balham, to house its trailer cars from 1915. The depot closed when trailer operation ceased in 1922.

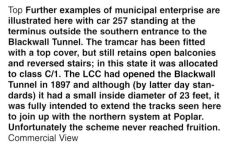

Top **Further examples of municipal enterprise are illustrated here with car 257 standing at the terminus outside the southern entrance to the Blackwall Tunnel. The tramcar has been fitted with a top cover, but still retains open balconies and reversed stairs; in this state it was allocated to class C/1. The LCC had opened the Blackwall Tunnel in 1897 and although (by latter day standards) it had a small inside diameter of 23 feet, it was fully intended to extend the tracks seen here to join up with the northern system at Poplar. Unfortunately the scheme never reached fruition.** Commercial View

Centre **The installation of conduit tracks was very labour intensive, involving as it did much excavation of the roadway and the soil beneath. Here outside St Alphege's Church, Greenwich we see the construction of the triangular junction for the Creek Bridge to Greenwich Church line which opened on 5th August 1911. The direct service from Greenwich to the 'Bridges' (Westminster and Blackfriars) had already commenced in January 1904 by way of the tracks in the foreground from Nelson Road into Greenwich High Road; these were to remain in use until the final day of London's tramways.** Commercial View

Right **The Elephant & Castle junction is pictured in 1904 with A class car 25 loading passengers whilst the conductor collects the fares on the top deck. B class car 104 moves sedately to the right of the scene, and it can be noted that the reversed stairs severely restricted the motorman's field of vision. Fitting of direct stairs to all cars in classes A to D began in 1906 and was completed in 1911.** LT Museum H/16381

LONDON'S TRAMWAYS

UNDER COVER ALL THE WAY

LONDON'S TRAMWAYS

UNKNOWN KING

DULL DAYS MADE BRIGHT IN THE MUSEUMS

The list below details the principal opening dates of the LCC electrified tram system:

15th May 1903	Westminster Bridge – Tooting (via Clapham)
	Blackfriars – Kennington Road (via Elephant & Castle)
	Waterloo Station – St Georges Circus
25th June	Kennington Church – Camberwell Green
7th July	Westminster Bridge Road – St Georges Circus
2nd August	Kennington Church – Vauxhall Cross
	Kennington Park Road – Brixton Road/(Handforth Road)
17th January 1904	Elephant & Castle – Greenwich (via Old Kent Road)
24th January	Elephant & Castle – New Cross (via Camberwell and Peckham)
21st May	Brixton Road – Brixton Station
30th May	Brixton Station – Water Lane
19th June	Water Lane – Streatham Library
1st August	St George's Circus – Southwark Bridge
	St George's Church – Elephant & Castle
	Southwark Bridge Road – Bricklayers Arms/Hop Exchange
	Westminster Bridge Road – Elephant and Castle
12th September	Bricklayers Arms – Tower Bridge
8th August 1905	Tooting (Totterdown Street) – Tooting Broadway
30th January 1906	New Cross Gate – Lewisham Obelisk
24th February	Islington (Angel) – Aldwych (via Kingsway Subway)
10th June	Lewisham – Rushey Green and Greenwich – Tunnel Avenue
18th June	Woolwich Road (Blackwall Lane) – Blackwall Tunnel
5th August	Tooting Broadway – Battersea (via Wandsworth)
	Vauxhall – Victoria
8th September	Vauxhall – Westminster (Stangate) (via Albert Embankment)
24th September	St George's Circus – Lambeth Bridge
13th October	Battersea (Princes Head) – Clapham Junction
	Battersea (Plough Road – Queens Road)
16th November	Islington (Angel) – Highbury Station
19th November	Camberwell Green – Dulwich Library (via Dog Kennel Hill)
15th December	Westminster Bridge – Blackfriars (via Victoria Embankment)
	Aldgate – Poplar (via Commercial Road)
22nd December	Battersea (Queens Road) – Victoria (via Nine Elms)
16th January 1907	Aldgate – Old Street – Clerkenwell – Holborn
4th February	Stangate – Westminster Bridge
6th February	Shoreditch – Stamford Hill (via Stoke Newington)
29th March	Moorgate – Old Street and Aldgate – London Docks
	Shoreditch – Great Eastern Street – Old Street
9th April	Shoreditch – Norton Folgate
	Shoreditch – Old Street
4th May	Lewisham – Lee Green
18th May	Shoreditch – Cambridge Heath (via Hackney Road)
29th July	Old Street – King's Cross (via Angel)
	Angel – St John's Street – Smithfield
13th October	Tooting Broadway – Longley Road (Mitcham boundary)
	Tooting Broadway – Tooting Junction Station
27th November	Islington (Angel) – Aldersgate (Goswell Road)
28th November	Highbury Station – Archway (via Holloway Road)
	East Dulwich (Goose Green) – Peckham Rye
5th December	King's Cross – Theobalds Road
4th April 1908	Lewisham – Greenwich and Vauxhall – Brixton (via Stockwell)
10th April	Aldwych (Kingsway Subway) – Victoria Embankment
17th April	Woolwich – Plumstead **
30th May	Hammersmith – Harlesden **
25th June	Whitechapel – Bow Bridge
9th July	Holloway (Nags Head) – Finsbury Park
26th July	Plumstead – Abbey Wood **
15th August	King's Cross – Holloway Road (via Caledonian Road)
21st November	Brixton – Camberwell Green (via Loughborough Jcn)**
10th December	Lea Bridge Road – Clapton (Leyton UDC Boundary)**
19th December	Dulwich Library – Forest Hill
23rd January 1909	Hammersmith – Putney Bridge (south side)**
25th January	Chelsea Bridge – Lavender Hill (via Queens Road)
11th April	Holloway – Camden Road Station
28th May	Camden Road Station – Tottenham Court Road
	King's Cross – Farringdon Road
30th May	Loughborough Junction – West Norwood (via Tulse Hill)**
22nd July	Tunnel Avenue – Charlton (Rainton Road)
	King's Cross – Mornington Crescent
31st July	Streatham Library – Norbury (part**)

	Islington Green – Essex Road (Balls Pond Road)
	Cambridge Heath – Hackney (via Mare Street)
10th September	Pancras Road – Hampstead Heath
14th September	Blackfriars – Southwark Bridge Road
23rd September	Vauxhall – Lavender Hill (via Wandsworth Road)
	Stamford Hill – Hackney (via Upper Clapton)
9th October	Lavender Hill – Clapham Junction (Falcon Road)
30th November	Camden Town – Chalk Farm (Ferdinand Street)
	Archway Tavern – Kentish Town
	Woolwich (Beresford Sq) – Woolwich Ferry (Nile Street)
15th December	Clapham Junction – Wandsworth (East Hill)
6th January 1910	Whitechapel Road – Cambridge Heath Road – Mare Street
26th February	Clapham (Plough) – Lavender Hill via Cedars Road
	Lewisham – Brockley Lane Station
25th March	Highgate (Archway) – Highgate High Street
14th May	Clerkenwell Road – Farringdon Street
1st July	Lower Clapton Road – Lea Bridge Road
23rd July	Woolwich (Beresford Square) – Eltham Church (Twin **)
5th November	Streatham – Tooting (Amen Cormer)
	Wandsworth (Garratt Lane) – Summerstown (Tooting)
25th February 1911	Brockley Lane Station – Forest Hill
	Tooley Street – Rotherhithe (Lower Road)
1st April	Charlton (Rainton Road) – Woolwich (Chapel Street)
20th May	Kentish Town – Parliament Hill Fields
22nd June	Rotherhithe (Lower Road) – Deptford (Creek Bridge)
	Battersea Park Road (Latchmere) – Chelsea (Kings Road)
5th August	Deptford (Creek Bridge) – Greenwich Church
30th January 1912	Putney Bridge – Wandsworth (Putney Bridge Road)**
	Hammersmith Broadway (Queen Street – Brook Green Road)**
5th April	Brixton Hill – Herne Hill **
1st July	Caledonian Road – Grays Inn Road (King's Cross link)
3rd August	Mildmay Park – Manor House (via Green Lanes)
3rd October	Lines either side of Creek Bridge joined up
26th November	Mildmay Park – Essex Road
	New North Road – Balls Pond Road
28th November	Tooley Street (Bermondsey Street – Stainer Street)
9th December	Tooley Street (Stainer Street – Duke Street Hill)
20th December	Poplar – Iron Bridge (West Ham boundary)
20th March 1913	Hackney (Mare Street) – Dalston Junction
	Norton Folgate – Liverpool Street Station
29th May	Forest Hill – Catford (Rushey Green)
26th July	Dorset Street from Essex Road to Southgate Road
6th March 1914	Dalston (Kingsland Road) – Islington (Southgate Road)
5th April	Woolwich Ferry – Woolwich (Chapel Street)
	Catford (Rushey Green) – Southend Village
25th June	Highbury Station – Canonbury Road – New North Road – Hoxton
16th July 1915	Wandsworth (Garratt Lane) – Putney Bridge Road
13th August	Forest Hill (Dartmouth Road – Park Road)
3rd June 1920	LCC and MET tracks joined at Stamford Hill
29th November	Lee Green – Eltham (Lyme Farm) (Twin **)
22nd March 1921	Eltham (Lyme Farm) – Eltham Church (Twin **)
28th July	Hackney (Well Street) – West India Docks Station **
4th August	Wandsworth (East Hill – High Street)
1st December	Hackney (Mare Street) – Junction to Graham Road and Well St
2nd May 1922	LCC and LUT tracks joined at Merton and Hammersmith
23rd March 1924	Stamford Hill – Seven Sisters Road **
14th July 1925	Southwark Bridge (southside – northside)
28th September 1926	Southend Village – Downham (Valeswood Road) (Part **)
4th November	LCC and SMET tracks joined at Tooting Junction
28th July 1927	Downham (Valeswood Road – Southover) **
15th November 1928	Downham (Southover) – Grove Park Station **
16th April 1931	LCC and LUT tracks joined at Summerstown
1st October	Eltham (Well Hall Road – Briset Road) **
30th June 1932	Eltham (Briset Road – Eltham Road 'Yorkshire Grey')**
	(** overhead power collection)

Authorised routes from Grove Park Station along Baring Road and along Westhorne Avenue northwards to Eltham Road at the 'Yorkshire Grey' junction had not been built by the time the LPTB took over, and were thus never constructed.

HAPPY DAYS AT THE ZOO
TRAVEL BY TRAMWAY

LONDON'S TRAMWAYS

F.P. Restall

CRICKET AT THE OVAL
TRAVEL BY TRAMWAY

In this view of New Cross Depot we observe lines of LCC trams featuring several C class cars with the first type of open balcony top cover. In the middle of the picture concealed by the car on the traverser is an eight-wheel D class tram. The traverser in the foreground was an essential piece of equipment in LCC depots and it provided efficient movement between the stabling roads in this large building which once held over 320 trams, making it the largest such facility in Great Britain.

THE LCC CARS (1900-1922)

The Watchword of the London County Council's tramway system seems to have been 'quality'. Quality of track, maintenance, staff, and cars. The LCC was also anxious that all firms it had contracted to work on its behalf, including those building tramcars and their associated equipments, adhered to strict working conditions for their employees, in respect of pay and hours worked.

The LCC was very influential in the design of its cars, eventually working in close association with several manufacturers like Hurst Nelson and Mountain & Gibson in the design of components like trucks.

Naturally a huge and standardised tramcar fleet like the one built up by the LCC required a well organised maintenance and overhauling system. In 1909 the Council opened its large new Central Repair Depot (CRD) in Woolwich Road, Charlton. Its opening coincided with the electrification of the Woolwich Road line. Of course the location benefited the larger southern LCC system rather than that running north of the River. Not until the works were enlarged in 1926 were north London's LCC cars sent south for refurbishment as the 'Pullmanisation' programme, which will be described later, got under way. Before that the CRD could only overhaul electrical components from the north area's trams because the only physical connection between the two systems – the Kingsway Subway – could only accommodate single-deck cars until 1931. Painting and body repair for north London trams was shared between Bow and Hampstead depots.

A rigid overhaul system was adopted by the LCC, with cars visiting Charlton, Bow, or Hampstead once a year, almost to the day. In 1931 this requirement was relaxed by the Metropolitan Police who changed the overhaul cycle to once every two years.

A thorough job was done. On arrival in the works, trucks and car body were separated and replaced straight away by newly overhauled equipment. All internal fittings were inspected and any requiring attention were removed; wiring was tested and the controllers inspected to see what level of maintenance was required. Latterly this process included the removal of seat cushions for re-upholstery. Meanwhile the trucks and motors removed from the tram on its arrival were being dismantled and made ready for overhaul. The newly assembled tram was then painted and varnished before being tested. It was then returned to its home depot. Blinds, route boards and number stencils were all manufactured at Charlton, which in 1932 employed 1,000 people from a wide area. A fleet of special trams was kept at the CRD to take them to and from the works at the start and end of the day.

The longevity of the LCC fleet, and the E/1 cars in particular, was due in no small measure to the care they received at Charlton. We now consider the LCC cars in detail.

CAR 101

Although not numerically the first car in the LCC fleet, car 101 was the first electric tram the Council acquired. This was in 1900, and the car had been used to demonstrate the conduit track system on the Westinghouse stand at the Tramways Exhibition held in London that year. The LCC having decided to adopt the conduit system for much of its tramway mileage later bought the tram and demonstrated it on a special section of track in the confines of Camberwell depot. No.101 was an open-top bogie car with a half-turn direct staircase. The G.F. Milnes & Co body was mounted on Brill 22E maximum traction trucks. In its later life the car was converted to single-deck and renumbered 110, taking the number of a B class tram badly damaged in an accident. (The B class car was later returned to service and numbered 101!). In its new form number 110 was a regular performer on the Queens Road (Battersea) local route until 1926 when it was withdrawn. It was eventually broken up at Charlton Works in 1931.

CLASS A	1-100	Total 100
CLASS B	102-201	Total 100
CLASS C	202-301	Total 100
CLASS D	302-401	Total 100

It was car 86 of the LCC's A class which carried the Prince and Princess of Wales when they formally opened the Council's electric system in May 1903. The car was painted in a special white livery bedecked with garlands and swags of greenery. Inside curtains and easy chairs ensured the royal party was spared the discomfort of wooden seats which awaited the citizens of London.

The first 400 electric cars ordered by the LCC comprised 200 bogie cars (Classes A and D) and 200 four-wheelers (classes B and C). They were delivered during 1903 and 1904 and their layout and design set the basic pattern for all the LCC's tramcars until the 'Pullmanisation' era of the mid-1920s. Even then very few cars built before 1906 benefited from even token attempts at comfort apart from fully enclosed top decks. Wooden seating formed by longitudinal side benches downstairs, and reversible garden-seats 'outside' was the order of the day. In the bogie cars, 28 passengers were accommodated downstairs and 38 on top, while the four-wheelers seated 22 downstairs and 34 on top. The lower decks of the bogie cars had four main windows each side, the ones nearest the saloon ends being divided into two. A strengthening partition was incorporated mid-way along the lower deck. The four-wheelers had three windows.

The upstairs was reached by a reversed staircase and was open to the skies. The upper deck side and rounded end panelling was topped with mesh to which a destination box was fixed at each end. At the top of the destination window in the box were three round coloured lenses. The coloured glass in each lens was changed as appropriate to form a code to denote the route the car was working. The design of the destination box was perpetuated right through until 1930, although the lights were no longer used after route numbers were introduced in 1913.

The livery chosen by the LCC was known as purple lake and primrose. The purple lake was applied to the waist panels the dash plates, staircase stringers and lower deck bulkheads. These areas where lined out in gold. The rocker panels and window pillars painted primrose, with the former being lined out in burnt sienna and black. Car numbers, and the large legend 'L.C.C.' on the side panels, were gold edged in black. The destination boxes were in polished wood. The lifeguard grilles below the dash and steps, together with the trucks, were painted red oxide. This livery was to remain standard on all LCC cars until the mid-1920s.

The bodywork for the first 400 cars was shared by four firms. The Preston based Electric Railway and Tramway Carriage Company built the entire A class and 80 of the class B cars; the remaining 20 Bs were ordered later from its parent company Dick Kerr but actually built by E.R.T.C.W. The four-wheel C class were all built by Brush of Loughborough. Brush also built the bodies for 75 of the D class (302-376), the other 25 (377-401) being supplied by the British Electric Car Company. The overall length of the A and D classes was 33ft 6ins, with that of the B and C cars, 28ft 9ins.

Electrical equipment was as follows:

Class A Mounted on Brill 22E bogie trucks, powered by Dick Kerr 30hp motors and Dick Kerr controllers. One truck on each car had the conduit plough carrier fitted to its inner end.

Class B Mounted on Brill 21E single trucks powered by Dick Kerr 25hp motors. The plough carrier was fitted centrally. Dick Kerr controllers.

Class C Mounted on Brill 21E single trucks powered by Westinghouse type 220 30hp motors. The cars had Westinghouse Controllers

Class D Mounted on McGuire bogie trucks powered by Westinghouse type 220 30hp motors and controllers.

All the cars were built to work on the newly constructed conduit lines in south London. Initially the As were used on the routes from Westminster Bridge – Tooting (via Clapham), Waterloo – St Georges Circus, and Blackfriars – Kennington, all of which began operation on 15th May 1903. The following month (25th June) brought the first Bs into use on the route from Kennington Church – Camberwell Green. Some were also fitted with gripper equipment specially for use on the Brixton – Streatham cable route. This proved to be a mistake as the weight of the cars put too much strain on the cable. The planned dismantling of the cable equipment, which had been expected to see a few more years of service, and its replacement by standard conduit was hastily brought forward.

The C class first saw service on the newly electrified routes from the Elephant & Castle to Greenwich, New Cross and Deptford, which began operation in January 1904. Two years later some of them were transferred to work on the Camberwell Green – Dulwich Library service which traversed the steep Dog Kennel Hill. The 100 bogied D-class cars were initially used on the New Cross and Greenwich routes, to augment the Cs during peak hours.

Class B car 106 now sports a fully enclosed top deck with direct stairs. Note the three lights above the indicator box, these were illuminated in different colour codes to denote separate services – this particular service, Catford to Westminster via Walworth Road, would have shown Green, Blue, Green. From 1913 they were replaced by service numbers. Car 106 later became a snow broom and was selected for preservation. It was subsequently restored to open top condition by the London County Council Tramways Trust, and the vehicle now resides at the National Tramway Museum, Crich, Derbyshire.

Dog Kennel Hill rises to a gradient of 1 in 11 near the summit and the motorman of C class 235 is probably aware of this fact as he ascends on his journey to Victoria. This view dates from November 1906. In order to get round the restriction of only one car on the up or downhill track at any one time, work was undertaken in 1912 on two additional tracks.

D class car 314 is very near the end of its working life as it passes the site works of the new Lambeth Bridge, shortly after the old structure was demolished in 1929. The original, purple lake livery on this tram had now weathered to a dull brown, however, the vehicle has still been well maintained. Note the unusual McGuire maximum traction trucks and the truck mounted plough carrier. *G.N.Southerden*

By 1905, with its electrification programme in full swing, the LCC was drawing up plans for a standard bogie tramcar, and placed an order for 300. The advent of the new generation of cars, which appeared during the mid-Edwardian period, influenced the later appearance of the first generation, the A, B, C and D classes. By 1907 all had received covered tops. The first cars to be fitted with them were Cs, and the tops were supplied by the firm of Milnes Voss, who became one of the chief suppliers of this now seemingly indispensable commodity. Eventually the LCC built its own top covers. This was to prove an intermediate step because it was soon decided to fit fully enclosed canopies at either end of the top decks. Finally the odd looking reverse staircases, which had caused problems, not least obstructing drivers' left-side vision, were replaced on older cars by a 'direct' version. The upper decks were also fitted with draught screens at the top of the stairs.

The rebuilding work was carried out in stages, and the whole programme was complete by the onset of the Great War. The bogie A and D cars saw yeoman service on the LCC system, spending much of their lives at New Cross and Wandsworth depots. They were withdrawn between 1929 and 1931 when new cars were delivered.

The B and C classes were less popular. By 1914 most of the Bs had been relegated to rush hour duties at New Cross and Streatham depots. Others were put into store. Some Bs were sold during the War to other UK operators including Sheffield, Rotherham, Newport, Southampton, and to Bexley Council whose system joined the LCC's at Plumstead. During the 1920s, when many of the Bs were withdrawn, 21 were converted to single-deck snowbrooms, to emerge during the depths of winter to sweep snow from the tracks lest it penetrate the conduit slots. Many were active in this capacity right up until the last winter of London's trams, 1951/52.

The Cs enjoyed a more active life than the Bs, and proved useful on the Dulwich hilly routes for which 60 were fitted with enhanced track brakes. One problem with the Cs as time passed was their unfortunate tendency to buck and sway when in motion, but this was overcome by equipping the cars with hydraulic suspension apparatus around 1926. Eighteen Cs were adapted for winter use as snow ploughs, 17 being converted to single-deckers for the purpose. One class C car was utilised as a stores van.

When the LCC projected new lines to Brockley and Forest Hill, agreement was reached with the local council to place the 'up' (London bound) line in Shardeloes Road and the 'down' line in Malpas Road. This view of car 229 dates from shortly after the opening of Shardeloes Road in February 1910. The use of single track in adjacent streets was pioneered by several London tramway operators, and many of these one way arrangements became permanent for other traffic as well as tramcars. The Shardeloes Road/Malpas Road layout was finally abandoned by London Transport in April 1952.

Every section of tram route had to be inspected by the Board of Trade before passenger services could commence and here, outside the Rose of Lee public house in Lee High Road in April 1907, class E car No. 497 takes the official party along the new section of route from Lewisham Obelisk to Lee Green, which opened the following month. The onlookers are no doubt marvelling at this novel intrusion into their horse dominated world.

CLASS E   402-551   Total 150
                     602-751   Total 150

The 300 E class cars, which the LCC ordered in August 1905, were the first of what came to be regarded as the standard LCC bogie tramcar. They set new standards in design, having fully enclosed top decks and direct staircases from new. As we have seen, their arrival heralded the retrospective updating of the A - D classes. The E class cars sat lower on the rails than the earlier cars in their rebuilt form. An A class car with rebuilt top deck was 16ft 4ins high, but an E was only 15ft 9ins. The length of the Es was 33ft 6ins, the same as the earlier bogie cars.

The first 150 Es had bodies by Hurst Nelson of Motherwell. Hurst Nelson were no doubt pleased to receive such a huge order since tramcar building was beginning to decline with most of the country's new electric tramway systems up and running by this time. The bodies were of a sturdier construction than the A and D offerings, in having a steel underframe. The strengthening lower deck central partition was not therefore needed.

The seating layout was the same as the earlier bogie cars, except the Es carried 10 more passengers. Thirty were accommodated downstairs with 46 riding on top. Mountain Gibsons provided the trucks to a design produced in consultation with the LCC. The first 25 Es (402-426) were powered by 30hp Westinghouse 220 motors while the remainder were fitted with more powerful 42hp Westinghouse 220 sets. All had Westinghouse controllers.

The first 150 Es came down to London from Scotland by rail in the early months of 1906. They were delivered in two halves, top deck on one wagon, bottom deck on the next,

and assembled at New Cross depot. The delivery schedule imposed on Hurst Nelson by the LCC required the Scottish firm to supply the first 80 cars by mid-February with the remaining 70 by mid-April. This caused some consternation in the Motherwell factory which normally provided a quarter of the output the LCC had ordered over the same period. Nevertheless the company met the target, and for its pains was rewarded with an order for a further 150 E class cars for delivery between July and October 1906. These were identical to the first batch except that some were fitted with upper deck draught screens from new. Most of the remaining Es received the screens by 1912.

The first batch of Es were used to upgrade the Tooting service, while the second inaugurated the LCC's double-deck electric services north of the river, working on routes from Poplar and Stamford Hill depots. The first of these began operation on 15th December 1906 when E class cars from Poplar depot began running between Aldgate and Poplar (Iron Bridge). On 6th February 1907 Stamford Hill's Es took over the route from Stamford Hill to Shoreditch.

Apart from some equipment alteration, including the fitting of more powerful 42hp motors between 1912 and 1923 to the cars not fitted with them when new, the Es stayed much the same throughout their lives. They were all treated to more comfortable interiors and a new colour scheme under the 1926 Pullmanisation programme, described later. A few also received a redesigned destination box with a deeper screen enabling three lines of route information to be displayed. These were most often found on the routes to Hampstead. The large display area occupied the space formerly used by the three coloured

route indicator lights. The class lasted until the arrival of trolleybuses in the mid-1930s. Scrapping of the Es began in 1935 and all had gone by early 1939, except one. The lower deck of number 420 was fitted with a new top deck following an accident in 1930. It was later fitted with the electrical equipment from an E/1 class car, number 1597, damaged beyond repair in an accident, and took its number. It was fitted with vestibule screens, and thus looked just like any other standard London tramcar. What gave away its Edwardian ancestry were the narrow corner pillars on the lower saloon. It managed to escape the breaker's until January 1951.

CLASS F   552-567   (Total 16)
CLASS G   568-601   (Total 34)

The F and G classes were the LCC's original single-deck tramcars built in 1906 specifically to run through the Kingsway Subway. The 16 Fs were built by the United Electric Car Company and the Gs by Brush. Both classes were very similar, the most noticeable difference between them being that the G class had glazed bulkheads. The 36-seater all-steel cars were 33ft 6ins in length and 11ft high. They had five windows each side, and clerestory roofs. The bodies were of an all-steel construction to make them as fire resistant as possible in the subterranean world they were built to inhabit. Both types sat on Mountain and Gibson trucks; the Fs being powered by Dick Kerr motors and controllers, while the Gs were propelled by Westinghouse equipment. The Fs and Gs spent all their lives running on 'conduit' routes, although the Gs had the necessary equipment to enable trolley poles to be fitted. They were all withdrawn in 1930 when the Kingsway Subway closed for enlargement.

CLASS E/1

752-1426 (Total 675)
1477-1676 (Total 200)
1727-1851 (Total 125)

The success of the E class led to LCC designers producing a revised version late in 1906 in anticipation of continued electrification schemes within the County, and through running agreements with its neighbours. The main difference between the Es and E/1s was that the latter had a slightly longer lower deck resulting in wider corner pillars downstairs, and dash plates which jutted out slightly below the limits of the upper deck. The longer wooden longitudinal benches in the larger lower saloon enabled two additional passengers to be accommodated, thus increasing the overall capacity to 78.

The E/1 proved to be the ubiquitous tramcar of London. An eventual 1,000 were built for the LCC, the main batches arriving between 1907 and 1912, with further deliveries in 1921/1922. Such was their success that similar cars were built in later years for the council services of Croydon, East Ham, Walthamstow and West Ham.

The bulk of the E/1s were bodied by Hurst Nelson. The firm built 752-1001 (1907), 1052-1226 (1908), 1227-1426 (1909) and 1727-1776 (1921). The LCC constructed fifty (1002-1051) during 1907/08 at its Union Road works in Leytonstone, which it had taken over from the North Met in 1906. The works remained under LCC control until the expiry of the lease in 1911. The remaining batches of E/1s came from Brush, which built 1477-1676 (1911/12) and 1777-1851 (1922).

The cars built at Union Road contained many steel components supplied by outside manufacturers, including Hurst Nelson, who provided the trucks for both this batch and the E/1s they themselves built in 1908, 1052-1226. Mountain & Gibson trucks had been used on Hurst Nelson's earlier E/1s, Brush built cars (1477-1676) had trucks by Heenan & Froude, of Worcester, and Hurst Nelson's final batch of E/1s (1727-1776) had the company's own design trucks fitted.

All E/1s built before 1920 were powered by the standard Westinghouse 220 42hp motors, and had Westinghouse control equipment. The post-1920 Hurst Nelson batch were powered by 50hp Metrovick 121 motors, while the Brush built 1777-1851 had Dick Kerr 31C sets giving 63hp, and English Electric control equipment. The new cars were thus faster than the older models. Such was the success of the higher powered cars that in 1923 the LCC bought 100 sets of new 60hp motors and controllers from Metropolitan Vickers (MV), with 200 more sets (100MV and 100 English Electric) coming in 1924. These greatly improved the performance of the older E/1s to which they were fitted, and put the cars on a competitive footing during the period of fierce competition from the buses. The motors displaced from the E/1s were fitted to the even older A and D classes enabling their own performance to be somewhat improved.

The ten year gap between the main deliveries and the 1921/22 batches did not mean the LCC had run short of ideas. In 1920 a competition had been proposed to help find a new design of tram, but as time was pressing and new trams were needed quickly the tried and tested formula was dusted off.

The E/1s were spread far and wide around the LCC system and reached all corners of the London tramway network. Most were eventually fitted with trolley poles for use on routes where they were required to work over other London systems, none of which operated the conduit track power supply principle. Cars 1350-1353 were fitted with double trolleys for the twin-wire Eltham route. E/1s could be seen as far from the County of London as Barking, Barnet, Enfield, Ilford and Waltham Cross, as well as in Croydon, Walthamstow and Edgware. They were the backbone of the LCC and subsequent London Transport tram fleets. All received redesigned interiors and the new red and pale yellow livery after 1926, and many were subsequently rebuilt and extensively modernised. As a result some were active until almost the very end of London's trams in 1952.

Above **Car 1076 and its crew pose at Church Street, Enfield before it begins the long return trip to Tottenham Court Road. Class E/1 cars were used on this joint service over MET tracks. In reponse to the loss of traffic due to motor bus competition, the LCC concluded agreements with other London tramway operators, and through services were operated in many areas of the capital.**

Below **Car 870 is an early example of what was to become London's 'standard' design of tramcar and it is pictured in Highgate shortly after the delivery in 1907. The LCC was alive to the revenue possibilities of advertising and the Albion House Clothing Co. would have paid £20 per annum for this whole, straight side advertisement on a bogie car. Commercial opportunities were also exploited by the use of transparencies on the ventilator top lights of the lower saloon.**

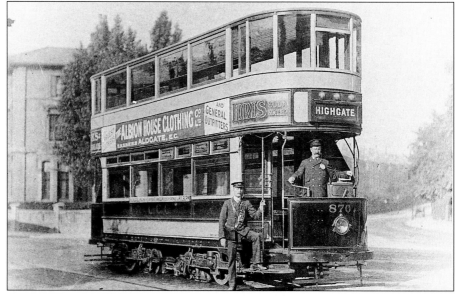

E/1 class trams were also to be found beyond the traditional LCC area as is proved by car 1185, caught on camera at Bakers Arms Corner, Leyton about 1911. At this location other tracks led to the neighbouring Walthamstow system and to the edge of Epping Forest. Trams also worked south from here through the closely packed streets of West Ham and onwards to termini adjoining the vast London docklands.

Stiff competition for the trams in Stanstead Road, Catford as a rival motorbus tries to poach customers. C class car 204 is now in its final state and is shown working service 58 to Victoria. This was one of the services to tackle the steeply graded Dog Kennel Hill.

Another tramcar employed to climb Dog Kennel Hill was this M class car 1680 seen at Goose Green on 17th March 1928. These sturdy vehicles were a four-wheel version of the standard E/1 class. Note the fares board below the top deck windows which offers a bargain ride at midday for only tuppence. G.N.Southerden

CLASS M   1427 (Total 1)
                      1428-1476 (Total 49)
                      1677-1726 (Total 50)

By 1910 it had become apparent that more four-wheel cars would be required, chiefly to operate on the newly electrified lines to Highgate Hill, between Woolwich and Eltham, and generally to augment the services on other hilly and lightly used routes in the LCC area. The result – class M, a four-wheel shortened version of the E/1. The class even had a prototype car, 1427, which was built by the LCC at its Leytonstone works in 1908. Oddly the car was to have been an open-topper, but the decision was later taken to build the car with fully enclosed top deck. Several tests were carried out on 1427, which was fitted with a special conduit slot brake at each end for working on the Highgate Hill route. Experiments continued, and the car eventually received a new truck and a centrally mounted plough carrier designed by Hurst Nelson. Westinghouse supplied the controllers and 220 series motors for this and the subsequent production M class. The body was supported with the aid of swing bolsters, like the E/1s. Once the design was perfected, Hurst Nelson received orders for 49 bodies and trucks. The bodies were identical to the E/1s, but with three windows each side instead of four, and thicker lower deck corner pillars. Sixty-two passengers could be seated in an M, 24 downstairs and 38 upstairs.

The first ten of the Hurst Nelson batch (1428-1437) were used on the Woolwich to Eltham service, which at the time it opened on 23rd July 1910 was separated from the main part of the LCC's electrification system, not becoming joined to the remainder until April 1914. This route was unique because the trams took their power from twin overhead wires and not from the usual conduit slots. This was due to the proximity of the Greenwich Observatory, where it was feared that the earth return current from the trams would disturb the precision instruments within. The twin-wire system on the route continued until the Observatory moved in 1927.

The remaining Ms from the first batch (1438-1476) stocked the Highgate Hill services. The final batch of 50 (1677-1726) built in July 1910 by Brush were used on the south side hilly routes centred on Dog Kennel Hill. The M class received 'Pullmanisation' treatment in the mid-1920s, including the new livery. Some Ms were transferred to the LCC-operated services in Leyton in 1930/31, and others were moved to Bexley on the formation of London Transport in 1933. Scrapping began in 1936 and continued until the last was withdrawn, at West Ham in 1938. Three M cars, 1441, 1444 and 1446, were 'stretched' in 1932/33 and converted to bogie cars, being reclassified ME/3. No. 1446 was later renumbered 1370, 1441 was destroyed in the war, but the other two survived until 1951.

Below **Twin trolley wires were employed at the behest of Greenwich Observatory, because it was alleged that stray electrical currents from a conventional single wire overhead would affect sensitive scientific instruments. M Class 1433 is seen at Woolwich Common.**

The board FULL above the motorman's head says it all as the rush hour one evening in 1913 is enlivened by the appearance of a packed E/1 car plus trailer. The operation of coupled cars on the Embankment to Tooting circular services was at first successful, but after the First World War it became apparent that the experiment had produced mixed results and the LCC announced on 19th April 1923 that trailers would be withdrawn from all services using the Victoria Embankment. LT Museum

| THE LCC | T1-8 (Total 8) |
| TRAILERS | T9-158 (Total 150) |

Around 1910 the LCC considered the vexed problem of how to provide extra capacity during the short period in the working day when trams got very busy, without having too many surplus trams standing around doing nothing at quieter times. The answer was thought to lie in the trailer car concept, which was already being used to great effect in many Continental cities. Board of Trade sanction was required before trailers could be used and the LCC had received permission in 1905 to run trailer stores vans, but only at the dead of night. At that time the idea was to run trailers through the Kingsway Subway by coupling together two single-deck cars, and although some experiments were carried out such a service never ran.

In 1912 the LCC received full powers to run trailers and quickly set about undertaking trials on the Woolwich – Eltham route

with a trailer rebuilt from a NorthMet horse car coupled to a standard M class tram. In March 1913 the first trailer service began on the Woolwich – Eltham route using three ex-horse cars. From July 1913, and for the next five years, these three, together with five others, worked on the Merton to Embankment route. As rebuilt the cars had deeper upper deck panels and steel under frames. They remained open-top. The experiment was deemed a success and the Council ordered 150 purpose-built open-top trailers from Brush in July 1914, for use on five routes in south London. The Brush cars had four windows either side and large destination blinds at each end.

The routes selected for trailer operation were not only heavily used in peak times, they also incorporated loop terminals, so the need for awkward reversing and shunting movements at termini were lessened. A tram/trailer combination, when it involved an E or E/1 car could carry 120 people, or up to 160 following the lifting of standing restrictions, a boon during World War 1. The problem was that the tram/trailers were slow in service, and when peacetime conditions returned and traffic settled down, they proved no match for the faster E/1s which arrived in the early twenties. As a result trailer operation was gradually phased out with the last running on route 70 (London Bridge – Greenwich) in April 1924. The ex-horse cars were scrapped, but the newer ones found a new lease of life in various parts of the country as chalets or greenhouses.

THE PETROL ELECTRIC CARS

Some of the local authorities in the LCC area objected strongly to the Council's intention to run electric tramcars in their localities, and constantly voiced their opposition to any proposals to introduce them. In particular three Metropolitan boroughs in east London, Hackney, Stepney and Bethnal Green opposed the electrification of the 2.75-mile line from South Hackney to West India Docks, because the LCC planned to use the overhead system of power collection on it. The LCC looked at ways of overcoming the problem and eventually decided to operate the route using three specially constructed petrol electric tramcars. The vehicles were adapted from ex-North Metropolitan horse cars. They had new, longer, platforms fitted at each end and deeper upper deck side panels. They remained open-top. The cars were powered by a 40hp petrol engine attached to a generator positioned under the stairs at one end; the engines were water-cooled. These strange vehicles, which could be driven from either end just like an ordinary tram, did see service, but never on the route they were built for. They started work in May 1913 on route 70 (London Bridge – Greenwich), but proved too noisy and expensive to run for the LCC to contemplate building any more. They were withdrawn after about six months of use, the bodies removed, and the chassis confined to shunting trailer cars in the Marius Road depot in Balham. They were scrapped in 1922 when the trailer car operation from Marius Road ended.

THE KINGSWAY SUBWAY AND THE BATTLE FOR CENTRAL LONDON

The geography of London, with the River Thames cutting a watery swath through the middle, meant that the embryo LCC tram network would for ever be in two distinct halves. But it wasn't just the Thames that formed a barrier to it linking up its services to the north and south, but the hostile attitude of the Cities of London and Westminster.

Nevertheless in 1898 the LCC saw an opportunity to bring its embryo tram network closer to the West End while at the same time unifying its own territory link up the two halves of London on each side of the Thames if only by a thin strand. The LCC was unable to exercise authority over either Westminster, which it did control, or the ancient City of London, which it did not, on matters of road transport, because it was not the designated highway authority; that power rested with the individual local councils.

But at the close of the nineteenth century the Council produced plans for a majestic new thoroughfare running down from Theobalds Road to the Strand, finishing in a crescent both ends of which ran into the Strand at its eastern end. This was Kingsway and Aldwych, and it was to be created by demolishing and clearing an area of slums. As the roadway was to be a completely new feature it presented an interesting possibility – the tramway could run beneath it in a subway. The LCC had considered the idea of tram subways as a way of winning its battle to serve the City and West End, but the new plan gave them a real opportunity to make a subway an integral part of a new development area thereby reducing its overall costs.

A delegation was despatched to America and visited tramway subways in New York and Boston. The group liked what it saw and detailed plans were drawn up for the subway which was to run beneath the whole length of Kingsway, under Aldwych to emerge on the Embankment beneath Waterloo Bridge. The idea was to link the existing tram service, which terminated at the southern end of Westminster Bridge, by securing powers for it to cross the bridge and link up along the Embankment with some trams running through the new subway and on to the northern system.

The subsequent parliamentary debate over the plan resulted in approval being given only for the subway as far as Aldwych. Thus the whole exercise was denied one of its most important features. The grand LCC scheme of running trams across Westminster Bridge and along the Embankment into the new subway and off to the north met considerable opposition. So a dead end subway was built with stations at Holborn and Aldwych. The subway was ready in 1904, but the LCC had not built the lines to link it with services to the north, which were still being operated under lease by the North Metropolitan using horse trams. In 1904 the LCC decided to buy out the Northmet's lease, which had another six years to run. Conditions for the buy-out took a long time to agree, but the LCC eventually won the day and assumed direct control of north London's entire tram system on 1st April 1906, by which time the Council had built a new stretch of line along Rosebery Avenue to the Angel, Islington, to link up with its new subway. The tunnels of the Kingsway Subway echoed to the sound of its first specially built single deck trams on 24th February 1906, but they ran only as far as Aldwych.

Later in 1906 the LCC won its right to operate trams across Westminster Bridge and along the Embankment, which it did from December 1906. Extending the subway and linking up the lines took another sixteen months and finally on 10th April 1908 the LCC launched an electric tram service from Kennington to Highbury over Westminster Bridge and under the strip of London which divided the shop and theatre world of the west end from the legal and commercial world of the Inns of Court and the City. Victoria, Moorgate, Aldwych and the north side of Southwark Bridge were the nearest the Council's trams ever got to the two most popular traffic objectives in southern England.

Trams had reached as close to central London as they ever would. The hostility which Train had encountered forty years before prevailed into the twentieth century. To counter it the LCC announced plans to run its own buses connecting the glittering thoroughfares of the West End with its tram termini on the fringes. Matters came to a head in March 1902 when the omnibus fraternity, fearing for the sanctity of its revenue, took the LCC to court over its plans and forced the Council to scrap them.

Above and Below **The Kingsway Subway before and after opening. Construction work is still proceeding in the view above and the demolition needed each side of the road to permit its widening here has not yet been replaced by the new buildings. In the lower view, an inspector stands at the entrance to the newly opened subway to see that no pedestrians or other traffic gain access.**

Above **The impressive, original portal of the Kingsway Subway is shown to full advantage in this scene taken on 24th April 1908, just two weeks after the inauguration of through services via this southern entrance and the Embankment. A very ornate street lamp bears the warning notice BEWARE CARS CROSSING. As traffic increased at this spot, an official was permanently stationed here. He would walk out into the carriageway with a red flag to alert other road users to the presence of an emerging tramcar.** Commercial View

Left **Car 556 slows for a trailing crossover in the Kingsway Subway. Other constructional details of the roof and walls will be noticed, together with the handily placed refuges for permanent way workers and LCC staff who had to dodge out of the way of the trams. In the 1911 Tramways Guide an intensive service at a seven minute interval was advertised on the Highbury to Tower Bridge and Angel to Vauxhall routes through the subway.** Commercial View

Car 552 was the prototype F class vehicle and is seen at Aldwych station. An official inspection of Kingsway Subway on 29th December 1905 was carried out using this tram. This view was probably captured on film shortly after 24th February 1906 when public service in the subway began.

THE MUNICIPAL TRAMS

The authorities running the Counties of London, Middlesex, and Hertfordshire were the only ones to take an active involvement in running trams for their inhabitants. The County authorities in Essex, Kent, and Surrey made no such move. There was no reason why they should, because apart from London and Middlesex the only tramways in Britain owned by any County Councils were the very small sections near Gloucester, Swansea, and Uddington (Scotland). It was left to the local councils around London, using the powers which they already had for compulsory purchase 21 years after the original construction, to buy out horse tram companies, and to plan and operate additional routes of their own. There was no lack of interest.

ESSEX
(Barking, East Ham, Ilford, Leyton, Walthamstow and West Ham)
By 1900 residential and industrial growth had pushed far into Metropolitan Essex, the south western corner of the county which lay within the Metropolitan Police District, and the local authorities were actively promoting plans for tramway schemes within their respective boundaries. The area was not devoid of tram services. The North Metropolitan was already active in Essex with its horse lines from Aldgate to Leytonstone and Manor Park, and the Lea Bridge, Leyton and Walthamstow was running services further north.

The area had seen experimentation in mechanical traction too, with the North Met's battery tram experiments between 1887/88. Not surprisingly, the plans drawn up by the respective municipal Councils were all based on electric traction.

EAST HAM (1901)
East Ham Council takes the award for opening the first municipal electric tramway service in the London area. This momentous event took place on 22nd June 1901, barely three months after the LUT had run London's first electric tram, but three years after East Ham Council had secured the powers to run trams in the borough.

Three routes opened on the first day:
Manor Park - Ilford UDC boundary;
Manor Park - Beckton Park (Manor Way);
Upton Park (Boleyn) - Barking boundary.
Even before services began the Council was granted powers to build more lines. On 27th March 1902 a short extension north from Manor Park opened as far as the City of London Cemetery. Later that year, on 29th November, a line from High Street North to Green Street via Plashet Grove opened. On 10th March 1903 the City of London Cemetery line was extended to Wanstead Park Avenue, and the Beckton Park line was extended south to the Royal Albert Dock. In 1904, when neighbouring West Ham's system opened to the joint boundary at Boleyn, the two authorities entered into through running between Canning Town and the Barking boundary, beginning a co-operation which would endure for almost thirty years. Also in 1904 the Urban District of East Ham was elevated to borough status.

Services began with a fleet of 15 four-wheelers. The first six cars arrived in March 1901, and all 15 were in stock by early May. They were 56 seater open-toppers with Electric Railway & Tramway Carriage Works bodies painted in a dark brown and cream livery. The dash plates and waist panels were in dark brown as were the staircases which were of the reversed type.

Such was the success of the first three East Ham routes that five identical cars (16-20) were ordered soon after services began, with another ten (21-30) being delivered in 1902. A further five (31-35) arrived in 1903 to increase the service on the Royal Albert Dock route. East Ham's pioneering success also spurred on other metropolitan authorities to electrify their horse car tracks and build extensions. In 1904 East Ham began through running on some routes in neighbouring West Ham. Later in the year five covered-top tram-cars (36-40) were ordered with 56 seat United Electric Car Co. bodies. They were delivered in 1905. Trucks, motors and controllers were the same as the original 35 except that they had a wheelbase of 7ft instead of 6ft, and although the cars had covered tops they retained reversed stairs. In 1910 a further five (41-45) were delivered. Their wheelbase was 7ft 6ins, six inches longer than 36-40, and this time direct stairs were included. They were also fitted with LCC conduit equipment for working the through services between Aldgate and Barking or Ilford.

Above **Looking very similar to the standard LCC E/1 class trams, we observe one of the 20 East Ham bogie cars supplied by Hurst Nelson in 1927/28. It is pictured at Stratford Broadway on joint service 63 which involved trams from three operators: the LCC, West Ham Corporation and East Ham Corporation. The last half mile of the route served Ilford Corporation territory, although none of that operator's cars ever participated on the trunk service to London. Car 56, shown here in its original livery, later passed to London Transport and was renumbered 86. It survived in south London until the end in July 1952. R.Elliott**

In April 1905 East Ham joined up its tracks to those of Ilford UDC at Ilford Hill and began running right to Ilford Broadway. A similar arrangement was agreed with Barking Council later in 1905, with the result that East Ham and West Ham cars now ran through to Barking Broadway. On 1st November 1907 a joint service between East Ham Town Hall and Stratford, via Plashet Grove and Green Street began, made possible by the joining up of the two authorities tracks at Green Street.

East Ham's trams worked from a depot in Nelson Street behind the Town Hall. By 1908 all main thoroughfares in the borough were served by electric trams except for the section of Romford Road which cut across the borough from west to east. This was still the province of the North Metropolitan's now seemingly outdated and very isolated horse car service, still trundling between Manor Park and Green Street. The LCC was already electrifying its east London routes and the idea of a through running agreement between East and West Ham and the LCC on a service to Aldgate was very attractive to the two authorities. East Ham therefore made representations to North Met to purchase its lines, a sum of £8,000 eventually changing hands in June 1908. After relaying the track and erecting the overhead a joint East Ham/West Ham service between Ilford and Bow Bridge began on 10th March 1909; four months later on 31st July the LCC began running electric trams between Bow Bridge and Aldgate. The three authorities now began discussing the possibilities of through running and following the adaptation of the necessary number of East and West Ham trams to work over the LCC's conduit system, a joint service between Aldgate and Ilford Broadway began on 11th May 1910.

Meanwhile the Corporation had been retrospectively fitting top covers to 31 of its earliest cars; the exceptions were 1, 2, 4, and 7. Fifteen trams were modified with conduit equipment in readiness for the through running services to Aldgate in 1910. These were additional to the five new cars (Nos 41-45) which had conduit equipment from new. They were also fitted with direct staircases since the LCC would not allow trams with reversed stairs on its tracks. The wheelbase of the cars concerned was increased to 7ft 6ins. Despite being equipped to run on conduit lines the East Ham trams were slower than West Ham's or the LCC's so they were fitted with General Electric 200 type 35 hp motors to improve their performance. In 1915 East Ham purchased a tram from the Barking Council fleet. This 54 seater Brush-bodied car had been built in 1911 and became East Ham's number 46.

By the end of the War many of East Ham's 46 trams, including some of the shorter wheelbase cars which had received top deck covers between 1905-1909, were in poor condition due largely to no compensatory strengthening work having been done when the tops were originally fitted. The situation placed the purchase of new trams high on the Council's agenda, but funds were very limited. It was decided to scrap nine of the cars in the poorest condition, renovate twenty of the original batches of 1901-1903 trams,

The East Ham tramcar of 1901 was a traditional 'Preston' product of the era with a Brill 21E truck, reversed stairs and open top. All over the country identically built vehicles were ushering in new municipal and company tramways. Many Londoners at the turn of the century paid day trips to East Ham just to admire these new wonders of transport science.
Tramway and Railway World

Car 16 rests at the terminal siding opposite St John's Church, Stratford Broadway, with a West Ham vehicle bringing up the rear. Note the distinctive shape of the domed roof top cover with the six-window layout. Many East Ham cars retained reversed stairs until they were scrapped by London Transport. One can only assume that the officials from the Metropolitan Police who objected to reversed stairs on LCC cars were unwilling or unable to stroll 'out east' and inspect what was going on in the Nelson Street depot of East Ham Corporation Tramways!
H.A.Whitcombe

and acquire some new ones, beginning in 1920 with an order for six (47-52) from Brush. These were 58 seaters built to the pre-war layout, except that the upper-deck roof was flat instead of domed, with an open balcony and direct stairs. They ran on Brush 21E trucks powered by GE 200K motors. The first arrived in spring 1921, and were followed by four others (37-40) in 1922. Some renumbering took place with the arrival of the second batch, three of which took the numbers of older scrapped cars, At the same time the former 38 became No.8. Six other cars were also renumbered, including 51 and 52 which became 36 and 46 respectively soon after delivery.

By 1925 much of East Ham was served by buses, and some were creaming off profitable traffic from the trams. For a time the Council toyed with the idea of running trolleybuses to challenge them, but the decision was finally taken to buy new large capacity bogie cars, ten of which (51-60) were ordered at the beginning of 1927. The LCC was already insisting that new trams bought for through running services should conform to the standards set by its E/1 cars, so the new cars, built by Brush, were virtually identical to the E/1s, which had first appeared in 1907, except they had a roller blind route number box. The smart new trams accommodated 71 passengers on cushion seating. They were fitted with double trolley poles and conduit gear, and ran on standard LCC maximum traction class 4 trucks powered by BTH 509c motors. A further ten (6170) were ordered in 1928. The bogie cars worked almost exclusively on Aldgate routes 63 and 67. When London Transport closed East Ham depot in September 1933, the bogie cars moved to the ex-LCC Bow depot, continuing to work on the 63. LT fitted them with windscreens and standard plough carrying equipment between 1938 and 1940, moving them over to south London, where most were still running on the last day of London's trams in 1952.

ILFORD (1903)

Further east, East Ham was bounded by the Urban Districts of Ilford and Barking. Both authorities were planning tramways as the nineteenth century drew to a close. In 1899 Ilford had obtained powers under the 1870 Tramways Act for four sections of route:

Ilford Broadway - Barkingside;
Ilford Broadway - Chadwell Heath;
Ilford Broadway - Loxford Bridge
(Barking UDC boundary);
Ilford Broadway - East Ham boundary at the foot of Ilford Hill.

However it was only when neighbouring East Ham opened its tram services in 1901 that local pressure in Ilford forced the Council to start track laying, which began early in 1902. The first routes, from Ilford Hill to Barkingside and to Chadwell Heath began on 14th March 1903. The depot was in Ley Street, on the Barkingside route.

The tracks down Ilford Lane to Loxford Bridge carried their first passenger tramcars a couple of months later on 27th May 1903. An enduring element of Ilford Council's Tramways policy was never to enter into through running agreements with neighbouring operators. Most operators viewed such arrangements as essential in staving off competition from the buses which were not hampered by restrictive barriers such as borough boundaries. East Ham Council, however, eventually persuaded Ilford to let its cars run the quarter mile up Ilford Hill to Ilford Broadway by agreeing to connect the tracks and paying 6d (2½p) per car mile for the privilege. The first East Ham trams crossed the Ilford boundary on 12th April

1905, after which Ilford's own cars never ventured west of Ilford Broadway. By 1910 Ilford had agreed to cars from West Ham and even the mighty LCC joining those from East Ham running up to the Broadway, each Council paying a fixed rate per car mile for use of the track.

Ilford's system was smart, efficient and, most important of all, consistently profitable. The Council's dogged aloofness from its neighbouring systems is therefore perhaps to its credit.

Ilford's thirty year history as a tram operator began with a fleet of 18 cars, twelve single-truck (1-12), and six bogie (13-18). All eighteen had Hurst Nelson bodies and trucks. The 27 foot long four-wheelers had three arched windows on each side and seated 57 passengers. The top deck was reached by reversed staircases, and the balconies extended over the platform area. The bogie cars seated 69 and, like the four-wheelers, were powered by General Electric type GE 54 motors and BTH K10 controllers. The bogie cars had four Tudor-arched windows each side and double-flight stairs. Ilford's livery was gold-lined red and cream, with the red being applied, as seemed general practice within the tramway fraternity, to dash plates, stair stringers and waist panels. A device similar to the crest of the County of Essex was carried on the waist panels.

Ilford pioneered the covered top in the London area. In 1903 the Council ordered a trial top from Milnes Voss and fitted it to car number 9. The trolley standard protruded through a hole in the roof. Eventually all Ilford's four wheelers had covered tops, the latter ones being supplied by Brush.

So successful were the first Ilford routes that the Council found itself in need of extra trams. Later in 1903 it ordered four more single-truck cars from Hurst Nelson (19-22), identical to the first twelve. The Council had experienced derailment problems with the bogie cars, and some subsequently had four-wheel trucks fitted, along with spiral staircases. In 1909 four covered-top four-wheelers were ordered from Brush. They arrived in 1910 and were numbered 23-26. They seated 54, had Brush 21E trucks, GE54 motor sets and BTH controllers.

In 1914 Ilford purchased a 1912 Brush built four-wheel covered top tram from Barking Council and the following year bought another one, this time one which Barking had purchased in 1911. The cars were numbered 27 and 28 in the Ilford fleet but retained the Barking livery. It was soon discovered that the livery on the Barking cars was more durable than Ilford's own so the decision was taken in 1915 to adopt Barking's colour scheme of sage green and cream with red oxide trucks.

Above **Ilford's trams contrived to be different from the mainstream of other London tramway operators. An early indication of Ilford's uniqueness is apparent in this view of car 1 which was fitted with a rather unusual Hurst Nelson cantilever truck. This separate approach was further compounded by the fact that the staff at Ley Street depot engineered a wheel profile which differed from the London norm, thus confirming Ilford's isolation. The signwriter of the route board above the Ilford crest slipped up in the spelling of Barkingside.**
National Tramway Museum

In the Indian summer of Ilford's tramways a brace of top-covered, four-wheel trams are caught on camera at the Broadway. The leading vehicle was built by Brush in the early 1920s and it retained open balconies. The tram outside Dunn & Co's hat shop is a more modern vehicle, with fully enclosed top deck, from the 33-40 series. G.N.Southerden

The last trams delivered to Ilford retained the 'tried and tested' look of the rest of the fleet. Concessions to modernity included sliding windows on the top deck and the long wheelbase Peckham P22 trucks. One member of this group of trams is depicted marooned in the middle of the road at Ilford Broadway, with the driver having an urgent chat to several other tramway officials. G.N.Southerden

In the period immediately after the First World War, Ilford UDC took stock of its fleet and as a result a handful of trams, chiefly those fitted with the early type of top cover, were deemed fit only for scrap. In 1919 six new four-wheel cars were ordered from Brush. They were to the standard open balcony covered top design, but larger than Ilford's previous deliveries of ten years before, seating 64 passengers. They rode on Peckham P22 trucks powered by GE 200 motors.

If Ilford was to have anything like a standardised tram fleet it appeared in the 1920s. The initial six new cars arrived in September 1920. Between then and 1930 Brush received orders for 17 similar trams, and by 1930 the design looked very dated. The cars were numbered in a new series (1-23), older cars remaining in the fleet being renumbered in a higher series. For such a small system the amount of renumbering was phenomenal, in fact one of Ilford's cars carried five different numbers during its lifetime.

In 1926 Ilford became a Borough, the new coat of arms replacing the Essex shield on the car sides. The same year car 16 of the new series was experimentally fitted with cushion seating. Naturally this proved popular with Ilfordians and the other fifteen were similarly treated. An overdue taste of modernity came to Ilford in 1932, when eight new cars (33-40) arrived. They had fully enclosed top decks and seated 68 passengers. They were built by Brush and had Peckham P22 trucks fitted with BTH 509c motors. When London Transport replaced Ilford's trams with trolleybuses in February 1938 the eight were bought by Sunderland Corporation on whose system they ran until 1954.

Car sheds often represented the acme of municipal pride and the West Ham depot at Greengate Street was no exception. Nearest the camera is No.1A, the water car used to damp down the dust in summer. Some of the rest of the open topped trams reside on the other roads of the depot. All in all the building had a capacity of around 150 vehicles, and it also contained paintshop and maintenance facilities to keep the fleet in tip-top condition.
Tramway and Railway World

WEST HAM (1904)

The next authority in Metropolitan Essex to begin its own tramway services was West Ham. Between 1904 and 1911, a total of 118 cars were built for its services which spread far and wide from the Corporation's own boundaries because of several through running agreements with its neighbours. The Corporation also built a few of its own trams.

The West Ham Corporation Act of 1898 granted West Ham the powers to operate the North Met's routes from the London boundary at Bow Bridge to the East Ham boundary and to Leytonstone, also an isolated section from Canning Town to the Green Gate at Plaistow. A further Act in 1900 gave the Corporation powers to build six new lines. The North Met was reluctant to sell and agreement was not reached until February 1903. This allowed North Met to continue to run its horse services until West Ham chose to electrify particular sections of route.

The initial order for fifty cars (1-50) was placed in 1903. The cars were open-top, four-wheelers with George F. Milnes 56-seater bodies. They had three windows on each side of the saloon, and were fitted with direct staircases from new. They were mounted on Brush type A trucks with a six foot wheelbase, powered by Witting motors and had BTH controllers. They were ready for service on the first day, Saturday 27th February 1904. The livery chosen was Munich lake and cream, elaborately lined out in gold. A red diamond was painted on the front of the dash plate around the headlamp. The words WEST HAM CORPORATION TRAMWAYS were applied to the rocker panels, and the Corporation's crest appeared on the waist panels.

The first route ran from Stratford Broadway down to the Abbey Arms in Barking Road. The local network grew steadily. Most of the system was built and opened before the end of 1905, and West Ham's maroon and cream trams were soon a familiar sight in most parts of the Borough, including Stratford, Canning Town, Upton

Park and the Victoria & Albert Docks. The London boundary at Bow Bridge was reached in August 1905, and Poplar in November 1908. This sowed the seeds for future through running with the LCC.

In 1905, as services expanded, a further 35 cars (51-85) were delivered. These had Brush 60-seater bodies with three windows each side. All except number 51, which was was fitted with an experimental Brush-Conaty radial truck, were mounted on Mountain & Gibson 21EM four-wheel trucks, fitted with Dick Kerr 25A motors and BTH controllers. Eight more four wheel open-toppers (86-93) came in 1906. These had 60-seater Milnes Voss bodies, M&G radial trucks with an eight foot six inch wheelbase and Westinghouse 200 motors and controllers.

Also in 1906 West Ham took delivery of its first covered top cars. These were seven (94-100) 60-seaters with Milnes Voss bodies, and the same trucks, motors and controllers as 86-93. The covered tops on 94-97 had three windows each side but was about four feet shorter than the saloon below, creating large open balconies at each end. The tops on 98-100 corresponded to the proportion of the lower saloon and thus had shorter balconies.

After delivery of the first covered top cars the Corporation fitted an open topper, number 51, with a covered top, later fitting cars 52-58 and several of the original trams with covered tops as well.

Still the new cars came. Six more four-wheelers with covered tops (101-106) were delivered in 1910. Their 58-seater United Electric Car Company bodies had six narrow windows each side of the lower saloon, and three either side upstairs. They also had some transverse seats in the lower saloon. The trucks were the Peckham R7 radial type, the motors were GE200K and the controllers Westinghouse. In 1911 West Ham took delivery of its first bogie cars, a fleet of twelve (107-118) 73-seater with open balconied Hurst Nelson bodies. The four large windows of the top deck were complemented by eight

smaller ones downstairs. The trucks were the LCC class 4 maximum traction type and the cars were powered by two 42hp GE203N motors, and English Electric controllers. The twelve, plus twenty six four-wheelers, were adapted for working on the LCC conduit lines to Aldgate. Until this time West Ham's cars had been fitted only with destination boxes, but the numbering of the LCC services from January 1st 1913 led the Corporation to introduce its own local route numbering system, necessitating the fitting of route number boxes at roof level to all its trams, although initially some had the route number placed on a board near the headlight.

In the midst of the First World War West Ham Corporation changed the livery of its trams to one of dark maroon and cream. It also laid plans to renovate many of the older tramcars in its 118 strong fleet. Work started in 1917 and several cars had body strengthening work carried out, or were fitted with new controllers and motors. The work became held up by shortages of steel and electrical equipment, and this contributed to the generally poor condition of the fleet by the War's end. Rehabilitation work, including remotoring, restarted in 1919 and continued for several years.

In about 1920 West Ham decided to give its entire fleet classification letters, although the information did not appear on any tram. As well as rebuilding its existing fleet, the Corporation had the capacity to build new cars at its Greengate Street works, and in 1923 turned out a four-wheeler with a fully enclosed top deck. It seated 58 passengers, was powered by BTH GE 200K motors, and had Westinghouse controllers. It was numbered 119 and was deemed to be a success. Over the next two years five similar cars were built at Greengate Street, all being grouped together in class E as Nos 60-63 and 65, the original one later being renumbered 64. The new numbers were released by renumbering two and scrapping four of the original Nos 60-65.

In 1924 the Corporation ordered six new 78-seater bogie cars with fully enclosed balconies, from English Electric. They had Hurst Nelson trucks powered by BTH GE 203N motors. BTH controllers were fitted and the cars were coded class F. They were delivered during the autumn of 1925, and were numbered 119-124. At the same time the Corporation was busy building a new bogie car at the Greengate Street works. It appeared during February 1926, and was numbered 125 of class G. It was something of a revelation, being the first London tram to have transverse upholstered seating on both decks. This reduced the seating capacity to 69, but the greater comfort resulting received much local acclaim.

Two similar trams were eventually built in 1926 at Greengate Street, and Brush received a contract for ten more. The new cars were justified because before the 1924 London Traffic Act reduced significantly the number of buses running parallel with trunk tram services the tram operators had to fight the competition with faster and more comfortable trams. The two home produced G cars (126 and 127) were ready in autumn 1926, those from Brush (128-137) arriving the following summer. BTH motors and controllers were fitted. In 1928 West Ham built another G class car (138) which was fitted with double trolley poles. It also ordered ten more new cars from Brush (76-85) which were delivered in November 1928. In 1930 seven more were built, six by Brush (69-74), and one by the Corporation (75). Another one appeared from the Greengate Street shops in 1931, incorporating a platform vestibule similar to those then being applied to the LCC fleet. This was number 68, the last new car for West Ham, and one of 134 it handed over to the new London Passenger Transport Board in 1933.

Above **Stratford Broadway, the hub of the east London tramway network, played host to the trams of various local authorities. Here on 'home' tracks is West Ham car 10 working service 10 which provided local residents and visitors with a circular tour of the borough. Note the service number stencil covering the headlamp of this vehicle which started life in 1904 in open top condition. The view dates from around 1913 and on a fine day like this the top deck of the bus to Seven Kings has already filled with passengers.** Commercial View

Left **Spring sunshine catches West Ham bogie car 121 shortly before it leaves the terminus at Barking. These trams did not follow the LCC practice of placing the service number indicator in the top deck front window, and therefore travellers in the upper saloon had an uninterrupted view of the landscape on the journey to Aldgate. This tram finally ended its days as London Transport No. 327, one of the staff cars at Charlton Works.** G.N.Southerden

The 'Napier Arms' was served by trams until 1939 and later by trolleybuses until 1960. In this view taken in the early 1920s car 20 of the original batch of 32 Brush bodied four wheelers makes ready to depart on the journey to the Essex/Middlesex county boundary at Ferry Lane. Commercial View

WALTHAMSTOW (1905)

Walthamstow Council obtained powers in 1902 to run four routes, the three which eventually began operation on Saturday 3rd June 1905 being:

Chingford Mount - Leyton (Bakers Arms);
Leyton (Markhouse Road) - Higham Hill;
Ferry Lane - Woodford (Napier Arms).

The Walthamstow tramway opened with 32 four-wheel open top cars. They were built by Brush and seated 52 passengers. The saloons had three windows on each side and the cars were fitted with direct stairs from new. The bodies were mounted on Brush 21E trucks and powered by Westinghouse (200 series) motors and controllers.

In 1910 Walthamstow ordered a further six trams (33-38) to run on the joint Leyton and West Ham Docks services. This time the order went to Hurst Nelson, who also supplied the trucks to the Brill 21E design. They too were powered by Westinghouse 200 motors and controllers. The 54-seater bodies were of the open-balcony type. They were painted in the Walthamstow livery of crimson lake and yellow, the latter being applied to rocker panels, window pillars and upper deck panelling. The legend WALTHAMSTOW DISTRICT COUNCIL appeared in gold, edged in red, on the rocker panels.

Walthamstow fared little better than neighbour Leyton during the War, and at its end was actively seeking second hand cars to buy so that it could begin a renovation programme on its own fleet. The LUT offered six bogie cars of class W, and these were hired for assessment, Walthamstow eventually deciding to buy them, although for some time both sides could not agree a price. While this was going on Walthamstow inspected and subsequently bought eight 1902 vintage single deck bogie cars from Rotherham Corporation. The 36-seater cars had ERTCW bodies on Brill 27G trucks and were powered by DK25A motors. They took the numbers 39-46 in Walthamstow's fleet. Meanwhile the LUT and Walthamstow Council had agreed a price of £570 each for the hired trams and they became Walthamstow's 47-52.

In 1921 it was discovered that Walthamstow's trams were losing £3,000 a month, a revelation which led the Council to ask the LCC if the Council would be prepared to take over the operation of Walthamstow's tramway, but the two authorities could not agree terms at that time. The financial situation improved, and Walthamstow entered into several route sharing agreements with its neighbours. In 1926 the Council ordered 12 new 69-seat bogie trams to the tried and

tested E/1 design. The cars had Hurst Nelson bodies and trucks and were propelled by BTH 504A motors. They took the numbers 53-64 in the fleet, and arrived in October 1927 as work began on fitting open balcony covered tops to Walthamstow's original four-wheel fleet. In 1931 the acquisitions of ten years before were showing signs of wear, and it was decided to purchase eight more bogie cars. The order was given to Brush who also supplied the trucks for the 69-seaters. The motors used were 57hp BTH 116AY type.

The new cars, numbered 39-46, arrived in July 1932 and were London's last new trams, all the Felthams having been delivered. Maybe it is fitting that the last new trams built for service in London were to a basically 25 year old design which had come to be regarded as London's standard. It is worth noting that in 1931 plans to link up Walthamstow's Ferry Lane service to the MET system over the Middlesex border had prompted Walthamstow Council to toy with the idea of buying some 'Felthams'.

Walthamstow's depot was sited in Chingford Road, and it continued to house public transport vehicles until 1991 when it ceased to function as a bus garage. The original council tramway offices still stand today, but housing now occupies the rest of the site.

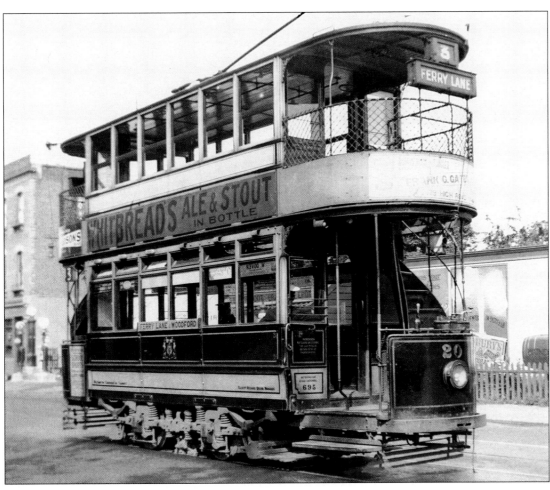

Left **Walthamstow Council didn't fit covered tops to their original cars until very late in the day, 1927 in fact. The work also included reposting the lower saloon windows so that the six-bay arrangement matched the new top deck. Car 20 shows off its new features in Woodford; the year is 1932.** R.Elliott

Below **Single-deck bogie car 44 is photographed at Higham Hill; the batch (originally numbered 39-46) was constructed for Oldham Corporation in 1902. They passed to Walthamstow via a spell in Rotherham ownership. They were mostly used on the Higham Hill to Markhouse Road service.** G. N. Southerden

LEYTON (1906)

The tram system run by Leyton UDC had its origins in two of the original horse tram companies, the North Met and the Lea Bridge, Leyton and Walthamstow Tramway Company. Leyton Council sought to promote the borough tramway service through the Leyton Tramways Bill 1898. This was successful but was dependent upon all sides agreeing to part with and acquire assets. The North Met, whose lines were due to fall for purchase in May 1899 was reluctant to sell. The Lea Bridge was keen, but neither terminal point of its route from Clapton to the 'Rising Sun' at Woodford lay within Leyton's boundary. Attempts to get the LCC and Walthamstow Council, the authorites actually responsible for the two termini, to agree to Leyton taking over the service were unsuccessful until Leyton, aware of Walthamstow's desire to run trams over a short section of track across the Leyton boundary withdrew its consent, thus forcing Walthamstow to agree to the construction of the Leyton line to the 'Rising Sun'. The LCC subsequently agreed to lease the Clapton section of the route to Leyton.

Leyton Council also wished to purchase and operate the North Metropolitan's route from Leytonstone 'Green Man' to the 'Thatched House' at the West Ham boundary. The North Met insisted the deal was only possible if Leyton also bought the Company's tramcar construction works and stables in Union Road, Leytonstone. Negotiations took over four years, and the Union Road works were eventually taken over by the LCC. Nevertheless on 1st December 1906 Leyton UDC opened four electric tram routes all running from its depot in Lea Bridge Road:

Lea Bridge - Woodford (Rising Sun)
Leyton (Bakers Arms) - Wanstead Park
Leytonstone (Green Man) - Bow Bridge
Lea Bridge - Bow Bridge via Whipps Cross

The section between Clapton and Lea Bridge continued to be worked by horse trams until the section was electrified and joined to the LCC system in 1908. The route from the Green Man to Bow Bridge was a short working of the main route to Bow from Lea Bridge and involved two miles of route right through West Ham territory to the LCC boundary. Both routes were operated jointly by West Ham and Leyton right from the start.

The trams ordered by the Council had covered tops from new. They were 40 four-wheelers with Milnes Voss bodies mounted on M&G 8ft 6ins wheelbase trucks and powered by Westinghouse 200 motors and controllers. The cars seated 56, the top-deck being reached by direct stairs. The 40 trams, numbered 11-50, were all delivered by the opening day. Cars 1-10 were ex-Lea Bridge, Leyton and Walthamstow horse trams which Leyton had taken over in 1905, and which were still running on the Clapton service. The Council soon realised that more cars would be required, and in 1907 ordered a further 20 (51-70), identical to the first batch. The horse cars were withdrawn in 1908.

Leyton chose a livery of dark green and cream for its trams. The cream was the dominant colour, appearing on rocker and between decks panels, window pillars and stair stringers. The green went on dash plates and the waist panels. The letters LUDC appeared in a gold monogram on the sides.

Through running was the hallmark of Leyton Council tramway operation, with the London County Council in particular running extensively within the borough from 11th May 1910 when Leyton was one of the local authorities the LCC approached with a view to co-operation along the busy routes to Aldgate. In 1910 cars 31-70 were fitted with plough carriers so they could run on the LCC conduit system.

The Great War was particularly unkind to Leyton, forcing it to renege on its joint working agreements because of acute rolling-stock shortages. After the war moves were made to sort out the problem. The result was an offer from the LCC to take over and run the system. This met with immediate and fierce opposition from Leyton Town Hall, but eventually it was decided that Leyton would renew all track and overhead within the borough, and the LCC would run the services under a joint committee from both bodies. This took effect from 1st July 1921.

The immediate effect was the drafting in of 20 standard LCC E/1 cars to Leyton, and the withdrawal of 19 Leyton cars, all of which were sent into long term store at Hampstead depot. The LCC gave heavy overhauls to Leyton's remaining 41 four-wheel cars at Holloway depot. They retained the Leyton green and primrose livery, even down to the LUDC monogram on the waist panels.

Leyton achieved borough status in 1926, after which the legend LBC appeared on its trams. Naturally, any new cars bought by Leyton needed to conform to LCC specifications, and when Leyton's original fleet was nearing the end of its useful life in 1930, a delegation from the Council inspected one of the LCC's new E/3 cars, deciding to buy fifty of them. The new cars were assembled by the LCC at Charlton and the first arrived at Leyton in September 1931. They had English Electric 74 seater bodies, mounted on Electro Mechanical Brake Co. (EMB) trucks, powered by 57hp BTH 116AY motors, and Metrovick controllers. They were painted in the then standard LCC red and cream livery and were numbered in the LCC series, becoming 161-210, but Leyton's crest appeared on the side panels. Around the same time LCC four-wheel M-class cars were drafted in to replace the last of Leyton's original four-wheelers. Leyton Council Tramways thus ended its days stocked entirely with standard LCC cars.

The 'Rising Sun' on the edge of Epping Forest was the starting point for many a rural ramble. In this meeting of two tramway systems we can imagine a colourful scene with the dark green and primrose Leyton car 70 stationed in front of the crimson lake and chrome yellow Walthamstow car 27. Despite the takeover by the LCC in 1921, many of Leyton's original cars survived until the arrival of redundant M class four wheelers in 1930.
Joel Kosminsky collection

BARKING (1903)

In 1898 Barking UDC obtained a Light Rail Order to run a tram service from Barking to the giant Gas, Light & Coke Company works at Beckton. Work began in 1902 on two lines which joined up making one through route from Beckton to Axe Street in Barking. As work on the line proceeded four more lines were proposed as well as a depot in Ripple Road. It was typical of this rather sad system that the depot and the route to it were never built. Barking's tramcars, when the service to Beckton eventually began, were housed in a large "temporary" corrugated iron shed hurriedly erected at the Beckton terminus. This remained the home of Barking trams from 1st December 1903, when the system opened, until it closed in 1929.

Barking's first seven trams were open-top four-wheelers with Brush 51-seater reversed staircase bodies having three saloon windows each side. The cars were powered by two 25hp GE54 motors fitted to Peckham 9A cantilever trucks, and BTH controllers (similar equipment was also fitted to the remaining three cars purchased by Barking during 1911-12). The livery was crimson lake and cream, the crimson being applied to the dash plates, waist panels and stairs. A special coat of arms depicting the tower of the town's famous 15th century Abbey adorned the waist panels. The cream rocker panels contained the words BARKING COUNCIL TRAMWAYS in gold. The first cars had been delivered to Beckton in March 1903 and, because no proper depot facilities had yet been provided, had to be assembled in the open. Four of the cars were later given Milnes Voss top covers. In 1906 the crimson lake livery gave way to brown, but this soon began to deteriorate so a sage green was substituted.

A unique feature of the Barking system was a bascule bridge built to take trams over the River Roding, which ran close to the western boundary of the borough, down to the gas works by the Thames. The bridge comprised three separate sections, one housing a huge wheel operated from a tower, which opened the centre section to allow river traffic through. It was not possible to run the overhead power lines across the bridge so trams glided over the bridge and the trolley pole was reunited with the overhead on the opposite side.

The Barking system expanded northwards. The Ilford boundary at Loxford Bridge was reached on 7th June 1905, and on 17th November Barking and East Ham tracks joined at the boundary between the two authorities and cars from East Ham and West Ham then operated a joint service to Canning Town from Barking railway station.

The lines to Axe Street were extended to Barking Broadway and joined to the tracks from Loxford Bridge and East Ham on 16th July 1907. This was to be the last stretch to be added to Barking's tramway. In 1910 Barking Council was persuaded to join East and West Ham Corporations in a through running arrangement between Loxford Bridge and Poplar Iron Bridge. For this the Council purchased two trams (8-9) with Brush 54 seater bodies in 1911. They had covered top decks, open balconies and direct staircases. The headlamps were set in the canopy screen. The two car were on Peckham R7A trucks. At about the same time Brush undertook to carry out some rebuilding work on car 7, which received a new top deck a direct staircase and a lengthened truck. Similar alterations were later carried out on several other Barking cars.

In 1912 the Council's last new car, number 10, arrived. It was identical to 8 and 9, except for its Peckham P22 truck. It was fitted with conduit collection gear as well as the standard trolley equipment. Six other Barking cars were fitted up for conduit working at the same time. These were needed for the extension of the Loxford Bridge to Poplar service to Aldgate, which began operation over LCC conduit tracks on Friday 20th September 1912. LCC cars now joined in the operation resulting in four different operators running on this one joint through service, a unique feature in London's tramways at the time. Barking's input into the Aldgate service was not a success and the Council lost money on it. It pulled out of the agreement with the other authorities on 31st May 1914 and to recoup some of its losses sold its newer cars, 8 and 10 going to Ilford, and 9 to East Ham. The Loxford Bridge route was cut back to Barking Broadway in 1914 and the abandoned section leased to Ilford.

Barking's sorry system tottered on. In 1922 the Council converted three (1-3) of its remaining seven trams back to open top, and fitted direct stairs to three others (4-6). By 1928 the Council was trying to persuade the London General Omnibus Company to take over the Beckton route. That year the Barking by-pass opened and the LGOC felt it was able to accommodate Barking's request to replace their trams with a bus service. The last Barking tram to Beckton ran on 16th February 1929, a week after the corrugated iron depot had been pulled down. The bascule bridge was made surplus by a bridge on the new by-pass and subsequently demolished.

Barking car 8 is depicted with side destination boards appropriate for the joint service with East Ham and West Ham which was inaugurated in 1910. Unfortunately Barking's dreams of grandeur did not last long and this particular tram was sold to neighbouring Ilford in 1915. The unusual looking truck was a Peckham Radial R7A, this was meant to give a ride similar to that offered by a bogie car, but in practice the aspiration did not match the technology, and this flexible axle truck was soon locked rigid by the depot staff. Brush

POPLAR (IRON BRIDGE) EAST HAM BARKING ILFORD (BOUNDARY)

BARKING COUNCIL TRAMWAYS

KENT
(Bexley, Dartford, Erith)

The LCC area to the south of the Thames was considerably more extensive than its counterpart to the north. But from the LCC's far south eastern boundary at Abbey Wood, which incidentally lay just 600 yards further west than the eastern extremity of trams north of the river at Chadwell Heath, it was possible by 1906 to travel deep into Kent by electric tramcar. Three systems were traversed before the tracks ended at Horns Cross two miles east of Dartford.

BEXLEY (1903)

Bexley, which had become an Urban District in 1894, bordered the LCC territory south of Plumstead. Various early schemes for horse tramways culminated in provision for six routes granted in the Bexley Tramways Act of 1901. The main route comprised a line from Plumstead 'Plume of Feathers', which lay within the County of London and which was also the terminus of the Woolwich & South East London Tramways Company, down to Welling and through to Bexleyheath Clock Tower, terminating just to the east of there at Gravel Hill, the boundary with Crayford Rural District. From Bexleyheath Clock Tower track was also laid in Erith Road as far as the boundary with Erith Urban District at Colyers Lane.

On Saturday 3rd October 1903 Bexley Council's tramways commenced with five and a quarter miles of route and twelve cars to operate on it. They were large, open-top, four-wheelers with five windows on each side of the saloon, and seating capacity for 52 passengers (22 in the saloon and 30 upstairs). The bodies were supplied by the Electric Railway & Tramway Carriage Works Ltd and had reversed staircases. Despite being electric trams the lamp on the dash plate was powered by oil. The cars were mounted on Brush Type A trucks with a six foot wheelbase. Dick Kerr supplied the controllers and DK 25A motors. The Council bought four similar trams (13-16) in 1904. These were in the same livery as the first batch, maroon and cream. The maroon panels, which as usual were the dash plates, stair stringers and waist panels, had gold lining, the cream panels were lined in sienna. The Kent County coat of arms with the legend BEXLEY URBAN DISTRICT COUNCIL appeared on the maroon panels.

The LCC wished to extend its services as far as Abbey Wood, which meant running over Bexley-owned tracks, a fact which prompted Bexley to seek running rights to nearby Woolwich in return. The LCC agreed and both systems served the busy road between Plumstead and Woolwich from 26th July 1908. This arrangement proved to be long lasting. Not so was the agreement between Bexley and Erith Councils which allowed Erith cars to run beyond the Erith boundary at Northumberland Heath down to Bexleyheath. The two authorities bickered over the rate per car mile, with the result that the arrangement terminated in 1909, after one year and although it was to resume again from 3rd January 1916.

Several munitions factories were located in the south eastern environs of London so

Horns Cross, two miles east of Dartford, was once the rather bleak, easterly outpost of the London system. Bexley car 16 waits hopefully for any passengers, whilst the crew huddle inside the lower saloon. This was the nearest point to another tramway system, the Gravesend and Northfleet metals being a mile or so down the road. Local politics and squabbles prevented connecting tracks being laid. *G.N.Southerden*

during the First World War efficient transport was essential. Despite the grievous situation there was still no workable agreement on through running payments between Bexley and Erith. The absurdity of the problem annoyed the Ministry of Munitions which arranged for a through LGOC bus service to operate. By late 1915 both sides had found common ground, but even then capacity on the cars was sorely stretched. For two and a half years in 1915-17 Bexley Council hired five E/1s from the LCC, these were eventually replaced at the end of 1917 by six B class trams which had been fitted with trolley poles. These cars were numbered 17-22 at Bexley and later purchased. In 1917 five other LCC class B cars were purchased by the Council and became Bexley's 23-27.

When the neighbouring Dartford system was destroyed by fire in August 1917, Bexley promptly hired 12 more class B cars from the LCC. Six of these were bought outright the following year and were given the numbers 28-33. After the War Bexley modified the livery of its trams, substituting chocolate brown for maroon. In 1919/20 Bexley returned six cars from the 1917 hiring agreement to the LCC, but the others remained in the locality until 1933.

Above **One of six former LCC B class trams bought by Bexley in 1918 is seen at Dartford.**

ERITH (1905)

In early 1902 Erith UDC announced plans for the construction of five sections of tramway, at the back of which was the fervent hope that one day it would be linked up with the LCC system at Abbey Wood, once the latter had acquired and electrified the Woolwich & South East London Tramway route as far as Plumstead. Erith's tramway vision didn't end at Abbey Wood, or even Woolwich, for the Council hoped that once its system was linked to the LCC lines, through running agreements would put much of south east London within its reach. Erith thus built its lines with clearances to allow use by the LCC's large bogie trams.

The first Erith route to open ran between Abbey Wood (Station Road) via Belvedere and Erith to Northumberland Heath where it met the Bexley system at Colyers Lane. A line also ran from Erith to North End. The first electric trams ran along this route on Saturday 26th August 1905. From then on the fortunes of Bexley and Erith trams are inexorably linked.

Fourteen single-truck cars had been ordered from Brush, seven open top (1-6 and 9), and seven open balcony covered top (7/8 and 10-14). Each type had four opening windows in the lower saloon, with the same number upstairs on the covered top examples. The open-toppers seated 52 against 48 on the enclosed cars. All fourteen had direct stairs. Mountain & Gibson 21EM trucks carried two Westinghouse 30hp 49B type motors. Westinghouse also supplied the controllers. The livery was apple green and primrose yellow, the green going on dashes, waist panels and stair stringers. All other areas were yellow. ERITH COUNCIL TRAMWAYS appeared in gold on the rocker panels. Erith's depot was situated in Walnut Tree Road.

In 1906 the Council purchased two single-deck demi-cars (15/16), which were 20-seater four-wheel trams worked by a driver only. They were used on the shuttle service along Crayford Road to North End. They had Milnes-Voss bodies, M&G trucks, two 27hp Westinghouse motors and control equipment; each cost about £675. The North End route closed in 1910, and the demi-cars were made surplus. It was some years before they were sold. One went to Dartford in 1915, the other to Doncaster two years later.

Erith's desire to join up with the proposed LCC route to Abbey Wood resulted in protracted discussions between 1906 and 1908, with each side failing to agree on through running payments and the level of service to be offered. As a result of this impasse, LCC tracks finished barely 25 yards away from Erith's at Abbey Wood, and there the matter was to rest. The tracks were not joined until the LPTB, which looked at the matter from a single viewpoint, linked them in 1933. However, Erith concluded a through running agreement with Bexley in July 1908, with the result that Erith trams ran through to Bexleyheath, but as time went on the two Councils disagreed more and more, the through running arrangements becoming like a stormy relationship ending and resuming several times.

Erith's original fleet soldiered on during the First World War, but by the end its trams

and track were in rather a sorry state. In 1919 the Council hired four 1902 vintage bogie cars from the LUT and eventually decided to buy them, numbering them 15-18 in the fleet. The cars received full length canopies and direct stairs as well as magnetic brakes. They joined a 76-seater ex-Hull Corporation bogie car which had been acquired in 1916 and which received the fleet number 19.

Like neighbouring Bexley, Erith altered the livery on its cars after the War, dispensing with the apple green in favour of dark red, fully lined, and cream.

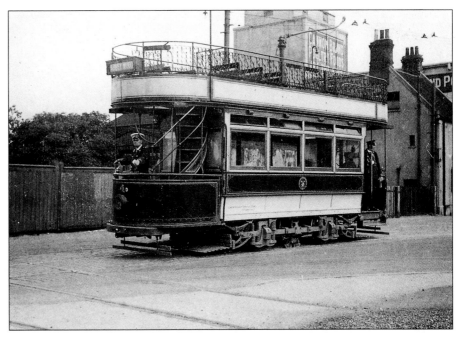

At the corner of West Street and Walnut Tree Road the Erith tramways crossed three standard gauge industrial railways on the level. Open top car 4 hasn't changed much since it was delivered from Brush in 1905; almost 30 years later and this tram now sports a dull brown livery instead of the original apple green and cream. From the looks of it only one passenger is on board to enjoy the ride through Belvedere to Abbey Wood. G.N.Southerden

Erith soon regretted buying bogie car 19 from Hull in 1916. It was very difficult to drive, derailed frequently and was heavy on electric current. In spite of this it performed wonders of crowd clearance during the First World War, when it was often observed packed with munitions' workers. Needless to say, this particular misfit did not last long in London Transport days. G.N.Southerden

DARTFORD (1906)

The Dartford Light Railways system was to form the only mileage on the Tramway network as inherited by London Transport to lie outside the Metropolitan Police District. Like other local authorities nearer London, Dartford UDC was actively considering building a tramway around the turn of the century, and hoped to secure powers to build a line to the Bexley boundary, thus completing a tramway linking Dartford with Woolwich. Only Bexley was successful in obtaining powers at this time. The Dartford authorities sought powers under the 1876 Light Railways Act and Dartford finally succeeded in getting a scheme approved in February 1902. The following year the Council obtained powers to extend its line to Horns Cross. Dartford's route, like those of many other local authorities, was single

track with passing loops. The rolling-stock consisted of twelve open-top, 54-seater cars fitted with 180 degree staircases. They were built by the United Electric Car Company and mounted on Brill 21E four-wheel trucks with a six foot wheelbase. Motors and controllers were by Dick Kerr. Dartford's livery was maroon and yellow, with the Kent County crest on the side panels. The cars, numbered 1-12, were joined in 1915 by one of the Erith Council Raworth demi-cars already described, which became, ominously as it turned out, number 13 in the fleet.

Trams began running from Gravel Hill, Bexley, through Crayford and Dartford to Horns Cross on Wednesday 14th February 1906, but not under direct Council control. They were run on Dartford UDC's behalf by J.G.White & Co. Ltd, who had built the line. Three years later Balfour Beatty & Co. Ltd, a

construction firm still flourishing in the 1990s, took over the running of all J.G. White's tramway activities both here and elsewhere.

On the night of Monday 6th August 1917, the Bank Holiday, all 13 Dartford trams were destroyed in a fire at their depot in Victoria Road. Bexley stepped in and on 9th August began to run Dartford's services using cars hired from the LCC. The following year Bexley purchased the hired cars from their owner. The question of who ran the Dartford system was resolved when, on expiry of Balfour Beatty's lease, which was for five years, twice renewed for a further five, a Joint Committee from Bexley and Dartford Councils was formed to run them starting from 1st April 1921. This arrangement survived until the takeover by London Transport twelve years later.

Built by Brush in 1906, Croydon car No.57 is seen at the Purley terminus. It was one of 30 new four-wheelers bought by Croydon between 1906 and 1911 similar in appearance to the Milnes-built trams that opened the service. Probably photographed soon after a repaint, the Munich lake and ivory livery was enhanced by the title of the undertaking in gold letters shaded blue on silver.
L. E. Brailsford

SURREY
CROYDON AND SMET (1901/1904)

By the end of the nineteenth century Croydon Corporation was showing increasing interest in acquiring the horse tram system of the Croydon & Norwood Tramways Company, and in 1897 built a line linking the main network with the isolated route to South Croydon. In 1899, after having already leased the new, albeit short, stretch of line to the Croydon and Norwood Tramways Company, the Corporation decided to acquire the rest of the Company's system and expand it. Croydon also sought to reach agreement with British Electric Traction Co. Ltd (BET), which several years later was to operate the MET on behalf of Middlesex and Hertfordshire County Councils, to electrify the system, and run it under lease for the Corporation. The service actually started, under Croydon's direct control, before the leasing agreement was formalised. The service opened on Thursday 26th September 1901 between Norbury and Purley, almost one and a half miles to the south of the old 'Red Deer' horse tram terminus.

Thirty five 52-seater open top, three bay, four-wheel cars had been ordered from George F Milnes. They had reversed staircases, and were propelled by 27hp General Electric GE52 motors fitted to either Brill 21E trucks (19 cars) or Peckham No.9 cantilever trucks (16 cars). All were fitted with BTH B18 controllers. The livery of the Croydon fleet was ivory and chocolate brown, or to give its proper name Munich lake, the darker colour being applied to the dash

plates, stair stringers, and waist panels, where the Corporation crest was displayed. The livery was lined out in gold. The words CROYDON CORPORATION TRAMWAYS appeared on the rocker panels.

On 22nd January 1900 the system was leased to BET, which set up its own subsidiary in 1904 with the intention of building lines elsewhere in the area. The new company was called the South Metropolitan Electric Tramways and Lighting Company Ltd (SMET). It was also in business to supply domestic power, but its tramway was obvi-

ously going to be a good customer. BET's lease with Croydon duly expired on 1st June 1906, and the Corporation reverted to controlling its own tramway system, and operating cars from its depots at Purley and Thornton Heath.

Ten more cars (36-45) joined the Croydon fleet in 1902. Built also by Milnes, they were very similar to the first 35 but rode on Milnes trucks. They belonged not to the Corporation but to British Electric Traction, and when the joint agreement between Croydon and BET ended in 1906 the cars passed to the SMET.

The date is 17th March 1927 and the conductor of Croydon car 48 takes a short break as he looks along an almost deserted lower saloon. The notice on the dash to the left of the head-lamp warns passengers to be alert for oncoming traffic – a problem virtually unknown in 1902 when this car was built. G.N.Southerden

The spendidly named South Metropolitan Electric Tramways and Lighting Company shows off one of its five bogie cars which worked the service from Croydon across the expanse of Mitcham Common to the county boundary at Tooting where they met up with LCC cars running on the conduit. The gold 'wheel and magnet' device of the British Electric Traction Company can clearly be seen on the waist panel. This vehicle is painted in the early holly green and cream livery.
R.J.Harley collection

The same year Croydon took delivery of ten bogie cars (46-55). These also had George F. Milnes bodies, seating 69 passengers (30 downstairs and 39 on top). They had double-flight staircases similar to those found on LUT cars to which they bore a general resemblance. They were powered by GE 52 motors fitted to Brill 22E trucks. Like the first 35 they had BTH control equipment. They were part of an order for 15 trams needed to increase capacity on the busy route between Norbury and Purley. The remaining five (56-60) were built in 1902 for the BET by Brush and were very similar to Croydon's new bogie trams. They seated 69 passengers and had the double flight staircases. Brush type B trucks, GE52 motors and BTH controllers completed the picture. Like 36-45 they passed to the SMET in 1906.

To the west the SMET built lines from West Croydon to Mitcham (Fair Green) and from West Croydon to Sutton, and to the east from South Norwood to Penge and Crystal Palace. All were working by the end of 1906.

Between 1906 and 1911 Croydon Corporation took delivery of 30 new open top, four-wheel trams, the first 15 of which took the numbers vacated by the ex-BET cars which were now working for SMET, (36-45

and 56-60). These, along with 61-75, were all built by Brush at Loughborough. They seated 54 passengers, and were very similar to the earlier single truck trams built by Milnes, who had now gone out of business. All were fitted with half turn stairs. The first batches, 36-45 and 56-60, came in 1906 and were mounted on Mountain & Gibson 21EM trucks. The remainder, 61–70 (1907) and 71-75 (1911) had Brill 21E and Brush 21E trucks respectively. All were powered by Westinghouse 21hp type 200 motors, and were fitted with Westinghouse controllers.

The SMET maintained three depots, Mitcham Road Croydon, Penge and Sutton, a large number for a relatively small system. However the SMET was not a united system. The bone of contention was West Croydon. The Corporation would not allow SMET cars to cross the main London Road in Croydon, although the line from West Croydon to South Norwood was connected to the SMET Crystal Palace and Penge lines before the leasing arrangement with Croydon ended. This ridiculous situation, at least as far as the provision of a service to the public was concerned, lasted until the creation of London Transport, although Croydon Corporation did enter into a through running agreement with the LCC in 1926 following the laying of tracks along a six inch section of road separating the two systems at Norbury. This brought LCC trams into Metropolitan Surrey and took Croydon's cars right up to Westminster.

The story of Croydon Corporation Tramways after the First World War is one of upgrading, both in the performance of cars and their comfort, but little was done before the mid-twenties, when many cars were given

new motors and received air brakes to replace the rheostatic braking equipment previously fitted. In 1927 the Corporation ordered ten new bogie cars (31-40) from Hurst Nelson of Motherwell, to run on the joint Croydon/LCC services from Purley to Embankment which had begun back in February 1926. Initially the LCC loaned Croydon 25 standard E/1s to use on the routes until the Corporation decided on which cars to purchase of its own for the service. The new 69-seaters were built to the general design of the LCC E/1 car. Two 65hp GEC WT32 motors, mounted on Hurst Nelson class 4 maximum traction trucks provided the power. GEC also supplied the controllers. The arrival of the new cars heralded a change in Croydon's livery. They were painted in ivory and a dark red called port wine. The red areas, which included dash plates and rocker panels, were lined in black. Also in 1927 Croydon sold eight four-wheelers to the SMET; two more were scrapped. Several older cars were subsequently painted in the new colours, and at the same time some renumbering took place.

Early in 1928 a further 15 bogie cars (41-55) were ordered from Hurst Nelson and these arrived later in the year sporting yet another new livery. This time the ivory was replaced by a pearl grey, and there was no black lining on the rocker panels. This was to become the standard livery of Croydon Corporation trams until the end. Also in 1928 top covers were fitted to the ten 1902 built bogie cars (46-55), which reduced the seating upstairs by seven to 32. The seats were cloth covered at the same time. The cars also received the new livery, and new fleet numbers (21-30).

Naturally, being a BET-owned company, the SMET went to fellow BET subsidiary Brush for its rolling stock. The first cars were 16 four-wheelers with 58-seat (28 inside and 30 on top) four-window open-top bodies with direct staircases. Brush, which was still reaping the benefits of the tramway building boom, bought the body shells from the United Electric Car Company simply because it couldn't fulfil the order itself in time. Otherwise the cars were an all-Brush product, powered by 40hp Brush motors mounted on Brush 9ft 6ins wheelbase trucks and controlled by Brush equipment. The cars were only six feet wide whereas most other London tramcars were seven feet across. This was apparently because the SMET believed their standard-gauge system might at some stage need to be converted to narrow gauge.

The new cars were numbered 1-16 in the SMET fleet. The following ten (17-26) were the 1902 Milnes-bodied four-wheelers which had come from Croydon Corporation. Numbers 27-29 together with 31 and 35 had also come from Croydon. These were the 1902 vintage bogie cars with Brush 69-seat double-flight staircase open-top bodies. The missing numbers, 30 and 32-34, comprised four bogie cars built for another BET subsidiary, the Gravesend and Northfleet Tramway, by the Electric Railway & Tramway Carriage Works in 1902. The open-top bodies were 68-seaters with reversed staircases. They ran on reversed Brill 22E series bogies powered by 30hp Dick Kerr DK35 motors and controllers.

Finally came cars 36-51 built for the SMET in 1906 by Brush. They were intended for the routes from Croydon to Tooting and Sutton and were delivered to Sutton depot. They were three-window open-toppers with seats for 50 passengers (24 in the saloon and 26 on top). Brush motors fitted to 21E trucks provided the running power. The control equipment was by BTH. These trams, like the rest of the SMET fleet, were painted in a dark green and cream livery, with green on the dash plates, side panels and stair stringers. THE SOUTH METROPOLITAN ELECTRIC TRAMWAYS COMPANY appeared on the rocker panels in blue lined silver, with the BET magnet and wheel crest on the side panels.

The SMET cars were eventually grouped into types common with the LUT and the MET, all of which were part of the Underground Group by 1912. While the MET cars were grouped into types A-H, and the LUT T-Z, the SMET cars were grouped thus: 1-16 (type J), 16-26 (K), 27-29/31/35 (L), 30/32-34 (O), 36-51 (M).

The SMET did not order any completely new trams after 1906. It continued to acquire second-hand vehicles and in July 1927 bought 12 cars from its neighbour Croydon Corporation. As only four were required for service the best were sent to Hendon (MET) depot, where the Underground Group had set up a centralised maintenance and overhaul facility. The remainder were cannibalised for spare parts. The four cars, which replaced a similar number of K-types, were eventually numbered 17, 21, 47 and 52, and given the code P. They had been built for Croydon by Brush in 1906/7 and were renovated to a high standard at Hendon, including the fitting of cushion seating, but retained their open tops.

In 1928 a start was made on refurbishing other SMET cars. Eventually cars from types J, M and O were rebuilt at Hendon. They were given flush side panelling and lower-deck transverse cushion seating but, as with the P-type, kept their open-top decks. When the LUT began a trolleybus service in 1931, the SMET took advantage of ten LUT surplus U-type covered-top cars to replace some of their L-types which went to Fulwell for scrap. The rebuilt SMET cars passed to London Transport in 1933, and many saw service until trolleybuses arrived at Sutton depot at the end of 1935.

Top **Car 39 was a regular on the Crystal Palace service which climbed Anerley Hill. As such it was equipped with Spencer track brakes to ensure that it did not run out of control. It was later classified type M in the SMET fleet.** G.N.Southerden

Above **Metal sheeting has now replaced the wire netting round the top deck in this view of car 46 taken shortly before the formation of London Transport in 1933. The location is Croydon Road at the Robin Hood junction. SMET car 46 will shortly take the tracks to the motorman's left, whilst the rails leading straight on carry the Penge service which was normally operated by Croydon Corporation trams.** R.J.Harley collection

THE UNDERGROUND GROUP

In November 1901 the LUT deposited the London United Electric Railways Bill in Parliament. It sought powers to build underground railways connecting Hammersmith and Shepherd's Bush with the west end of London. Underground railways were another popular transport innovation of the age. The first two deep level 'tube' railways, the City & South London Railway and the Central London Railway, were already running successfully and others were planned. The LUT's Bill was just one of many advanced at the time, and a Lord's Committee was formed to consider them all. As the Committee began its work a firm of bankers called Speyer acquired the majority shareholding in the LUT. Speyer's were also involved with American businessman Charles Tyson Yerkes, himself a banker, who was promoting tube railways in London. Speyer's withdrew the LUT's Bill to put further weight behind Yerkes' proposals which included several lines destined to form part of today's Underground network.

One of Yerkes' schemes was the Great Northern, Piccadilly and Brompton Railway, which was similar to the LUT plans to connect Hammersmith with central London. It opened in 1906, the year after Yerkes died, and because of its close association with the LUT, through fares were available on both tubes and trams. By 1908 most of what now comprises the central London area Underground network had opened and the various operating companies, finding themselves locked in competition with the buses, moved towards closer co-operation, trading jointly under the name 'Underground'. Out of this emerged the Underground Electric Railways Company of London (UERL) which comprised the three tube lines built by Yerkes, who had also bought the District Railway and the LUT.

In 1911 the London General Omnibus Company, which had continued to expand, merging with or buying out other companies, approached the UERL on the possibility of fare pooling. The result was a rationalisation of bus services with the General running feeder routes to Underground stations. This angered the Metropolitan Railway which announced plans to run its own buses, a move which prompted the UERL and the LGOC to merge and form the Underground Group, or 'Combine' as it was often called, so they could best deal with the competition.

Meanwhile the MET had been considering how to fend off competition from the buses. In 1911 a decision was reached which in essence was 'If you can't beat em, join em'. The MET persuaded the British Electric Traction group (BET) to finance a bus operating venture and early in 1912 The Tramways (MET) Omnibus Company Ltd was formed. An order for 100 buses with bodies built by BET subsidiary Brush was announced, followed by an order for another 100 a few months later. Maybe the emergence of a new competitor worried the LGOC, which was also planning expansion in north London, because in 1912 the MET was invited to join the 'Combine', which it did at the end of the year.

Already in place at the Underground Group was Albert Stanley (1874-1948), a man destined to shape the future of London's transport. Stanley, a native of Derbyshire who had spent the early part of his business life in the United States – his last job there being General Manager of the Public Service Corporation of New Jersey – joined the UERL as General Manager in 1908 becoming Managing Director in 1910. By this time, Frank Pick (1878-1940), another transport professional who was to exert a strong influence in London, was Traffic Officer with the Group.

With the LUT and the MET now part of the same Group, ironically one which had growing bus and railway interests as well, the only privately owned tramway still operating in the London area was the SMET, in the south. Here too buses were on the agenda. The BET, which also controlled the SMET, decided to create a bus subsidiary in the area to compete with the LGOC. Eventually common sense prevailed and in 1912 the Underground Group was invited to be a shareholder in the venture which was reconstituted as a tramway undertaking called London & Suburban Traction Company Ltd into which were transferred the holdings the BET had in the MET, and the Underground Group had in the LUT. This in effect brought the SMET into the same arena, and its ownership was transferred to the London & Suburban in June 1913. The LUT, MET and SMET were now part of the Underground Group, which had adopted the circle and bar emblem of the General as its logo. Thus 20 years before Albert Stanley, who became Lord Ashfield in 1920, and Frank Pick steered the Group towards their goal of a unified public transport system for London, the embryo London Transport was in existence.

By 1921 all the cars owned by the three tramway companies were grouped into a common classification structure and all were painted in the Underground Group's red and broken white livery. This apart, each company kept very much to its own territory, and there was little re-allocation of cars.

Above **The Official Board of Trade inspection of the new LUT service through New Malden in May 1906 has drawn a small crowd at the point where Kingston Road passes beneath the London & South Western Railway. The line became single track at this point, and the rubble on the left was no doubt the spoils of road lowering.**

LONDON UNITED TRAMWAYS

The honour of giving the capital its first daily electric tramway service falls to the London United Tramways, which in 1898 secured parliamentary powers to electrify its lines and build power stations to generate the electricity. On Thursday 4th April 1901 the first LUT red and white electric trams began running on the previously horse tram routes from Shepherd's Bush to Acton, from Shepherd's Bush to Kew Bridge, via Chiswick, and from Hammersmith to Kew Bridge.

On 6th July 1901 the Shepherd's Bush to Kew Bridge route was extended to Hounslow (Bell) and the route to Acton was extended to Southall on the 10th. The official opening ceremony involving dignitaries from local councils took place on this latter date also.

New electric routes were developed in Hounslow, Richmond and Twickenham in 1902, with extensions to Hampton Court in April 1903. The Uxbridge Road route was completed in June 1904 when the extension from Southall to Uxbridge opened. No new lines opened in 1905, but in March 1906 extensions opened from Hampton Wick to Winters Bridge via Kingston and Surbiton, from Kingston (Clarence Street) to Kingston Hill and from Surbiton Station to Tolworth.

May 1906 saw lines open between Brentford (Half Acre) and Hanwell Broadway, Kingston and Richmond Park Gates, and between the junction of London Road and Cambridge Road and Malden Fountain.

The LUT's network was completed in 1907 with new tracks from Malden Fountain to Wimbledon Broadway via Raynes Park Station, Wimbledon to Tooting and the LCC boundary and from South Wimbledon to Wimbledon Stadium

The LUT system, like that of the LCC, served both sides of the River Thames, but only crossed it at one point, Kingston. There was no less interest in tramway building in Middlesex and Surrey than there was elsewhere. The LUT had sought sanction under the 1896 Light Railways Act to build lines in south-west Middlesex and north-west Surrey, but then so had several local authorities in the area. By 1900 opposition to the LUT was on the wane, spurred on apparently by straw polls conducted amongst the local population which showed most people favoured the LUT proposals.

Not all the lines proposed in the various LUT Bills were sanctioned, and LUT met considerable opposition to its plans from some of the local authorities in the area, notably Kingston, Ealing and Richmond, the latter objecting to the electrification of Kew Bridge to Richmond horse tram service. The matter was finally resolved by the LUT, under its new General Manager Albert Stanley, suggesting Richmond Council electrify the line themselves. Richmond did not agree, and the line closed in April 1912, as a direct result of its having three and a half months earlier come under the same ownership as the LGOC, whose bus route 27 had already covered the route since three weeks before that.

The only major change to the network came in May 1922, when the LCC bought the four stretches of LUT routes which lay within the Metropolitan Borough of Hammersmith, although LUT cars continued to serve both the Hammersmith Broadway and Shepherd's Bush terminals.

The LUT's main depot was Chiswick, transferred in about 1910 to Fulwell, where all maintenance of the company's fleet was carried out. Other depots were at Acton, Chiswick, Hanwell and Hounslow. The depot at Chiswick was used by the LCC from 1922 to 1932.

METROPOLITAN ELECTRIC TRAMWAYS

Events further north were moving too. In 1901 Middlesex County Council took the decision to involve itself with tramway operation, chiefly to serve the busy developing suburbs within its boundaries. Rather than run trams itself it turned to British Electric Traction which had been created in 1896 to promote electric tramways up and down the country. BET had as part of its group the Metropolitan Tramway and Omnibus Company Ltd (MTOC), which had been set up in November 1894 to build tramways in Hertfordshire and Middlesex, and was still in the process of securing the necessary powers. In 1901 the County Council, using the provisions of the Light Railway Act, obtained powers to lay track with the MTOC providing the rolling stock and depot facilities. Powers were granted for four routes; Tottenham – Friern Barnet, Archway – Whetstone, Cricklewood – Edgware and Harlesden – Stonebridge Park. The lines of the North Metropolitan in Middlesex and the whole of the Harrow Road & Paddington Company's tracks were absorbed into the new company, the latter by agreement with the LCC in whose area much of the route mileage lay.

Eventually Hertfordshire County Council associated itself with the scheme, and the MTOC changed its name to the Metropolitan Electric Tramways Ltd, remaining a subsidiary of BET.

The Metropolitan's system grew steadily between 1904 and 1911. Its area embraced all the principal towns in north Middlesex including Edgware, Edmonton, Wembley, and Enfield. It reached Hertfordshire at Barnet and Waltham Cross. Through running agreements with the LCC resulted in the MET's trams being seen in central London locations like Holborn and King's Cross. Opening dates were as follows:

22nd July 1904	Finsbury Park – Wood Green and Manor House – Seven Sisters
20th August	Wood Green – Tottenham (Bruce Grove)
24th August	Seven Sisters – Tottenham (Brantwood Road)
3rd December	Cricklewood – Edgware
12th April 1905	Stamford Hill – Edmonton (Angel Bridge) (Through service)
7th June	Highgate – Whetstone
19th July	Edmonton (Angel Bridge – Tramway Avenue)
6th December	Alexandra Palace West – Turnpike Lane (The Wellington)
22nd December	Highgate – Archway Tavern
11th March 1906	Cricklewood – Willesden Green
11th April	Wood Green – Alexandra Palace East
	Bruce Grove – Tottenham High Road
4th August 1907	Whetstone – Hertfordshire County boundary
10th October	Harlesden – Stonebridge Park
28th November	Wood Green – Bounds Green
22nd December	Harlesden – Paddington (Lock Bridge)
28th March 1907	Hertfordshire boundary – Barnet
10th May	Bounds Green – New Southgate Station
7th June	Wood Green – Palmers Green
31st October	Edgware – Canons Park
11th December	Edmonton (Tramway Avenue) – Enfield (Freezywater)
23rd December	Willesden Green – Craven Park
15th April 1908	Stonebridge Park – Wembley
17th April	Enfield (Freezywater) – Waltham Cross
30th June	Willesden Junction Stn – Harlesden (Jubilee Clock)
1st August	Palmers Green – Winchmore Hill
8th April 1909	New Southgate Station – North Finchley
3rd July	Winchmore Hill – Enfield
7th October	Harlesden – Acton
17th December	North Finchley – Golders Green
21st February 1910	Golders Green – Hampstead (LCC boundary)
	Cricklewood – Childs Hill (The Castle)
14th July	Paddington (Lock Bridge – Warwick Avenue)
24th September	Wembley – Sudbury
6th December	Warwick Avenue – Paddington
20th February 1911	Ponders End – Enfield

THE LUT FLEET

Moving to the vehicles, the LUT's fleet was composed entirely of bogie cars, and during the company's 39-year history almost 400 electric trams were built and operated. The LUT ordered one hundred 69-seater open-top cars (1-100) from Hurst Nelson for its first services in 1901. The lower deck had six Tudor-arched windows each side. The top deck, which did not overhang the platforms, was reached by a double right-angle staircase at each end. The cars were powered by BTH GE58 motors mounted on Peckham 14D.2 maximum traction (MT) swing bolster trucks, and BTH B18 controllers. The livery was red and off white, the dash plates and waist panels being red. Subsequent deliveries sported various colour schemes depending on the routes worked, a reversion to horse tram practice which lasted until the LUT became part of the Underground Group in 1913 when red and off white was adopted as standard.

Later in 1901 the first of a further batch of 50 cars (101-150) arrived. These had McGuire maximum traction swing bolster trucks and Westinghouse 49B motors and controllers. The 69-seater bodies were by George F. Milnes and were very similar to the first 100, except that the decency boards around the upper decks were shallower. The cars were in an all-white livery and nine of them were used in the official parade to mark the opening of the LUT electric system on 10th July 1901. The white cars were used on the Southall service, while the original red and white cars ran from Shepherd's Bush to Acton and Kew Bridge.

Numbers 151-300 came in 1902, and formed a single class, all being mounted on Brill 22E maximum-traction side bearing trucks. They were bodied by two different manufacturers, George F. Milnes (151-211 and 237-300) and the British Electric Car

Car 117 was placed on the Uxbridge Road service in 1901, but subsequently migrated in 1906 to become one of the three Hanwell to Brentford shuttle cars. This batch of LUT trams (101-150) was brought out first in a very fetching livery of yellow and cream, however by 1908/9 a more serviceable vermilion had been substituted for the yellow. The view was taken at Brentford, Half Acre and we also witness the trolley being swung for the return journey along Boston Manor Road. Commercial View

LUT car 295 negotiates the curve into St George's Road, Wimbledon. These particular trams epitomised the height of Edwardian elegance with interior furnishings of blue Utrecht velvet seating in a flowered pattern with matching curtains at the lower saloon windows. The complete tram cost £669 when new! The external colours were royal blue and cream. The two 25hp motors will help to convey this load of passengers on their trip to Hampton Court. Commercial View

Company (212-236). The appearance of the 150 cars followed the same pattern as 101-150. All 150 had Westinghouse 49B motors and Westinghouse controllers. The cars were needed for the new services to Hounslow, Twickenham, Richmond Bridge and Hampton Court.

Covered tops reached the LUT in 1906 with a batch of 40 United Electric Car Co bodied trams (301-340). The cars also had the top deck balconies built out over the driver's position. The roof extended out to this point too, but the balcony thus created was open.

The 74-seater bodies (30 downstairs, 44 on top) were mounted on Brill 22E MT trucks, and powered by Westinghouse motors and controllers. They were the last new cars to be delivered before the LUT began fitting covered tops to its older trams. In 1911, 102 cars were given covered top decks. For some reason none of the side windows in these were glazed, although later most and eventually all were. In 1912 the LUT issued classification codes for its trams: 1-100 became type Z, although the 52 cars from the class fitted with top decks were coded type Y, 101-150,

none of which were given top covers, became type X, 151-300 became type W, except for the 50 which received covered tops which were classified U, and 301-340 became type T.

There is one passenger car in the LUT fleet worth noting. This was the luxury saloon for exclusive use by the Company General Manager, Sir James Clifton Robinson. It was even stabled in a special siding at Robinson's Hampton home. Robinson retired in 1910 and befittingly died riding on a tram during a visit to New York later that year.

THE MET FLEET

On Friday 22nd July 1904 the first trams ran on the Metropolitan Electric Tramways system. The MET, having taken over all of the North Metropolitan's horse-car lines west of the River Lea and north of the County of London boundary, was set to expand and serve the developing suburbs to the north and north-west of London, and, by through running agreements, into London.

The first orders were for 130 open-top, bogie cars divided into two classes. Numbers 1-70 were classified type B, and were built in 1904/5 by Brush, the manufacturing part of BET. They had eight windows on each side of the lower saloon, two narrower ones at each end and two larger ones in the middle. The windows were fitted with roller blinds. The lower deck seating on cars 1-35 was of the longitudinal bench type and accommodated 30 passengers, but on 36-70 some transverse seats were added which reduced the seating capacity in the lower saloon by six. The capacity of the top deck, which was reached by a direct staircase, was 38. Thus cars 1-35 seated 68, and 36-70, 62. As a result the 62-seaters were classified B/1. All were powered by two 28hp GE58 motors mounted on Brush type BB reversed MT trucks. These had the larger of the two wheels innermost under the car with the smaller, or 'pony' wheels at each end. The MET relied heavily on BTH control equipment, fitting it almost exclusively to its trams throughout its 30-year existence.

Cars 71-130 were designated type A and were also delivered between 1904/5. Although they too had Brush bodywork they looked completely different from the first 70, resembling more closely the early cars of the LUT system. This was apparently the design preferred by Middlesex County Council. The A type trams were thus always known as the MCC cars. The saloons had six tudor-arched windows on each side, and the top deck was reached by two divided double-flight stair-cases. The top deck did not extend over the platforms. A large headlamp was positioned on the dash plate on earlier cars and on the bulkhead above the platform on later deliveries. The lamp would be in an equivalent position on all future MET tram deliveries up to 1912. The cars seated 68 passengers, 30 in the saloon, which when new had cush-ioned covered seats, and 38 on top. The trucks and motors were the same as on the B type trams.

Above Right **Bogie car 60 belonged to type B/1 and was one of the workhorses of the MET system, and it proved reliable right up to the end of company operation. Its last resting place after withdrawal by LT was Acton Depot; the type finally became extinct in the winter of 1935.** R.J.Harley collection

Below **Another example of the same type, after being fitted with a covered top deck and mismatched glazing. This late-1920s view at the Paddington terminus also shows car 19 of type A on route 62. The livery used by the MET was vermilion and ivory. Although situated well into LCC territory the Harrow Road end of these two services was operated exclusively by MET cars.** G. N. Southerden

In 1905 the MET took delivery of 20 single deck bogie cars for the Alexandra Palace service. They were numbered 131-150 and formed type E. They were powered by 28hp GE509C motors mounted on Brush Conaty four-wheel trucks. The bodies had clerestory roofs and six windows either side of the saloon. They seated 36 passengers on longitudinal rattan covered benches. The saloon was divided into two compartments, a smaller 12-seater area being provided for smokers. In the event smoking on these trams was banned by order of the police. The headlamps were fitted to the roofs over the platforms. In 1907 four were deemed to be surplus to requirements and were sold to Auckland Tramways in New Zealand, another BET subsidiary.

Twenty-five four-wheel open-toppers were supplied by Brush in 1906. They were incorporated into type D and numbered 166-190. The bodies were 54-seaters with four arched windows on each side of the saloon. Brush Conaty trucks gave a six-foot wheelbase and the cars were powered by two 28hp GE58 motors. The Ds were allocated to Wood Green and Stonebridge Park depots when new. Car 191 was a one-off, classified D/1. It had been a demonstrator car and its first owner had been Leicester Corporation. Because it would not have been standard with the main order of Leicester cars, which were supplied by Dick Kerr, it was returned to its builder Brush who sold it to MET in July 1904. After three years of training duties it entered revenue earning service in 1907. It was very similar to the D type except for its reversed staircase which was replaced with a direct one.

In 1906 Brush supplied fifteen 74-seaters with six Tudor-arched windows on each side, mounted on Brush BB MT trucks and powered by GE58 motors. The upper decks, which had full-length canopies, were reached by direct stairs. Five of the cars, which were classified C (151-165), were allocated to Hertfordshire County Council and carried the county name and crest on the waist panels.

Before Bluebell and the Felthams came along, car 233 of type H with its all-enclosed top deck represented the most modern cars of the MET. All of this type were modernised in 1928/30 and received new upholstered seating and other improvements. R. Elliott

MET E type single decker No.150. The two routes which served Alexandra Palace and Park were only worked by this type of tram. Traffic was very light, and the service only really came to life when special events were being held at the Palace. Dave Jones collection

Above **A tram of MET type H at Kings Cross.**

Above Right **The traditional lower saloon of car 122 contrasts with the modern methods of cleaning as demonstrated in this photograph. Bell punch tickets are sucked into the hose after the end of another day's work. Notice the handrails and straps which were needed by standing passengers during the rush hours.** LT Museum U6077

In 1908 the MET ordered 25 new cars with a new type of bogie truck. The first 20 of the order (192-211) came to be classified C/1 and were delivered in 1908. They soon became a familiar sight in Finchley and along the Harrow Road. Their open-top 74-seater Brush bodies were almost identical in appearance to the earlier cars but they sat on Mountain & Gibson type 3L MT bogies powered by GE58 motors and BTH B18 controllers. One truck on each car was fitted with conduit equipment for operating over LCC lines. The LCC stipulated that cars which ran on its system had to be powered by 40hp motors and have magnetic brakes, so from 1912 the 28hp GE58 sets were replaced by the 40hp GE67 motors.

The prospect of running alongside the LCC's modern fully canopied E/1 cars caused a late design change as production of the C/1s was ending, when it was decided to give the last five fully enclosed top decks, in similar style to the LCC E/1s. This was achieved by reducing the height of the lower deck; as a result the five (212-216) were grouped into a new F type. The fully enclosed top covers had six windows per side. The seating capacity was thereby increased by four to 78. Oddly these were squared windows while those on the lower saloon were still tudor arched, making it look like the tops had been added as an afterthought. Like the C/1s the Fs were remotored in 1912, and fitted with conduit running equipment.

The MET surprisingly reverted to open-top for the next batch of 20 bogie cars which comprised type G (217-236). They arrived from Brush in 1909 and were very like the C/1s, except they were fitted with 40hp GE67 motors from new. They worked initially from Finchley and Wood Green depots. Covered top

decks came back with a vengeance between 1909 and 1912 with the delivery of the 80 cars of type H (237-316). These were similar in appearance to the F type cars, even down to the Tudor-arched windows in the lower saloon. Like the Fs they seated 78. In common with other recent MET bogie cars, the first five were mounted on M&G type 3L trucks. Mountain & Gibson went into liquidation in June 1909 so Brush provided the trucks for the remaining 75 cars to a design almost identical to the M&G original.

In 1912 the MET began a programme of modification to upgrade its fleet, including fitting open balcony top decks, built by the MET, to type B and C trams. The work was carried out at Hendon depot and by the outbreak of World War 1, all the Cs and 16 of the Bs had new tops. The Bs were reclassified B/2 and the Cs, C/2. The cars had also been remotored with 40hp GE 67 sets. The War halted further work, the remaining 54 B-type cars retained their open tops for the rest of their lives.

In later life, MET type B/2 No. 30 is seen at North Finchley a few days after passing into LPTB ownership in July 1933. This tram subsequently became London Transport's No. 2478 and was withdrawn in October 1935. The ugly plain sheet metal panelling replaced the wrought iron balcony ends (as seen in an earlier view of another B type tram on page 68) in 1931.
G. N. Southerden

In 1921 the MET built another open-top G type car and gave it the number 317. The following year E-type car 132 was rebuilt for driver only operation following a collision with a steam lorry. The body was shortened to five bays, and longer platforms with vestibule screens were fitted. It thus became London's first vestibuled tram. Passengers boarded and alighted from the front platform and the driver dispensed the tickets. The tram passed to the LUT in 1922, and continued to be used as a one-man vehicle. It was renumbered 341 and classified type S/1. It was joined later in 1924 by three others (342-344), rebuilt from W-type double-deckers, fitted with similar electrical equipment to 341, and classified S/2. They worked on LUT route 55 (Brentford–Hanwell) for several years.

Refurbishment was the keynote of the LUT and MET during the twenties. In the early part of the decade much of the scarce available funds went on track renewal rather than new or rebuilt cars. The MET undertook some experimentation to increase capacity

using two C/2 type vehicles coupled together running between Golders Green and North Finchley. This met with strong police opposition. Further experiments involving a cut-down B-type car coupled to an H-type, a combination which offered seating and standing accommodation for 124 passengers, still got a cool reception from the police so the idea quietly died. An LUT X-type was acquired by the MET in 1921 and rebuilt at Hendon as a works car. In 1924 the MET built six new tram cars of type H. Four years later top covers, supplied by Underground Group sister company the LGOC, were fitted to cars in types A, C/1 and G, the latter two types also receiving lower-deck transverse seating. The five F-type cars were also re-seated downstairs. In 1929 the MET began a re-motoring scheme whereby many cars were fitted with new 60hp BTH B509 motor sets. Many H class trams received vestibule screens.

In 1928 the LUT's 40 T-type cars of 1906, together with 49 U-types, were re-motored (with Westinghouse WT28 sets) and fitted

with magnetic brakes. At the same time the T-types were given new transverse upholstered lower deck seating which reduced the capacity by three. New T-style top-deck covers were fitted to five type W cars which became type WT and had their seating capacity increased to 74.

The former MET A type tram, although having been fitted with a top cover, is seen in a bad light when compared to the allegedly 'more flexible' motorbus. The truth of the matter is that with the notable exception of the Feltham type trams, investment in new tramway technology had been at a minimum.
A.B.Cross collection

TRAM V. OMNIBUS

In the early 1900s, while the LCC was busy trying to unite its northern and southern systems, London's legions of bus operators were looking at new means of motive power. The horse had been a faithful servant, and in 1902 many thousands were still actively employed hauling over 3,700 omnibuses around London and its environs. But by 1905 excitement was running high about its successor, the motor bus. Like the tramcar, the omnibus had been the subject of countless experiments during the second half of the Nineteenth Century, mainly with steam. But now all attention was on the petrol engined motor bus, and most bus companies had at least one or two to try out. Makes like Milnes Daimler, De Dion, Leyland, Crossley and others, were being assessed.

The LGOC did not immediately enter the motor bus fray, preferring to wait and let the competition make trials and errors. The General also continued with its policy of buying out and absorbing most of its main competitors when the opportunity came up. In London, buses were going from strength to strength but trams were still more profitable, at least until the outbreak of World War One. Buses were losing the tag of being transport for the better off; they were starting services earlier in the day, and issuing "workmens" fares. They were also trying to cream off revenue from the trams by running along the same routes. The tramway operators were thwarted by this kind of competition and unable to retaliate, their conditions of operation not allowing them to run bus services.

It seemed as though the bus was getting the upper hand. It was not bound by fixed stopping places as was the tram; people could board and alight wherever they wanted. It did not have to worry about crossing council or county boundaries and was not disrupted by track maintenance or renewal works. Indeed, if buses had to make diversions from their usual routes for road works or other emergencies they occasionally stumbled on new markets and opened up new territories which the track-bound trams could not. Apart from making the most of through running agreements with their peers, all the tram operators could really do in retaliation was cut fares, which few of them could afford to do. The LCC did however reduce some fares during 1923 and 1924 and introduced the famous 'Shilling All Day' ticket in 1925.

After the First World War, in which tram fleets and track had become run down as circumstances forced patronage upwards, the bus continued to outdo the trams in many respects. In 1913, 3,664 buses had been registered in London, on January 1st 1924 the total was 5,311. A large number of "pirate" buses came onto the streets to compete not only with trams, but also with the LGOC whose bus design ability was now reaping rewards. Having designed and built the famous 'B' type from 1910, it was time for the 'K' and 'S' types to make their debut. New more advanced designs were rolling off the drawing board with increasing speed to serve new and developing areas outside the now seemingly limited LCC boundaries. The Underground Group, which included the LGOC, still wanted some form of working relationship with the tram operators, particularly the LCC. The fact that tram operators were now facing some stiff competition from faster, more modern, buses and electric railways undermined the LCC's position.

However help was on the horizon, in the shape of the 1924 London Traffic Act which, among other things, placed restrictions on the number of buses which could run along congested and busy streets. The Act pinpointed 695 such streets, and deemed all roads served by trams as "congested". The Act concluded that more buses were being operated than the public needed. In 1926, just before the Act took effect, the number of buses running in London had reached 5,500. The competition was thus diminished significantly at a stroke and the ailing fortunes of the trams revived at a time when in other parts of the country some smaller tram systems were being closed down. Indeed, some stretches of London tramway were closed during the 1920s; Hounslow Heath (LUT) 1922, Richmond Bridge (LUT) 1924, Addiscombe (Croydon) 1927, together with the Barking system mentioned earlier.

Generally speaking the 1920s proved a mixed bag for tram operators' fortunes. The all-important balance sheet was all too often written in red ink. True, deficits could be made good from the rates, but it demonstrated that the heady years of Edwardian mobility that the electric tramcar had brought to countless thousands.

In 1929 the tramcar took another knock when the LGOC unveiled LT 1, an AEC Renown LT-type double decker. The advanced style and performance exhibited by the LT and its shorter wheelbase counterpart, the ST, made many of London's trams look positively archaic, even when set against 'Bluebell' and 'Poppy', the two experimental cars the LGOC's sister company the MET built in 1927/8. They had demonstrated that improvements could be made to the traditional tramcar design to enhance comfort, make boarding and alighting easier and improve performance standards in the face of new and better buses. But tramcar design was about to surpass even this.

THE PULLMANISATION PROGRAMME AND MORE TRAMS FOR THE LCC

After speeding up many of its services, particularly those in south London, with more powerfully motored trams, the LCC decided to make the cars themselves more comfortable and pleasant to ride in. The basic LCC tram had changed little since Edwardian times, but by the early twenties the world had moved on. While buses were winning the comfort battle hands down with padded seats, and better suspension, London's tram passengers were still resting their more tender regions on wooden slatted benches. So the LCC acted, and in 1926 one of the 1922 E/1s, 1817, received the 'Pullman' treatment, new upholstered transverse seating downstairs and cushioned seating on top; brighter interior decor with better lighting finished the job. Outside a new rich red and cream livery replaced the original primrose and purple lake. All panelling beneath the lower deck windows, and the upper decks, was red, with the window surrounds in pale yellow. A number of different versions of the new livery had been tried, including simply replacing the purple lake with crimson. An E class car even appeared in orange.

Following the success of car 1817, which was allocated to Clapham depot, the LCC began a major programme to update the E, E/1, and M classes. Just as this was finishing more new cars began arriving. All embodied the concession to greater comfort from the beginning.

CLASS HR1   1852   Total 1
CLASS HR2   1853   Total 1

In the late twenties the LCC set about designing the replacement for the pre-1906 cars still in service. Two prototypes were built at Charlton in 1929 and were classified HR (Hilly Route). The purpose was to replace the C and M cars working on the services which included steep gradients like those around Dog Kennel Hill and Highgate Hill. HR1/1852 and HR2/1853 had a revised style body which was to become the LCC's new standard design. They differed from earlier cars, especially in the design of the top deck which had repositioned window pillars at each end. As a result there was one large window which housed the route number stencil box, and three narrow, instead of two wider, windows on either side before the vertical sliding windows. While 1852 had tapered lower deck side panels, 1853's lower deck side panels were flush straight with the body side and did not taper in like those on earlier models. The lower-deck window pillars were wider. The body was an all-metal construction with the top deck composed of aluminium alloy.

Above **Although the LCC Pullmanisation project concentrated on providing new, transverse seating in the lower deck, those 'on top' weren't entirely forgotten as this picture proves. Cream paint has brightened the interior and new lighting provides sufficient illumination for newspaper readers. The group of people posed here sits on newly upholstered seats. All the passengers look very middle class, somewhat out of character with traditional view of the top deck crammed with workers and artisans on their way to the daily toil!** LT Museum H16076

Left **During the last few years of the LCC tramways further research programmes were instituted into improving current collection. Car 1172 is seen at Grove Park underneath overhead which has been designed for trolleys, bow collectors and in this case pantographs. Car 844 was similarly fitted with a pantograph, whilst sister vehicles Nos. 835 and 1360 sported a bow collector. Had tramway development continued unhindered, it is interesting to speculate that the expensive conduit system might have been replaced by overhead wires.**
R.J.Harley collection

Also 'Pullmanised' were the three M class trams that were extended in 1932/33 and reclassified ME/3. The lower saloon of 1444 is shown here; this car lasted in service until 1951. LT Museum

Heralded as 'one of 150 new and better trams' HR/2 class car 1863 poses for the official photograph in August 1930. These particular vehicles will always be remembered for their climbing abilities and the seeming ease with which they could tackle Dog Kennel Hill and Highgate Hill. Although traditional in shape when compared to the Felthams, most of class HR/2 performed sterling service well into the twilight years of the London system. LCC

The E/1 series 552-601 easily stood out from the rest of the fleet by virtue of the double width centre window pillars in the lower saloon. This view was taken at the corner of Wickham Lane, Plumstead, shortly after the series was introduced, and it shows quite clearly the truck mounted plough carrier, salvaged with all the rest of the undergear from redundant F and G class cars. R.Elliott

Inside, 1853 embodied some of the principles of 'Pullmanisation'. It had padded moquette covered transverse seating downstairs, with maroon leather padded transverse seating on top. The new red livery was applied. Both 1852 and 1853 were mounted on two Hurst Nelson trucks which had wheels of equal diameter all round, rather than the usual arrangement of two large and two small wheels per bogie in order to accommodate two 35hp MV 109 motors (instead of one), and to put the whole of the car's weight onto the driving axles. Each truck was powered by two 35hp Metrovick motors. Both cars had twin trolley poles and Metrovick controllers. They were allocated to Camberwell depot and were there on the night of 7th/8th September 1940 when the depot was all but destroyed by bombing and most of the trams inside, including 1852 and 1853, were blasted beyond repair.

CLASS E/1   552-601 (Total 50)
Fifty new cars were built in 1930, and although they were incorporated into the E/1 class they were easily distinguishable from the 1,000 E/1s already in service. The bodies were built by English Electric and they resembled the restyled design first seen on 1852, except that the lower deck side panels

sloped inwards as on earlier E/1s. Also, as on 1852 the central window pillar on the lower deck was considerably wider than those either side of it. These new E/1s were not built with windscreens, but were fitted with them later on.

The 50 cars were given the same stock numbers as the F and G classes which had only recently been withdrawn, because they utilised the trucks and electrical equipment displaced from them, although the numbers applied to the trucks changed within the batch. They were fitted with Westinghouse controllers and 220 type motors and allocated far and wide across the LCC area. All received windscreens during the latter 1930s and some lasted until the end of London trams in 1952.

CLASS HR2   1854-1903   (Total 50)
              101-160   (Total 60)
Production of the HR2 class began in 1930 with a batch of 50 (1854-1903) being supplied by English Electric. They were the last LCC cars to be built without platform windscreens. They were mounted on two EMB trucks and were powered by Metrovick 109 motors. The second batch (101-159) were built by Hurst Nelson, and were intended for the Highgate Hill service. The two EMB

trucks on these housed Metrovick 109Z motors. The cars were fitted with Metrovick control equipment and a driver's windscreen was fitted to the Hurst Nelson cars. This batch was equipped for conduit operation only. The vestibule overhung the dash plate and increased the length of the cars to 34ft 8 ins. The trucks earmarked for car 160 were instead fitted on the LCC's 'Bluebird' car (see later), and 160 received the later type of EMB maximum traction truck similar to those fitted to E/3s, into which class No.160 was assimilated.

It was in 1931, at the time the Hurst Nelson HR2s were being built, that the Metropolitan Police, which licensed every passenger carrying vehicle in London, had finally relaxed its time honoured objection to buses and trams having windscreens, which it had always advocated was on the grounds of safety. Nonetheless the welcome decision meant the end of numb cheeks and watery eyes for London's tram and bus drivers some years after their provincial counterparts had enjoyed the protection of glass screens. Many older trams were retrospectively fitted with windscreens, although those which were thought to have only a few more years of service remaining, like the E class, most of the Ms and many E/1s, never got them.

Above **E/3 No.1936 emerges into a damp Southampton Row at the northern end of the Kingsway Subway. Traffic is heading south on both sides of the tunnel entrance, and includes an open-staircase NS bus along with a more modern ST/LT fully enclosed double-decker on the right. Today the tunnel entrance, together with its rusting conduit track, is still visible.**

Right **At the official re-opening of the Kingsway Subway on 14th January 1931, we witness the excited throng of invited guests, some of whom have alighted from the special car. This E/3 class tram, appropriately numbered 1931, was painted in a white livery lined out in blue and is seen on the right of the picture. In many ways this occasion and the construction of the new Westhorne Avenue tramway in Eltham marked the swansong of the LCC tramways. After 1933 the new owners had very different ideas on tramway operation and investment.** Museum of London

Below Right **Another view of the same event, showing the art deco columns and light fittings and four special cars.** Capital Transport Collection

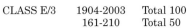

CLASS E/3   1904-2003   Total 100
                161-210   Total 50

The first 100 E/3s (1904-2003) had Hurst Nelson 74-seater bodies, and were delivered concurrently with the first batch of HR2s in 1930. They were built primarily to replace the last of the original A and D class bogie cars, and to work through the rebuilt Kingsway Subway which opened in its enlarged form on 14th January 1931 amid much celebration. The centre of attraction on the day was car 1931 which had been painted in a special white livery lined out in blue. A few weeks earlier car 1930 had received the same treatment when it was anticipated the subway would be open again before the end of that year. The first double-deck passenger trams went through on 15th January. Numbers 1904-2003 were mounted on EMB trucks, and were fitted with English Electric controllers and EE126A motors. Numbers 161-210 were built by English Electric, fitted with Metrovick controllers and powered by BTH 116AY motor sets. These cars were built for the Leyton Council services.

BLUEBIRD No.1

After designing, building and operating tram-cars for almost 30 years, the chapter was about to close when the LCC built a new car which was bang up to date in looks, appoint-ments and performance. This was 'Bluebird', so called because it appeared in a striking new livery of dark blue and ivory. It was also given fleet number 1, and it is widely believed to have been the first of an intended batch of 100 cars, a notion reinforced by the fact that stock numbers 2-100 were also vacant at the time.

Number 1 was built at Charlton works in 1932 and was a notable departure from even the still very new HR2 and E3 cars which still had the look of trams built a quarter of a century before. The overall effect was stream-lined, in line with blossoming 1930s practice. The car was 36ft long, 1ft 4ins longer than the vestibuled E3/HR2s. The top deck tapered inwards very slightly on both sides, as did the front ends, to below window level. There were jack-knife entrance doors instead of open platforms, and the car was devoid of beading

and protruding 'add-ons' like destination boxes and route boards, route information being housed in a glazed side panel at the nearside front of the platform area, and under the front upper-deck windows.

'Bluebird' seated 28 downstairs and 38 upstairs in sound-proof splendour on reversible seats covered in blue moquette. Movement around the car was made easier by a lower entrance/exit step and floor, and an absence of compartment doors in the upper and lower saloons. The car was powered by the same electrical sets as the HR2s, two EMB trucks and four MV109Z motors. It was fitted with MV controllers.

It entered service at Holloway depot in July 1932, and was used on the Kingsway Subway services. Its unique livery disap-peared early in 1938 when London Transport painted it red and cream and it was trans-ferred to Telford Avenue depot. In December 1951, when London's trams were being with-drawn for scrap, it was sold for further service to Leeds Corporation where it remained, along with the ex-LUT/MET 'Feltham' cars

which Leeds had also purchased, until the Leeds system closed in November 1959. Today it resides at the National Tramway Museum at Crich in Derbyshire.

The Bluebird car took the LCC Tramways into a new era of comfort and performance. Unfortunately the prevailing debate on unifi-cation for London's transport made it an era of uncertainty for the LCC and the capital's other tramway operators. It was obvious to the Council that, with the bulk of its rolling-stock approaching its quarter century some decision would soon be needed on upgrading or even replacement. Several options were considered, and some cars were rebuilt to test the options out. One idea was to stretch the four-wheel M class into bogie trams, and (as already mentioned) three were duly adapted in 1932. More experiments were carried out. Several new seating styles were assessed and an E/1 car was repanelled in aluminium. Eventually it was decided to recondition up to 1,000 existing cars, but the final decision was not taken by the LCC; by then the trams had been taken over by London Transport.

Above and left **Bluebird was a natural for the new Kingsway Subway services and is seen in these views whilst work-ing service 33 to West Norwood. Special crews were chosen from the staff at Holloway Depot to man the new vehicle, and by all accounts they took great pride in it.** LT Museum/R. Burrows

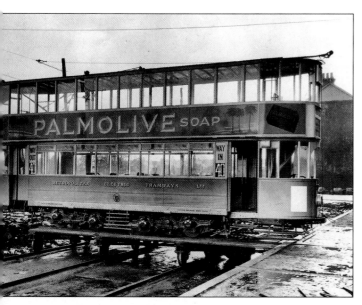

LUT AND MET MODERNISATION

Meanwhile the MET had been giving some thought to the next generation of tramcar, and in 1927 unveiled its home-produced 'Bluebell', number 318, a 71-seater so called because it was clad in a light blue and cream livery. The distinctive body, which had a less pronounced taper at each end, was fully enclosed being fitted with platform doors and vestibule screens. It was mounted on Brush M & G trucks and powered by MV 101 motors. BTH B49 controllers were used and the car was fitted with air brakes. The step height was lower than usual, a feature which endeared it to passengers. It was used on route 40 between Barnet and Cricklewood, but in June 1927 was involved in a serious accident in which the driver was killed when it collided with a lorry. It returned to service the following year, rebuilt with wider entrances. In 1929 it was given an aluminium roof. Two years later it received the MET's standard red livery.

Another new car, numbered 319 and nicknamed 'Poppy', appeared in 1928; not from an established tramcar builder, but from of all places the LGOC workshop at Chiswick. This was probably why the car looked like two General NS-type buses joined back to back. In fact the driver's cab jutted out from the main body line at each end. Like 'Bluebell', 'Poppy' was fully enclosed, although the driver's cabs were not fitted with windscreens. It had seats for 64 passengers, fewer than most cars of the same size, as the accent was on more space and comfort. It had double transverse seating on the lower deck. Poppy had identical trucks and equipment to Bluebell. Not surprisingly it appeared in the LGOC red and broken white livery, which included red panelling around the upper deck. It started life with the MET but was soon transferred to the LUT where it became number 350.

Above **Bluebell made an immediate impact on the streets of north west London when it was put through its proving trials in 1927. The length of the car is apparent in this view taken on the traverser at Hendon Depot. It was also one of the first public transport vehicles in London to have a themed advertising livery – in this case light blue for Palmolive Soap. The interior view of the lower saloon shows the moquette upholstery.**
LT Museum

Left **LUT car 350 (Poppy) was built for the MET, but after only a few months in service during 1927 it transferred to the LUT. This view shows it at Chiswick, passing the LGOC works where it was built.**

Right **Interior of Poppy 350, showing the plushly upholstered seating fitted throughout the tram.**
LT Museum

THE FELTHAMS

In 1929 the powers that be at the Underground Group's new headquarters at 55 Broadway, Westminster, demonstrated a well placed faith in the role of the tramcar in London's transport structure by authorising the construction of two new-design trams by the Union Construction Company. The UCC had been registered in 1901 by Charles Tyson Yerkes. It had existed on paper for many years, but blossomed in the 1920s, building many Underground train carriages for the Group. Its excursion into tramcar building was a first for the Company, and was to result in the production of the ultimately very successful Feltham car.

The first of the two prototypes was delivered to the MET in April 1929, and went into service from Finchley depot on route 40 (Cricklewood–Barnet). It was a revelation. The car, number 320, was in the Underground Group's standard red and ivory livery broken by broad black bands above and below the window lines and around the middle. The full name of its owner appeared on the ivory panelling above the lower deck windows. At 40ft 11½ long its lightweight metal framed aluminium panelled body, built as one integral unit, was about six feet longer than the standard bogie tramcar. Its height, 15ft 0¼ins, was 5¼ ins lower than normal cars, and it was streamlined. The top deck windows tapered inwards up to a domed roof

and long curved glass windows rounded off the top-deck corners. The domed roofed driver's cab at each end jutted out Poppy-style, thereby increasing passenger space in the lower saloon and on the platforms. The driver had a seat, and the new-type English Electric control equipment was enclosed in a cabinet. Despite its size the new tram seated only 64 passengers, 22 downstairs, 42 on top, but its roominess was not in doubt and the resulting comfort was one of its many plus features. Numerous others included special panel linings to reduce noise, stylish recessed lighting and sprung seating.

The MET-designed trucks had equal-radius wheels. Power came from four axle-mounted 35hp Metrovick 105 motors specially designed for smooth and rapid acceleration.

The second new tram, number 330, arrived in October 1929. It closely resembled the earlier car but it had the more standard Brush maximum-traction trucks powered by two BTH509 motors. The use of standard equipment had meant the underframe had to be redesigned with different stress points and reinforcement plating. It was thus possible to keep the overall height as low as the earlier car. Modified BTH controllers, classified B 527B, were fitted. Number 330 was kitted out for Pay As You Enter operation, which meant it had reversed staircases so every passenger had to pass the conductor who

stood by a ticket machine in the lobby area, a feature which reduced the standing accommodation of the car. The new tram, which also worked on route 40, was in the same livery as 320, except that it had METROPOL-ITAN in gold on the side panels. This later became standard for the whole MET fleet.

In 1930 came car 331. It retained the basic design principle of its two predecessors, but the driver's cabin was redesigned to enable standard controllers to be used, and to make the eye-level position the same as on an ordinary tram where the driver had to stand up. As a result the cabin was higher than on the prototypes. The trucks were equal-wheel UCC types and the motors were 35hp GEC WT18s. The controllers were BTH B49. The car had a centrally-positioned entrance/exit with a straight staircase placed to the right of each. This resulted in the lower deck being equipped with longitudinal seating, except for two transverse seats attached to the bulkheads, and a mixture of transverse and longitudinal seating upstairs. The tram seated 70 passengers, 28 downstairs and 42 on top. The driver's cabins were reached through a door in each bulkhead. The centre doors were air-operated and were opened by the driver as the car drew to a halt. The conductor closed them again when the tram was ready to proceed. The car appeared in a modified livery with the centre panelling painted red instead of ivory.

Facing Page **MET cars 320 and 330 posed near Finchley depot. No.330 was equipped for 'Pay As You Enter' operation, with a seated conductor by the entrance.** LT Museum

Left **The third experimental Feltham car was sponsored by the MET rather than the parent Underground group. Car 331 was the precursor of the eventual standard Feltham shape, and to some observers it presented a more elegant appearance with its centre entrance than the later production models. The joys of car 331 can be experienced today at the National Tramway Museum where this pioneer vehicle now resides.** LT Museum

Below **Interior view of 331. A family resemblance to the Underground Group's trains can be seen.** LT Museum

A side elevation of the production Feltham car. The magnificence of the modern design must have been something of a revelation at the time, especially when the inhabitants of LUT and MET were still riding around on vintage open-toppers like the example seen in the background of this view taken in 1930 in the Fulwell depot yard. LT Museum 8492.

All was now ready for the new design to go into full production. In August 1930 it was announced that 100 new trams had been ordered, 46 for the LUT and 54 for the MET. The first ones arrived from the UCC's factory in December 1930, and almost immediately they became known as the Feltham cars. The body shells were jig-built and taken to Fulwell depot for assembly. To keep the costs down, standard maximum traction trucks were used. The MET cars, which were numbered 319, 321-329 and 332-375, were fitted with EMB trucks, BTH509 P1 motors and BTH0K 33/B controllers, while those destined for the LUT (351-395) had trucks by English Electric, GEC WT29 motors and GEC KB5 controllers. The last LUT car, number 396, had DK 131 motors and English Electric CBB2 controllers. All the motors were designed to give good acceleration. All the cars had air brakes.

The body layout was similar to that used in the very first prototype, 320, and the livery reverted to the basic black band lined broken white, with red lower side and dash panels as seen on the first two prototypes. But there were differences, and the result was a fine design which was the last word in style, comfort and spaciousness, features which until then had not generally been associated with tram travel. The overall shape of the vehicle, including the taller cabin, was similar to the last of the prototypes, number 331, but there were two doorways either side, a double one at the rear for entry/exit and a single exit door by the driver at the front. The spaciousness of the vehicles, including a total absence of upper deck bulkheads, reduced boarding times and made it easier for the conductor to collect fares. A designated lower-deck standing area soon became popular with short-distance riders. The 'Felthams' were the first London trams to boast heaters. The inside livery was blue rexine panelling with white ceilings. Upstairs the seating was covered in red rexine, while downstairs seats were covered in green lozenge moquette, although some MET cars had grey lozenge. The driver's cabs were glazed, apart from an odd gap in the frontmost screen which let in the rain. The design was quickly modified.

The MET cars worked from Finchley depot on routes 21 and 40, and Wood Green on route 29, which they shared with lower powered LCC E/1s. Their size and restricted clearance limited their use. The LUT used them on trunk route 7, and on the 55 on Sundays.

Below Left The upper deck of MET Feltham No.321 when new, showing the leather seating which was dark red. In its later guise as London Transport No.2067, the car was seriously damaged in a collision in the late 1940s and was scrapped in Purley depot in 1949. LT Museum

Below Right The lower deck of a new Feltham in 1930, displaying the more comfortable moquette-covering seating. The design is very reminiscent of the tube cars being built by the UCC at the time for the Underground, particularly the advertising frame on the bulkhead, and the quarter-light pull-in opening windows. LT Museum

Finchley Depot on 28th October 1931 and the Felthams have arrived in style. Car 330, the second prototype, sits on the traverser waiting to move sideways past five standard production models and the very distinctive car 331. This depot was modernised in 1930 to give extra shed and stabling space for the new trams.
LT Museum U9862

Left **An MET Feltham at Kings Cross. The 'running number' is visible in the windscreen.**
G. N. Southerden

This 1933 photograph spans the divide of London's tramway history created by the formation of the London Passenger Transport Board that year. The Underground Group, the largest partner in the new LPTB family will have branded appropriate publicity with its 'Tramways' emblem, but traces of the old regimes, including the fine illuminated LCC tram stop beneath Hungerford Bridge, and of course class E bogie tramcar 622 of 1906 seen on a late evening journey to Wimbledon, live on. Museum of London

LONDON TRANSPORT'S TRAMS

The London Passenger Transport Board came into operational existence at midnight on Friday 30th June 1933. The setting up of the Board's Tram and Trolleybus operating department brought together tramway professionals from across the constituent undertakings to fill various roles. As many staff as could be were absorbed into the new structure. Immediately on takeover Mr T. E. Thomas, former Manager of the LCC Tramways, took over the new south-east division, which included all the former LCC network as well as the municipal undertakings in Essex and Kent; Mr C. J. Spencer, former General Manager of the LUT, MET and SMET, took control of the north-west division; LUT, MET, SMET and Croydon. Later in the year Mr Spencer left to join Northmet Power, leaving Mr Thomas to manage the entire London tramway network.

By first light on Saturday 1st July all 2605 passenger trams taken into the Board's ownership had new legal ownership stickers fixed to their rocker panels. All evidence of origins, such as borough coats of arms or inscriptions, were soon painted over in the respective livery colour of the now defunct company or council operator. Before long suffix letters were added to the dash plate stock numbers of the trams from the smaller systems to denote their origins; Bexley cars were given the letter C; Erith, D; Croydon, E; Ilford, F; East Ham, G; West Ham, H; Walthamstow, K; and SMET, S. The wholesale renumbering of non-LCC trams began a few months later.

Inevitably more visible changes were on the way, and for tram travellers in the extremities of south east London they came sooner rather than later. The poor condition of both trams and track in Bexley and Erith alarmed a group of LCC officials who visited the area prior to takeover day in the knowledge that it was to be added, for operating purposes, to the LCC system. Trials using redundant four-wheel M-class cars were carried out over the Bexley/Erith tracks during May 1933 and the result was the extraction from store of twelve four-wheel M class cars which were given a heavy overhaul at Charlton.

The Ms emerged in the standard LCC red and cream livery with distinctive blue interiors and cushion seating on both decks. When they entered service from Bexley depot on 3rd July they bore LPTB ownership legal lettering. Strict instructions were issued that they should not be operated at more than half power. This situation arose because of the poor state of the track work in the Bexley, Erith and Dartford areas. Urgent work on the overhead, which in places was slack and untensioned, also necessitated speed restrictions. Their arrival at Bexley enabled twelve of Bexley's open-toppers to be withdrawn and taken into store at Abbey Wood. Many more Ms, 35 in fact, were taken from store and overhauled, although not so lavishly as the initial twelve, and drafted in to Bexley and Erith depots by the end of October 1933, enabling older cars, including all of Bexley's ex-LCC 'B' types, to be withdrawn.

The Ms were not the only cars to move to new pastures in the early days of London Transport, as the LPTB soon popularly became known. Eight ex-LUT U and U2 type cars moved over to MET territory at Stonebridge Park in July to replace life expired ex-MET open-top B class cars on route 62. London Transport continued the work begun by the MET of fitting canopy windscreens to some of the G and H class trams. Eventually 21 Gs, 34 Hs and two class F cars were fitted with driver's screens.

On 16th August the Board closed East Ham depot with the consequent reshuffling of trams and route responsibility. East Ham's twenty standard bogie cars moved to Bow, along with East Ham's duties on route 63. Most of the East Ham 4-wheelers went to West Ham, but twelve cars were withdrawn. West Ham depot took over the duties on routes 1, 67 and the Wanstead Park service, losing its own allocation on route 8, together with seven 4-wheelers, to Leyton.

Top **Among the vehicles destined for a short life under the new regime were the 17 ex-LCC B-class trams working with Bexley Council like 23c setting down its passengers in Bexleyheath during the summer of 1933. Car 23 is on a special working and will shortly reverse for the journey back to Woolwich.** C. F. Klapper

Right **Invading new territory is former LUT U2 class car 288 (LPTB 2405) running on ex-MET route 62. By the time this view was taken the panels of the top deck cover had begun to work loose making travel a draughty experience.** M. J. O'Connor

An event occurred about this time which suggests that London Transport was considering using bogie cars on some busy suburban routes normally operated by four-wheelers. One Sunday morning in August an ex-West Ham bogie car was dispatched to Ilford and driven to Barkingside to see if the lighter Ilford tracks would present problems for larger cars, Ilford of course operating only 4-wheelers at this time. The resulting wheel spin and overheated motors gave the inquisitive engineers the answer they were seeking and bogie cars never again traversed the territory beyond Ilford Broadway. However, the eccentricities of Ilford's track did not preclude the operation of West Ham four-wheelers in the town, and during the same month number 53H was allocated to Ilford depot to maintain cover while Ilford cars were taken to West Ham works for repainting following the closure of the Ilford paint shops. Ilford was not the only guinea pig for bogie cars. An ex-LUT U-type car was tried out at Erith but kept derailing.

During September Walthamstow's twenty standard bogie cars were exchanged with a similar number of ex-LCC 1930 series E/1s from Holloway, the latter finding it difficult keeping pace with the ex-MET Felthams with which they jointly worked route 29. The faster motored Walthamstow cars soon proved their worth, even against the Felthams. Holloway also received ten ex-Leyton E/3s (161-170) for use on the 29. The E/3s also appeared on the Kingsway Subway routes but were not fitted with the 'Via Kingsway Subway' screen above the destination indicator until 1950. As compensation Leyton depot received some standard E/1s in their place.

With trams moving around to 'foreign' territories it soon became imperative to introduce some form of common stock numbering system. A provisional list was drawn up using the existing LCC numbering block as its nucleus. It ran like this:

1, LCC (Bluebird); 5-44, Ilford; 45-100, East Ham; 101-160, LCC; 161-210, Leyton; 211-344, West Ham; 345-399, Croydon; 402-2003, LCC; 2004-2065, Walthamstow; 2066-2098, Bexley; 2099-2117, Erith. No provision was made at that time to renumber the ex-Company cars.

The establishment of a unified numbering system did not mean that the Board intended to keep all its trams. A scrapping programme began soon after takeover and within the first year some 69 cars, all four-wheelers from the council systems, were dismantled. They included 33 from Bexley, seven from Erith, thirteen from Croydon, twelve from East Ham and four from Walthamstow. Thus many cars did not survive long enough to carry their new

LPTB numbers. In the summer of 1934 twelve ex-MET B type bogie cars were scrapped and more followed in ensuing months with the last B being withdrawn in November 1935. London Transport attempted to convert one B type car, 2516 (ex-MET 63), into a staff car but encountered problems fitting it with a plough carrier. It ended its days as a storeroom in Wood Green depot, finally being disposed of in April 1936.

The early indication of how the unified fleet was to be numbered was accompanied by an interesting experiment in livery styles. Ex-Leyton E3 car 192 appeared in a pale blue and cream livery, complete with a gold legend 'London Transport' on the side in a flash-style type. Ex LCC E/1 (1930 series) 583 also received a blue and cream livery.

Above **The arrival at Holloway of the ex-Walthamstow standard bogie cars for use on route 29 enabled a faster service to be operated on the route, which it shared with Wood Green's Felthams. A representative of each type is seen at Enfield in this view taken in 1937 when 31 trams (19 from Holloway and 12 from Wood Green) were scheduled to operate the Monday to Friday service.** Capital Transport Collection

Left **Ex-Leyton E3 192, seen passing through a leafy section of route 61 near Whipps Cross, is in the experimental blue livery it wore in 1933/34. The tram was painted in medium blue and cream with the words London and Transport separated by a lightning flash** D. W. K. Jones

The arrival of the M class cars did not entirely overcome the rolling stock problems in Bexley and Erith. Further help came in the form of ex-Croydon open-top four-wheeler number 5E of class W1, which was taken into Charlton works and overhauled, emerging in the new livery and with a new number, 349. It was taken to Erith during the autumn and found to be satisfactory in operation, prompting the engineers to exchange the trucks from seven ex-Croydon cars awaiting scrapping at Brixton Hill with those from the remaining former Erith four-wheelers. The work was carried out at Abbey Wood where the bodies from the seven Erith cars were mounted on the specially lengthened Brill 21E trucks from the Croydon vehicles. The cars were then overhauled and painted red and cream but kept their original numbers; 7, 8, 10, 11, 12, 13 and 14. They returned to Erith to join number 349 and two former East Ham four-wheelers, numbers 53 and 58, which had also been repainted and fitted with magnetic track brakes. These two were not a success in their new home and saw little service. Back in Croydon cars 1-3 were renumbered 345-347, number 19 became a snowbroom, while cars 4, 6-18 and 20 made the final journey to Brixton Hill, one of the depots being used to break redundant cars. They were joined there by all the former Bexley and Erith cars languishing in Abbey Wood depot, including Bexley A class Nos 1-16, Bexley's ex-LCC Bs Nos 17-33, Erith Nos 1-6, 9, 15-18 and the ex-Hull car No.19.

As 1933 entered its last quarter it became evident that the red and cream livery adorned by the LCC trams was to be the standard for the whole fleet, Croydon and Walthamstow cars being among the first to carry it along with their new stock numbers. The first route withdrawal of the new regime occurred on 1st November when ex-LCC route 80 (Blackfriars – West Norwood) was replaced by a diversion and extension from Brixton of tram route 48.

Even the most ardent tramway enthusiast could not deny that the LUT's trolleybus network in the Kingston area had been a success, so it came as no surprise when during November the Board confirmed its intention to seek powers to begin the lengthy process of replacing London's trams with trolleybuses, starting with 90 route miles mainly north of the Thames.

Top **M class car No. 1725 heads for Dartford on the route which was to become number 96 in the route numbering changes introduced on 3rd October 1934. A notice to this effect can be seen pasted on the rocker panel next to the entrance. However, for some reason Bexley's Ms never carried stencils for the 96 or 98, so the route number holder fixed to the front upper deck window of 1725 was destined to remain empty until it moved across to east London late in 1935 and began work on the Leyton and West Ham local services, which did carry proper route stencils.** C. Carter

Right **The era of London Transport has truly arrived in this corner of south-east London, as the gloss from a newly applied coat of scarlet paint on former Erith Council four-wheeler No. 13 testifies. Now numbered 13D in the LPTB fleet, it is seen here in 1934 in front of a standard ex-LCC E/1 car at Abbey Wood, working on what was to become route 98.** Dave Jones collection

From Mitcham to West Croydon there was plenty of opportunity for the motorman of Car 427 to ride flat out on 'top notch'. This picture was taken just before service 30's conversion to trolleybuses. Alan B. Cross

One of London's longest tram routes was created on 6th December when former LCC route 30 was joined to ex-SMET route 6, the new service being numbered 30. The 14-mile route from Harrow Road / Willesden Junction to West Croydon required forty trams and mostly veteran ex-LCC E cars operating from Hammersmith depot were used. Thornton Heath supplied 1930 series E/1s, drafted in specifically for the purpose. At the same time the service on ex-SMET route 5 (West Croydon – Crystal Palace) was strengthened with ex-Croydon cars 1E–3E being fitted with magnetic track brakes to enable them to safely descend the steep Anerley Hill. Route 4 (West Croydon – Penge) was withdrawn. Some former LUT cars which had been working on route 6 moved again, this time to Sutton, joining ex-SMET J-types on route 7 (Sutton – West Croydon). The SMET trams were numbered in the series 1S-16S. Although the renumbering of trams had begun, the LPTB had decided by this time not to renumber remaining cars from the former SMET, Bexley or Erith systems, a sure indication of their limited life expectancy. The tramcars from these fleets which were still running retained their original numbers until withdrawal, although a few survived long enough to receive a new coat of red and cream paint.

During the night of 18th December 1933 the long-desired connection between ex-LCC and Erith tracks at Abbey Wood was made. It was not used for passenger services, but to facilitate more conveniently the transfer of trams from the area to Abbey Wood depot and Charlton Works. It was used ten nights later when all Erith depot cars were transferred to Abbey Wood, after which Erith depot closed and the premises returned to the local council.

Renumbering of London's trams into a common series was well advanced by the end of 1933. The final groupings embraced vehicles according to origin and type:

LPTB number		Former number	Remarks
1	Ex-LCC		'Bluebird'
5-27	Ex-Ilford	1-23	Open balcony 4-wheel
28-30 & 32	" "	24-26 & 28	" " " "
31	" "	27	4-wheel (Originally Barking 10)
33-40	" "	33-40	Enclosed-end 4 wheel
41-44	" "	29-32	Domed-roof open-end 4-wheel
45-64	Ex-East Ham	1-35	(Only nine actually renumbered)
65-69	" "	41-45	(Only 44 & 45 actually renumbered)
70	" "	35 (second)	4-wheel (Originally Barking 9)
71-80	" "	36-40 & 46-50	Flat roof (all others were domed)
81-100	" "	51-70	Standard bogie cars, enclosed ends
101-159	Ex-LCC HR2	Retained	Equal wheels All-metal
160	Ex-LCC E3	existing	Max. traction bodywork
161-210	Ex-Leyton E3	numbers	" " enclosed ends
211-258	Ex-West Ham	1-26,28-43,45-50	Open balcony 4-wheel
259-267	" " "	51-59	" " " "
268-273	" " "	60-65	Enclosed ends 4-wheel
274-288	" " "	86-100	Open balcony 4-wheel
289-294	" " "	101-106	" " " "
295-312	" " "	68-85	Standard bogie cars
313-324	" " "	107-118	Open balcony bogie cars
325-330	" " "	119-124	Standard bogie cars
331-344	" " "	125-138	" " "
345-364	Ex-Croydon	1-20	Class W/1 open-top 4-wheel
365-374	" "	21-30	Class B/2 bogie cars uncanopied
375-399	" "	31-55	Standard bogie cars
400-401	Not allocated		
402-551	Ex-LCC class E	Retained	Standard bogie cars
552-601	" " " E/1	existing	Formerly single-deck
602-751	" " " E	numbers	Standard bogie cars
752-1426	" " " E/1	"	" " "
1427-1476	" " " M	"	4-wheel enclosed ends
1477-1676	" " " E/1	"	Standard bogie cars
1677-1726	" " " M	"	4-wheel enclosed ends
1727-1851	" " " E/1	"	Standard bogie cars
1852	" " " HR1	"	Experimental bogie car
1853	" " " HR2	"	
1854-1903	" " " HR2	"	Equal-wheels all-metal
1904-2003	" " " E/3	"	maximum traction bodywork
2004-2024	Ex-Walthamstow	1-32	Open balcony, long wheelbase
2031-2041	" "	Nos. intermixed	" " short "
2025-2030	" "	33-38	Open balcony 4-wheel
2042-2053	" "	51-62	Standard bogie-cars, unvestibuled
2054-2061	" "	39-46	" " " vestibuled
2062-2065	" "	47-50	Ex-Rotherham single-deckers
2066-2119	Ex-Met Felthams	319, 321-329, 332-375	
2120-2165	Ex-LUT Felthams	351-396	
2166-2168	Ex-Met	320, 330, 331	Experimental Felthams
2169-2247	Ex-MET class H	237-314 & 316	Covered top, enclosed ends
2248-2253	" " class H	2, 12, 22, 31, 46 & 82	" " " "
2254	" " class H	315	" " " "
2255	" "	318	'Bluebell' experimental car
2256-2260	" " class F	212-216	Covered top, enclosed ends
2261	" " class G	317	" " " "
2262-2281	" " class G	217-236	" " " "
2282-2301	" " class C/1	192-211	" " " "
2302-2316	" " class E	131, 133, 134 137-142, 145-150	Four-wheel single-deckers
2317	Ex-LUT	350	'Poppy' exp, originally MET 139
2318-2357	Ex-LUT class T	301-340	Covered top, open balcony
2358-2402	" " class U	151-300 (many gaps)	Covered top, uncanopied
2403-2405	" " class U2	155, 199 & 288	" " "
2406-2410	" " class WT	157, 161, 211, 243 & 261	Covered top, open balcony
2411	" " class UX	247	Covered top, uncanopied
2412-2466	Ex-MET class A	71-130 not in sequence	" " "
2467-2482	" " class B2	1-70 with many gaps	Covered top, open balcony
2483-2497	" " class C/2	151-165	" " "
2498-2521	" " class B	1-70 with many gaps	Open-top, open balcony
2522-2529	Ex-LUT class W	165, 173, 182, 185, 200, 240, 254 & 259	Open-top, uncanopied

Also taken over by London Transport were 78 miscellaneous works cars, snowbrooms, snow ploughs, water cars, rail grinders, sand carriers, breakdown vans, wheel carriers and stores vans. Fifty-four such vehicles came from the LCC, with the bulk of the remainder coming from the LUT and the MET. The SMET and each of the council systems provided one vehicle apiece. All the non-LCC works cars were disposed of before the war, while four of the ex-LCC snow ploughs were converted to snowbrooms by the LPTB. In this form both they and the remaining ex-LCC works fleet survived until the closedown of the London tram system which began at the end of 1950.

An essential part of London's transport unification strategy – that of providing transport by the most appropriate means – was demonstrated on 19th April 1934 when the one-car, one-mile Dartford-Wilmington route was replaced by the existing Country Bus route 401. On 16th May the former LUT Merton-Summerstown route was replaced by an extension of bus route 67. Also in May the first vehicles bearing the newly designed gold underlined LONDON TRANSPORT fleetname, which was to be a familiar feature of London Transport road and rail vehicles for the next fifty years, appeared on the streets.

The end of June brought the LPTB's first year to a close and the Annual Report for the year, which was in fact published simultaneously with the second report on 31st October 1935, makes interesting reading. In June 1934 total tram route mileage stood at 327. A staggering 1.2 billion passenger journeys had been made by tram, and the 2560 cars had between them travelled over 102 million miles. £10 million of capital expenditure had been allocated to the tramways, of which £6.3 million went on track. The staff total was given as 19,558, but this included those working on the Kingston area trolleybuses.

An ominous event took place in 1934. The LPTB Act (1934) received Royal Assent, and gave the Board, among other things, its first powers to replace trams with trolleybuses on the whole of the surviving LUT, SMET, Erith, Bexley and Dartford systems, as well as MET routes 21, 29, 62, 64, and 66. In August two new trolleybuses designed by London Transport arrived at Fulwell depot to begin trials. They were numbered 62 and 63, following on from the LUT series. Number 62 was a 70-seater with a Metro-Cammell body mounted on an AEC 663T three-axle chassis, while number 63 was a 4-wheeler with English Electric body and AEC 661T chassis. The smooth, graceful lines of number 62 were to set the style for the massive fleet of trolleybuses which over the next six years would remove virtually all the trams from north of the Thames and many from south of the river too.

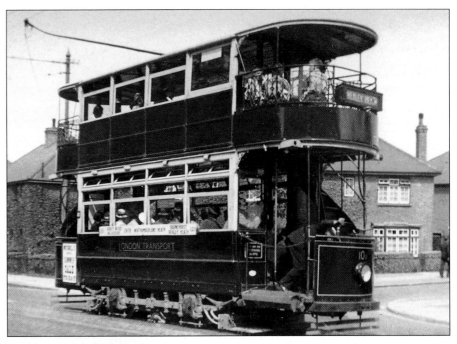

Above **The red and cream livery of the LCC was soon adopted as standard for London's unified tram fleet, and appeared on many trams whose life with the new Board was destined to be short. One such is Erith car 10D seen in April 1934. It was withdrawn for scrap in October 1935.** D. W. K. Jones

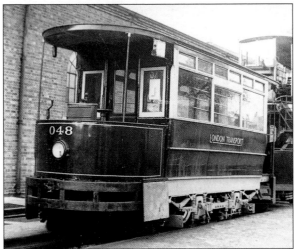

Left **Snowbroom No. 48 converted from former ex-LCC C Class 4-wheeler No. 258, seen at Hanwell.** D. W. K. Jones.

Two former West Ham routes renumbered in 1934 were the 2 and the 6 which became the 1A and 69 respectively. This view at Stratford Broadway shows four-wheelers 247 and 236 in the new red and cream livery, but minus a fleetname. On the rocker panel of each car is a notice advertising the sixpenny (2½p) evening tourist fare which was introduced on 16th April 1934. It allowed unlimited tram travel between 6pm and midnight.
Capital Transport Collection

In just 15 months the LPTB had attacked many of the problem areas besetting its inherited tramway. Many improvements had been made to the infrastructure, especially track, worn-out cars had been withdrawn, and a standard livery and numbering system had been adopted. Now it was the turn of the route numbers to be rationalised to avoid duplication. Some routes were renumbered, others received numbers for the first time.

The route numbers were altered as follows; Croydon route 2 became 42; Walthamstow 2, 3 and 5 became 97, 23 and 85; Leyton 7 and 8 became 97 and 87; and West Ham 2, 5, 6 and 9 became 1A, 95, 69 and 99 respectively. Surprisingly West Ham routes 1 and 10 were not altered. Five ex-MET routes were also renumbered; 18 (39A); 26 (49A); 32 (37); 34 (39); and 40 (45).

Five previously un-numbered ex-Council routes were also now given numbers; the former East Ham route from Wanstead Park to the Royal Albert Docks was numbered 73, the two Ilford routes became 91 (Barkingside – Barking) and 93 (Chadwell Heath – Barking), the Bexley route (Woolwich – Horns Cross) became the 96 and the Erith route (Abbey Wood – Bexley Heath) was numbered 98. Despite this attempt at rationalisation some duplication of route numbers between former Company and Council services remained; for instance three routes still carried the number 7. The Board obviously thought it not worth renumbering SMET routes 5 and 7, LUT 7, 55, 57, 63 and 67 and MET 60, 62, 66 and 68, all of which were scheduled for conversion to trolleybuses within the next two years, and West Ham circular 10, which was duplicated entirely by other tram services and was discontinued six months later. The numbers 50, 76, 80, 82, 86, 88, 90, 92 and 94 remained unused.

The appearance of new route numbers meant that the East Ham four-wheelers and all Ilford cars had to be equipped with route number stencil plates. All other surviving ex-Council cars already had these or roller-blind boxes. The M class four-wheelers on routes 96 and 98 did not receive stencils bearing the new numbers, and continued to run displaying the blank white-painted LCC stencil-holder back plate.

The new service numbers took effect from Wednesday 3rd October 1934 to coincide with the 1934/35 winter schedules, which reduced running times on many routes. The Ilford cars were fitted with ex-LCC Westinghouse magnetic track brakes in place of their BTH T2K equipment, to enable them to work the faster schedules safely.

The scrapping of redundant trams continued during the autumn. Between September and December the 34 stored ex-LCC M cars which had not been recalled for service in south-east London were broken-up, along with several four-wheelers drawn from other erstwhile systems; a total of 46 trams in all.

At the end of 1934 the LPTB deposited another Bill in parliament seeking powers to convert a further 148 miles of existing tramway to trolleybus operation. This however came amid preparations to give a facelift to some lucky members of what had become London's standard tramcar, the E/1.

While the Board was striving to make much needed improvements to London's unified tram system, the business of maintaining the fleet went on. Charlton Works was still the principal establishment for this activity, at least as it affected the former LCC fleet; soon it would widen its sphere of responsibility to embrace the overhaul of 'foreign' cars as well. Despite the plans for a new

trolleybus network there was obviously going to be a sizeable tram fleet in existence for perhaps a further ten years, a fleet that had to be able to withstand increasing demand.

A number of options for improving the condition of the rolling stock were considered by the Board. These included, building a completely new fleet of trams, mounting new bodies on existing trucks, fitting new style top decks to existing cars, and reconditioning to a high standard complete existing cars. Whichever way the final decision went it was thought that around 1,000 trams would need to be treated. Eventually the refurbishment option was decided upon, but it is interesting now to speculate how the fleet might have looked if 1,000 cars had been fitted with new top decks. In fact little speculation is required because a handful of cars did receive new top decks around this time, usually as part of an accident repair. The top decks were tapered and had domed roofs reminiscent of that fitted to the LCC Bluebird car of 1931. The E/1s fitted with domed roofs during 1934 and 1935 were 982, 1103, 1260 and 1373. Two of the hybrid ME/3 class, 1444 and 1446, also received them. Car 1446 was later renumbered 1370, taking the number of a tram written off in an accident in June 1933. This event has a bearing on the subsequent refurbishment policy, for London Transport eventually built a new body which was fitted to the trucks from the erstwhile 1370 and given the number 2. This tram appeared in February 1935 and it shows us what might well have been the result if the Board had plumped for the new bodies for old option for the 1,000 strong 'new' fleet. Although London's tramcar fleet now had a vehicle bearing the stock number 2, numbers 3 and 4, as well as 400 and 401, were never allocated to an LPTB tram.

E/1 1260, seen in Holloway depot, shows off its new tapered aluminium top deck complete with domed roof. It also has the neater panelling, a hallmark of London's refurbished trams. It was one of several trams used as guinea pigs in 1934 prior to the full-scale refurbishment programme which began in the autumn of 1935. In addition to the evening tourist ticket it also advertises the famous shilling all day facility.
W. A. Camwell

The standard style of E/1 refurbishment is reflected in this side-on view of 1517, rebuilt in January 1936. Note the list of via points on a board attached to the lower deck corner panel by the entrance. The use of this panel lapsed after the war, which sadly 1517 did not survive, having been scrapped following an accident in 1941.
R. Elliott

The rehabilitation target of 1,000 trams was soon reduced dramatically to 250, but things were already under way. In fact in April 1934 class E number 467 and E/1 962 had their top decks repanelled and received new flush lower deck panelling without a collision bar. The destination boxes were removed and the apertures in which they had sat adapted as a recessed destination screen. A route number blind box was cut into the panelling above the screen. In June a more extensive refurbishment was carried out on E/1 1397. Flush side panelling and vestibule windscreens were fitted, and a ventilator was installed at each corner of the lower saloon.

All this tinkering culminated in the autumn of 1934 with the rehabilitation of E/1 car 1038. This was to form the basis of the scaled-down rehabilitation programme which eventually took place. In its new form, 1038 had vestibule screens supported by the canopy ceiling which sat on deeper dash plates, flush side panels, new upper-deck panelling with recessed, three-line destination screen, and single advertisement positioning strip on each side. Gone were the four curved corner poster panels. (Where was Mr Oakey to advertise his household abrasives in the future?).

As passengers entered the car they passed the route board in its new position on the lower-deck corner panel. Inside was a revelation. Sprung cushion seating, improved lighting assisted by chrome reflectors and new white-enamelled plywood ceilings, fire resistant linoleum flooring and brighter interior finishes all conspired to make 1038 a popular vehicle with passengers when it entered service at Telford Avenue in March 1935. Three more E/1s, 936, 1001, and 1144 were refurbished in much the same way except that, for some reason, 1001 did not receive a windscreen and retained its horizontal route boards.

During the summer Lord Ashfield inspected 1038 and the Board authorised the expenditure of £100,000 for the refurbishment of 250 trams from the E/1 fleet. The result was something akin to a new tram costing ten times as much. Each car was stripped down to its frame which was strengthened and repanelled. Then the new features which now graced 1038 were applied, including a recessed route-number aperture above the destination screen, which, although incorporated in earlier experiments, had been omitted from 1038. The result brought a touch of contemporary style and comfort to at least a small segment of London's tram fleet.

The cars selected for rehabilitation were those fitted with 60+hp motors. They were taken from the trams arriving at Charlton for the standard overhaul, so cost economies had a bearing on the end result which was that cars across the E/1 spectrum were rehabilitated, although almost all were south London cars because they were the ones with the more powerful motors. Most north London E/1s were still running with their 42hp sets.

The first cars emerged from their transformation in October 1935, E/1 1191 being the first completed. The refurbishment rate continued at about 11 per month until the autumn of 1936. By early the following year the pace had slackened considerably and the last 'rehab', 1922 series E/1 1771, left Charlton in February 1937. A total of only 145 trams, made up of 126 original E/1s, fifteen 1922 series E/1s and four ex-Croydon standard bogie cars received the production line refurbishment which, when added to the prototypes and four HR2s which were partly rebuilt in the same style, brought the total to 164. In a separate exercise carried out in the late 1930s, many of the trams which had not been treated to the full rehabilitation but which were deemed to have a reasonably healthy life expectancy – 400 in all – received driver's windscreens. The total was made up of over 320 E/1s, including all of the 1930 series E/1s, 21 ex-Croydon standard bogie cars, five ex-East Ham and three ex-West Ham standard bogie cars and all non-rehabilitated HR2s in the 1852-1903 series. During the overhaul cycle many cars received new upper deck panelling similar to that on the 'rehabs', and the new 'K-Ray' style angled destination indicator box which first appeared on the 1930 series E/1s, E/3s and HR2s.

Aside from car improvements, evidence of modernisation of the track layout was apparent with the opening on 25th August 1935 of the new roundabout at the Yorkshire Grey, Eltham. Automatic points were fitted, so that the motorman of each tram could select his route by applying power or coasting under an overhead contact. These often failed however, especially in later life.

Despite this small renaissance the system was still contracting. On Tuesday 3rd April 1935 ex-Walthamstow route 2 and West Ham circular route 10 were withdrawn, the former being replaced from the following day by a weekday extension of route 87. A number of ex-West Ham four wheelers were scrapped as a result. Leyton depot lost its allocation on peak hour route 55EX which became the exclusive property of Hackney.

A short route extension over existing tracks occurred on 26th September, when service 6 was prolonged from Tooting Junction to Mitcham Fair Green.

When the Board's second Annual Report was published on 31st October 1935 it was able to show that the improvements to tram services made up to 30th June had attracted 11 million extra passenger journeys to the system. There were 2,473 tramcars in service, a decrease of 87 over the previous year. Although the total route mileage of the system had fallen from 327 to 324, the last year this happy state of affairs would prevail, car miles had fallen by 466,183 to 101,576,367, a staggering figure nevertheless. A further £488,400 had been spent on track. The Report also carried a brief eulogy to the trolleybuses, then beginning their first onslaught on tramway mileage since 1931; they would be, 'of considerable assistance in relieving traffic congestion and attaining safer and more efficient operation'.

Later in July Royal Assent was given to the LPTB (Agreement) Act 1935, offering up 148 more tramway miles to the trolleybus, chiefly in north and east London. These included sections of route not previously served by trams. The process of seeking powers to substitute trolleybuses for trams

was to continue until the Board had obtained authority to substitute all London's tramway mileage with trolleybuses, a process which began on the night of Saturday 26th October when trams on former LUT route 57 from Hounslow depot, together with those on routes 63 and 67 from Fulwell, ran back to their depots for the last time. At these locations 52 gleaming new trolleybuses, built in the style of prototype number 62, were waiting to make the first assault of London Transport's wholesale tramway abandonment programme. It had been decided to place the new trolleybus route numbers in the 6xx series, with the last two digits, so far as was possible, duplicating the replaced tram service number. Thus routes 657 and 667 ran from start of services the following day. One important change associated with this conversion was the withdrawal of ex-LCC route 26 between Hammersmith and Kew Bridge.

Over fifty trams were displaced. They came mainly from former LUT types T, U, U2, and WT. The remaining eight type W cars were withdrawn as was the unique number 2317 'Poppy', but a number of ex-LUT trams were transferred to former MET depots where they replaced 25 type As and all the B/2 types. Many redundant trams were scrapped at Hampstead and Fulwell depots. The Board's policy of cascading redundant cars in better condition to replace worn out trams on routes still running was to continue throughout the replacement programme.

After the first sortie it was only a fortnight to the next round of changes, which took place on Sunday 10th November. Route 98 (operated by Abbey Wood depot) was replaced by trolleybus 698 working from a

huge new depot in Erith Road, Bexleyheath. As it turned out this was to be London's only completely new trolleybus depot, all others being converted from former tram installations. Route 698 ran right through to Woolwich thereby forging the link across the Erith/London border about which much agonising had taken place in earlier years. This replaced the need for route 40 to run between Woolwich and Abbey Wood and Abbey Wood depot ceased to run trams on the 40 as a result. Interestingly, it soon became obvious that the new trolleybus routes 696 and 698 plus the original tram services 36 and 38 were unable to cope with passenger traffic demands between Woolwich and Plumstead. Therefore on 21st May 1936 service 40 was reinstated at peak hours to terminate at Wickham Lane, Plumstead.

Below **The money allocated, but not in the event used, for E/1 refurbishment was utilised to partially update many other vehicles. This E/1 seen at the Epping Forest terminus of route 81 has had new panelling bolted over the old, between the decks. It has also been fitted with a Kay-Ray route destination indicator.**
H. B. Priestley

Right **The much heralded tram to trolleybus conversion programme is under starters orders as the last (ex-LUT) 57 of all waits to depart from the Shepherds Bush Green terminus on the night of 26th October 1935. In just a few hours trolleybuses on new route 657 will be circumnavigating the Green and this ex T type 'palace' tram will be taken on its final journey.** LT Museum

Left **Time is running out for the M class cars in the Bexley and Erith area. At Bexley depot shortly before the changeover an LT tower wagon is parked awaiting another foray to check the new overhead wiring needed for the trolleybuses, which would be housed about half a mile away in a brand new depot.**

Two weeks later on 24th November it was farewell to Bexley tram route 96, which became trolleybus route 696 working from the new Erith Road depot. The old Bexley depot which had run the 96 closed and was returned to Council ownership. The trolleybuses did not proceed beyond the Market Place at Dartford, the Dartford – Horns Cross section of the 96 being replaced by the existing Country Bus route 480 to Gravesend.

The 696 and 698 between them required 38 trolleybuses. The vehicles allocated were 60-seat short-wheelbase versions of number 62. Forty-seven four-wheel ex-LCC M class trams were rendered surplus, most crossing the Thames to West Ham depot where they replaced all remaining East Ham four-wheel trams and several more West Ham four-wheelers too, 35 cars in all. The other surplus trams at Abbey Wood and Bexley depots were not so lucky. All remaining former Erith cars and the Croydon four-wheeler 349, a total of eight trams, went for scrap. The two exiled East Ham four-wheelers had been broken up during the summer.

Former SMET route 7 was replaced by new trolleybus route 654 on Sunday 8th December 1935. The intention was for the 654 to combine routes 7 and 5, creating a new service from Sutton through to Crystal Palace and thus forging another of those controversial links, this time across London Road, Croydon. The 5 however was able to see in the first chimes of 1936 for neither the new overhead wiring on the Crystal Palace section, nor all the 30 new trolleybuses ordered for the 654 (short-wheelbase 60-seaters fitted with special braking equipment in case of dewirements up the steep Anerley Hill) had been completed. It was not until Sunday 9th February 1936 that the fully fledged 654

became operational and route 5 was withdrawn. This conversion brought the end of the former SMET tram operation centred on Sutton depot, which from then on ran only route 654. Penge depot was closed, the cars from route 5 being broken up there. The 5 and 7 conversions resulted in the scrapping of thirty trams, 27 of the former SMET type J and M cars and the three ex-Croydon class W/1 vehicles, the last open-top trams in London. The ex-Sutton cars were scrapped at Brixton Hill depot; however six of a batch of ex-LUT type-U cars (2376, 2382, 2384, 2393, 2396 and 2401) which had been working from Sutton were moved to Stonebridge Park to allow more ex-MET A type trams to be withdrawn.

Ex-SMET type J bogie car No. 1, complete with LPTB 'S' suffix, waits at the Croydon terminus to begin its route 7 journey to Sutton. The London Road and North End behind were no-man's-land for the SMET. This location at the top of Tamworth Road was destined to see trams again 65 years later. Author's collection

Oddly ex-Croydon open-topper No. 2 (LPTB 346), dating from 1901, carries new style fleet numbers but no London Transport transfer along its side panels. It waits at the terminus by the Crystal Palace, one of London's best known and unique landmarks, tragically engulfed by fire in November 1936.

Now that the tramway replacement programme was gaining momentum a number of depot locations were being employed in breaking redundant cars. These included the former SMET depot at Aurelia Road, sometimes referred to as Mitcham Road, which was specially re-opened for the gruesome purpose, and also Brixton Hill, Fulwell, Hampstead and Purley.

April 1936 was to be an eventful month. On Sunday 5th former LUT/LCC route 89, operated jointly by Acton and Hammersmith depots, was replaced by trolleybus route 660, running from Acton depot. There were alterations to ex-LUT routes 7 and 55 as well. The 55 now ran from Acton depot instead of Hanwell, Acton henceforth sharing the Sunday operation of the 7 with Hanwell. A handful of ex-LUT type T and U cars were withdrawn. The former MET overhaul works at Hendon was closed, its work being transferred to Charlton. Accident damaged cars from the area were now repaired at Hampstead. Hendon then took on a new, more sinister role, that of scrapyard for the trams displaced from the next three conversions which brought the first intrusions of trolleybuses into former MET territory.

The first of these took place on Sunday 5th July when routes 66, operated by Acton and Hendon, and 68 operated by Acton, together with the fledgling trolleybus route 660, were replaced by new trolleybus route 666 (Hammersmith – Edgware). Route 64 was demoted to running in peak hours only. The last mile of the 66 from Edgware to Canons Park was totally abandoned, although reinstated two years later by an extension of trolleybus route 645.

Four weeks later, on Sunday 2nd August 1936, came the turn of Finchley's route 45 and the 60, operated by Finchley and Stonebridge Park. These were replaced by routes 645 and 660 both to Edgware only, the latter number having been in use twice within three months. Route 64 reverted to all-day working and gained a peak hour extension to Edgware. But only briefly, for just three weeks later on 23rd August, the 64, run by Hendon, became trolleybus route 664, running to Edgware all-day, and the 62 from Stonebridge Park became route 662. The peak hour extension of ex-LCC route 28 to Wembley (from Victoria via Scrubs Lane) was withdrawn as well.

Within just seven weeks the whole of the west side of former MET territory hummed with trolleybuses, 160 of them. All remaining LUT cars which had transferred to Stonebridge and Hendon, a total of 69, were scrapped. These included all that was left of small types U2 and WT, the solitary UX number 2411, as well as the last 41 Us. Eighteen type T trams were also broken up, along with all 15 former MET type C/2 cars, a handful of C/1s, and the last 20 A types.

While the 'Silver Lady' brought a touch of modernity to the A-class, most of them ended their days in much the same condition as they had appeared when new, like No.111 (LPTB 2436) seen during 1935 loading up at Paddington before setting off on a journey to Sudbury.

Above **A casualty of the August 1936 tram to trolleybus conversions was ex-MET A-class car 77 (LPTB 2412). She had been rebuilt with a new deep-domed aluminium painted top-deck at Hendon works in 1929, and was thus dubbed 'The Silver Lady'.** D. W. K. Jones

Below **Busy King Street Hammersmith proves precarious for those having to step into the road to board type T car 2326 (ex-LUT 310) as it begins its journey to Hanwell. Trams used a one-way system to circumnavigate Hammersmith.**

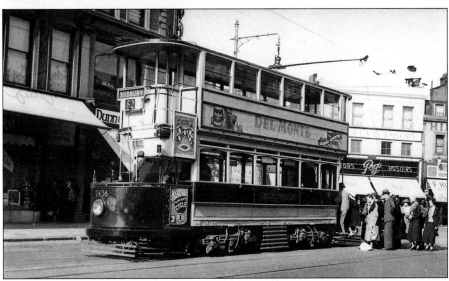

Above **The Bluebird car, No.1, in LPTB days working on route 35A. It still carries its original blue and ivory livery, but now sports LT-style fleet number and fleetname. The unique livery survived until 1938, when the car was repainted into the standard red and cream livery and moved from Holloway to Telford Avenue Depot.** A. W. V. Mace

Above Right **Experimental Feltham No.2168 (ex-MET 331), working on route 45 at North Finchley, displays a unique split variation of the London Transport fleetname. Note also the 'Centre Exit' notice on the dash plate.** A. D. Packer.

Below **A selection of London tramcar motive power at Finchley in the mid-thirties made up of LPTB 2404 (originally LUT U2 No.199), ex-MET Feltham 346, No.2090 in the LPTB fleet, and an unidentifiable ex-LCC E/1. Such was the variety to be enjoyed on the London tramway scene at the time. The Finchley tram station and new track in adjacent streets was opened by LT in January/February 1935.**

Bluebell (ex-MET 318) and No.2255 in the LPTB fleet, reposes at North Finchley during 1935. It has lost its unique blue livery in favour of the now standard red and cream livery of the LPTB. Despite being a relatively new vehicle Bluebell was an early victim of the Board's rigid standardisation policy and, along with route 45, was withdrawn in the July 1936 tram to trolleybus conversions in north west London.
G. N. Southerden

Two unique cars, 2166 the experimental Feltham of 1929, and 2255, 'Bluebell', were disposed of as well, after an attempt to unite the trucks from 2255 with the chassis of 2166 had failed. Stonebridge and Hendon depots no longer ran trams, and a big dent had been made in Finchley's allocation.

One effect of the 45 and 60 conversion was the transfer of ex-MET Felthams 2099-2107 and 2113/4, along with prototype Feltham 2167, four ex-MET Gs and a C/1, from Finchley to Wood Green depot to work on routes 29 and 39A. The other experimental Feltham, 2168, was offered for sale and was bought by Sunderland Corporation in 1937.

It was during this period that London Transport commenced a renumbering programme for a few of the standard E/1 class trams. The reasoning behind it has several possibilities, but whatever the aim the plan was never carried through to a logical conclusion. The effect was that many of the early cars with high-powered motors exchanged numbers with higher-numbered trams with low-power motors. Many of the recipients of 'new' numbers were rehabilitated E/1s then emerging from Charlton Works. It may have been that the Board wanted to withdraw block numbers of trams, indeed before the war most E/1s numbered under 1000 had either been scrapped or were in store. By

August 1940 only about 23 low-numbered E/1s were still in service. Another possibility is that the Board wished to avoid any future confusion with trolleybus numbering, as trolleybuses numbered 750 upwards were due to make their appearance during 1937/38. Eighteen of the 38 rehabilitated E/1s originally numbered below 1000 were renumbered, but twenty were not and retained their original pre-1000 tags until the early 1950s, along with a handful of unrehabilitated examples. The renumbering programme also involved a few higher-numbered trams exchanging identities, but this may have been to reallocate numbers from accident victims for insurance purposes.

At East Ham High Street South, by Roman Road crossover, car 72 reverses for the return trip to Wanstead on service 73. The trams here perished in October 1936 when a strengthened bus route 101 took over the duties. D.W.K. Jones

Walthamstow four-wheeler No 36 (LPTB 2028) was typical of many cars built for British tramway systems in the early 1900s by Hurst Nelson of Motherwell. 2028 is picking up passengers for a journey on route 23. Of interest is the dual-route slip board which could also be used for journeys on route 85.

While all the havoc had been taking place in north-west, west, south, and south-east London, the close-knit east London tram network had largely carried on unaffected. Its turn finally came on Wednesday 7th October 1936 when former East Ham route 73 (Royal Albert Docks – Wanstead Park) was withdrawn and replaced by additional buses on route 101 which paralleled the 73 for its entire length. Seven ex-West Ham four-wheelers were displaced. The trolleybus made its debut in east London on Sunday 18th October when route 623 replaced tram route 23. Another of those unmade links of years past was finally welded with this conversion, for the 623 carried on beyond the 23's terminus at the Ferry Boat Inn, penetrating deep into former MET territory, through Tottenham Hale and Seven Sisters before terminating at Manor House. The conversion left just 27 trams scheduled at Walthamstow, which was gradually to become a trolleybus depot. Nineteen ex-Walthamstow four-wheelers were scrapped as well as the first member of the surviving ex-LCC M class. The twenty 1930 series E/1s, drafted to Walthamstow in late 1933 moved on again to various depots, seven going to Leyton, which had an increased allocation on route 57. Some went to Thornton Heath, eventually allowing all ten former Croydon Corporation B/2 class bogie cars 365-374 working on route 42 to be scrapped, a task carried out at Mitcham Road depot.

In November 1936 it was the turn of the former LUT route 7 to go over to trolleybuses. The Board planned to relocate all Felthams, both LUT and MET in origin, to Telford Avenue depot, but before the move the ex-LUT examples needed equipping with plough carriers so they could work on south London's conduit lines. All the ex-MET Felthams had plough carriers, and during the summer two of these were drafted in from Wood Green to Hanwell depot to act as a buffer while the LUT Felthams went off, two at a time, to Hampstead depot, by way of Acton, Finchley and Archway from whence they were towed to Hampstead to have the plough equipment fitted. Two of Holloway's E/3s, 163 and 164, were drafted to Wood Green as replacements for the Felthams on loan. They were none too popular with the Wood Green crews, used to the comfort of the Felthams, and apparently every opportunity was taken to find fault with the pair and run them back into the depot out of service. The plough fitting job was completed in October, and on the night of Saturday 14th November Hanwell's Felthams made the move south after tram route 7 ran for the last time, the long haul from Shepherds Bush to Uxbridge henceforth being made by trolleybus route 607.

Route 28 was cut back from Craven Park to Harlesden on the same night, resulting in the first large-scale withdrawals from the 300-strong fleet of ex-LCC E class bogie trams of 1905/06 vintage. Four weeks later, on Saturday 12th December, almost the last traces of the pioneering London United Tramways system were erased when route 55 was withdrawn. Trolleybus route 655 took over the following morning and the last fifteen ex-LUT T-types made the journey south to Aurelia Road depot to be broken up.

Above **Route 42 was to
survive until April 1951,
unlike 1902 vintage
ex-Croydon B/2 bogie
car No.23 (LPTB 367)
which was withdrawn
and scrapped following
the introduction of newer
and more modern
ex-LCC cars on the route
during October 1936. The
route was then operated
by Thornton Heath depot
and required 11 trams for
its Monday to Friday
schedule.** O. J. Morris

Left **Long ex-LUT route 7
was home to the modern
Feltham cars from 1931,
but older vehicles like
the ex-LUT T-type (LPTB
2353) still appeared right
up until the route was
replaced by trolleybuses
in November 1936. At
this conversion, Hanwell
became an all-trolleybus
depot.**

Tram replacement during 1937 centred almost entirely on the former Essex systems. The year was just 17 days old when new trolleybuses on new route 685 from Walthamstow depot replaced trams on the 85, making 13 more cars, ten ex-Walthamstow four-wheelers and three ex-LCC Ms, redundant. This was offset by a brief revival on Wednesday 17th February, when new route 97EX, together with extra trams on route 97 replaced the Leyton Garage to Stratford section of bus route 34.

Springtime in 1937 was a busy period for the trams. A four-week-long bus strike between 1st and 27th May placed an incredible burden on the unaffected trams and trolleybuses. Wednesday 12th May was the Coronation of King George VI, the crowds making full use of the many tram routes which got anywhere near the regal activity at Westminster.

On Sunday 6th June the Board wielded the axe over five more local east London tram routes, affecting three depots. The routes were the 69 (West Ham), 87 (Leyton and West Ham), 97 (Leyton, Walthamstow and West Ham), and 99 (West Ham), which were withdrawn in favour of trolleybus routes 669, 687, 697 and 699. Additionally route 55 was withdrawn between Leyton Station and Bakers Arms, and the 57 no longer ran north of Bakers Arms to Chingford Mount. Walthamstow lost its allocation on the 57, and for the next 23 years was to be a trolleybus depot. However it was still connected to the east London tram system and indeed regularly saw trams, albeit the ones destined to be broken up in the yard behind, for Walthamstow had now joined the other depots listed previously as a tramcar graveyard. Among the victims of the 5th/6th June conversions were the last of the Walthamstow four-wheelers, 33 more former West Ham four-wheelers and 45 ex-LCC M class cars. The following month the oldest Ilford cars, numbers 30 and 41-44, were scrapped at Walthamstow. They were replaced at Ley Street by West Ham four-wheelers 261, 265, 273, 275, 279 and 282.

Another tram to motor bus conversion took place on Wednesday 8th September when Clapham-operated route 32 (Clapham Common – Chelsea Bridge) was replaced by bus route 137. To compensate, extra trams appeared on route 34. At the same time route 66 was diverted from Embankment to Victoria and introduced on Sundays.

Top **A couple of ex-LCC four wheel M class cars, 1437 and 1684, wait at the Victoria Docks terminus of route 87. Both met up with the scrapmen at the back of Walthamstow depot following the June 1937 tram to trolleybus conversions in east London.** A. D. Packer

Right **Route 97EX and its route 97 counterpart were withdrawn on 6th June 1937. E/1 car 1348, which has been repanelled between decks but retains an original pre-1929 destination box, has just been repainted and will survive until January 1939.** Alan B. Cross

Four days later, on the night of Saturday 12th September, nineteen more east London cars, fourteen West Ham four-wheelers and five ex-LCC Ms, were withdrawn for scrap when West Ham's routes 1, 1A and 95 were replaced the following morning by new trolleybus routes 685 and 689. The outer ends of the 1 and 1A were joined together by a new section along Barking Road to create a new circular service 689, very different from the earlier circular tram service 10 in the same area.

This conversion coincided with the introduction of four new trolleybus routes in south-west London from Sunday 12th September. Three tram routes were drastically shortened, although only one was completely withdrawn in the process. This was the long route 30 (Harrow Road – West Croydon), operated jointly by Hammersmith and Thornton Heath depots, which was replaced by trolleybus 630. Thornton Heath, now with spare capacity, took over Purley depot's allocation of 21 trams on routes 16 and 18, allowing Purley to be closed as an operational shed, its duties as a scrap site continuing. The arrival of the 630 brought with it the end of the former SMET tramway system as well as the last section of MET in west London (just the tiny half mile in Harlesden High Street). Other tram routes affected by these changes were the 12, which was withdrawn between Wandsworth and Tooting Junction, this section becoming part of new route 612 based at Wandsworth, which now became a combined tram and trolleybus depot. Route 26 no longer ran between Hammersmith and Clapham Junction, and Hammersmith's daily allocation on what was left of it was replaced by a weekday one from Clapham. Route 28 was withdrawn between Clapham Junction and Harlesden, Wandsworth and Hammersmith depots no longer providing trams for it, leaving it all to Clapham. Hammersmith bade farewell to life as a tram depot, becoming in one fell swoop the base for 52 scheduled trolleybuses on routes 626 and 628 as well as the 630. At the same time route 655 was extended from Hammersmith to Clapham Junction, and the 14 and 31 trams were withdrawn between the Princes Head, Battersea, and Wandsworth. Over sixty ex-LCC E class trams were scrapped following this changeover.

Another route withdrawal took place on 12th October. Peak hour and Saturday route 25 (Tottenham Court Road – Parliament Hill Fields) was taken off without replacement.

Top **Chingford Mount is the setting for this front-on view of 1930 series E/1 car 566. Route 57 was cut back to Leyton (Bakers Arms) from 6th June 1937. The bigger aperture destination box, similar to those fitted to some E class trams towards the end of their days, allowed three lines of type to be displayed. It is not being used here to its full effect.** Alan B. Cross

Left **The fate of cars made redundant from the route 1A conversion, illustrated by this view taken behind Walthamstow depot, needs little in the way of graphic description. To the right is the truck from a recently scrapped class M car. Scrapping continued at Walthamstow until 27th May 1938. In total 293 trams perished at this location** Author's collection

Above Left **One route which did not fall to trolleybuses was the 32 run by Clapham depot. Instead bus route 137 provided the replacement service following its withdrawal on 11th September 1937. E/1 1045 is seen at the Chelsea Bridge terminus.** J. Bonell

Above Right **Car 775 nears its terminus in Wandsworth. Road works for the new trolleybuses and the new overhead wiring herald the imminent arrival of route 612.** Alan B. Cross

Below **Outside Ilford depot ex-Ilford car 30 (LPTB 42) prepares to enter service on route 91. This tram was delivered new to Ilford in 1909. It was scrapped in 1937, seven months before the end of the Ilford system.** A. D. Packer Collection

During the autumn of 1937 Ilford car 38, one of the 1932 batch of eight built with fully enclosed top decks (33-40), was dispatched north to Sunderland for evaluation by the Corporation. London Transport had offered all eight for sale and Sunderland had shown an interest, eventually buying the other seven following the closure of the Ilford system on the night of Saturday 5th February 1938 when routes 91 and 93 were withdrawn and 1910 vintage car number 32 closed the service. Trolleybus routes 691 and 693 ran out from the now tramless Ilford depot in Ley Street the following morning. While the remaining seven 1932 Brush-built cars were dismantled and prepared for transportation

to Sunderland, the other Ilford cars and the West Ham four-wheelers which had been allocated there latterly, made just one more trip, this one being to the Walthamstow scrap yard.

On Tuesday 22nd February 1938 London's last single-deck tramcars made their final trips on Wood Green local routes 37 and 39. Route 37 was withdrawn completely, and the 39 altered to run from Wood Green to Bruce Grove with double-deckers. The section of reserved track through the grounds of Alexandra Palace, which at the time was being used by the pioneering BBC television service to broadcast to the small London reception area, was lifted. There was no

trolleybus replacement. A new road through the grounds of Alexandra Palace was completed and from 1st June London Transport used it to extend bus route 233 from Muswell Hill to Wood Green station, thus covering both the 37 and 39 tram routes. Tram route 51 was diverted from Muswell Hill at Turnpike Lane station to run instead to Wood Green Piccadilly Line station, thereby making the tracks in Turnpike Lane and Priory Road redundant, and buses now used the tram island in Turnpike Lane and its subway down to the tube station. The former MET type E single-deckers 2302-2316 were towed to Walthamstow depot for scrap, the first ex-MET cars to be broken-up there.

It's the evening of Saturday 5th March 1938 at Finchley depot, and in a few hours the new trolleybuses standing ready for service inside will have replaced all the depot's tram routes and trams, including vestibuled ex-MET H-class car No.2169, one of the last runners on route 19. D. W. K. Jones

Over the next twelve months the remains of the MET's north London system were obliterated. A big swipe took place, not only at former MET depots, but at the giant ex-LCC Holloway depot as well on Saturday 5th March when routes 9, 11EX, 13, and 17, (all worked by Holloway), route 19 (Holloway and Finchley), route 21 (Finchley and Wood Green), route 35A (Holloway), and routes 39A and 51 (both Wood Green) were withdrawn and replaced on 6th March by trolleybus routes 609, 517/617, 521/621 and 651. Changes were made to route 27 which now ran every day; the 41, which was extended from Manor House all day instead of only at rush hours to Winchmore Hill; and the 71 which was withdrawn between Wood Green and Aldersgate.

Finchley depot ceased to run trams. All its windscreened ex-MET Hs together with three type G cars and four Felthams went to Wood Green, the Hs returning there after an absence of seven years. Six of Finchley's Felthams went to Streatham. Wood Green sent 16 Felthams south to Streatham where

they were used on routes 8/20, 10, 16/18 and 22/24. Seven of Wood Green's C/1s were scrapped, but four found further service at Edmonton. Wood Green took over the whole of route 29 from Holloway, and gained an allocation on route 41. G and H type cars now ran on the 41, the Hs also appearing on route 29. The ex-Walthamstow bogie cars were henceforth used on routes 27, 41 and 53. The use of ex-MET cars on the 41 necessitated the provision of new destination blinds, for a period of just nine weeks. After this conversion the last MET works car, sand van number 05, was scrapped at Hampstead.

This conversion made large inroads into the former LCC fleet at Holloway depot, with the remaining class E cars there going for scrap and redundant E/1s going east to Hackney and Stamford Hill depots to replace more Es. During March and April 1938 no fewer than 73 E class cars had a rendezvous with the scrapmen. It was also the end of trams at Finchley depot, whose remaining H-type cars were transferred to Wood Green for their final months' work. Only four ex-MET

C/1s remained, Nos 2294, 2296, 2297 and 2301, and these moved to Edmonton.

Also during March the final West Ham four-wheelers together with the last ex-LCC class M car, number 1691, all of which had remained at West Ham depot just for the 99A dog racing special service, went for scrap. One, number 290 (ex-West Ham 102) was spared, and was taken to New Cross depot to be stored as a possible preservation exhibit. Today it can be seen, restored to West Ham livery, at the London Transport Museum in Covent Garden.

Early in April 1938, ex-LCC number 1 'Bluebird', resplendent now in London Transport red and cream, moved south from Holloway to Telford Avenue where it joined the Felthams. Officially, it had been a one-car-only allocation on route 35EX (Monday – Friday) and 33EX (Saturday and Sunday). Its main use however was on route 33. It was never a very popular tram during its subsequent fourteen-year stay at Streatham and, initially anyway, was only used during peak periods.

At the end of the tramway era outside Wood Green tube station, the line of tramcars still looks deceptively permanent. At the front of the queue is a fully enclosed car, 2279 (ex-MET G type car 234). Note the interchange of passengers between tram and Underground. LT Museum.

A Feltham in its new territory; No. 2318 (ex LUT 301) passes a locked and darkened Tooting Broadway station in September 1938 while on a night service to Embankment. Night routes were not given numbers until 1946. LT Museum U27718

On Sunday 8th May another large-scale tram to trolleybus conversion took place. This time it was the turn of routes 29 (Holloway and Wood Green), 39 (Wood Green), and 41 (Holloway and Wood Green) to disappear, and it meant the end of tramway operation at Wood Green depot. Routes 29 and 41 were directly replaced by trolleybus routes 629 and 641, but the routeing of the 39 was incorporated into new trolleybus route 625 which continued into new territory along Chesnut Road, Tottenham Hale and then across the Lea to Walthamstow and Woodford.

Wood Green's ex-MET G and H cars moved over to Edmonton and the last ex-MET Felthams, 31 in all, journeyed south to Streatham. The four remaining ex-MET C/1 and some unvestibuled H-type cars were withdrawn and became the last trams to be scrapped at Walthamstow, the yard closing on 25th May. After this, scrapping of redundant trams was largely carried out at Hampstead and Purley depots. More E/1s were transferred from Holloway to Stamford Hill in place of Es. With the 8th May conversion trolleybus mileage surpassed that of the trams. The LPTB Annual Report for 1938 set the mileage figures at 198 for trolleybuses and 175 for trams, although there were still 642 more trams in the fleet which now stood at 1668, against 1026 trolleybuses. Only 152 of the 198 miles were ex-tram; 46 were said to be new trolleybus extensions.

On Sunday 15th May Ex-LCC No.1 'Bluebird' returned to north London on hire to the Light Railway Transport League. It made a 25 mile trip down the length of London's tramway system from Waltham Cross to Purley while such a trip was still possible. Bluebird was also one of the first trams to negotiate the revised layout at Vauxhall, where new rails had been laid in Parry Street and along the eastern side of Vauxhall Station inaugurated to conform with a one way traffic scheme. May was the last time east Londoners could ride on one of West Ham's original bogie cars for all twelve (313-324) went for scrap during the month.

Above **Wood Green depot plays host to MET E types and the familiar form of type UCC – the Feltham. In contrast to LCC depots, Wood Green did not have a traverser. Access to stabling roads was via the track fan in the foreground.**

Below **A chapter of London's tramway history closed in May 1938 when the capital's last open-balconied trams were withdrawn. Here is ex-West Ham No.114 (LPTB 320) of 1911 vintage, at Barking on route 67, which in 1938 required 37 trams to work its Monday-Friday schedules.**
W. A. Camwell

Former MET 330 in London Transport livery and now numbered 2167 is seen at Wood Green shortly before the withdrawal of route 39. Dave Jones Collection

The date is May 1938 and Feltham car 2120 is in new surroundings at Victoria terminus. The ex-LCC cars behind look distinctly archaic. R.S. Carpenter.

Hampstead closed as an operating depot on the night of Saturday 9th July when routes 3, 5, 7 and 15 were replaced by trolleybus routes 513, 613, 615 and 639, all working from Holloway. More class E cars went for scrap, along with the first members of the huge E/1 class. Hampstead depot continued with its two other activities, that of scrapyard and redundant tramcar store. Among its first occupants were three ex-East Ham and four ex-West Ham standard bogie cars displaced at West Ham depot by ex-LCC E/1s. Hampstead remained linked to the rest of the system by way of a single track through Junction Road and Kentish Town to Holloway depot.

On Wednesday 3rd August the last of the 'dog specials' on route 99A from West Ham depot was replaced by an ad hoc bus service. Latterly the service had been worked by standard bogie cars.

Right **The junction at Camden Town finds 1906-vintage E class car 538 en route to Parliament Hill Fields.** H. B. Priestley

Below **At the Hampstead terminus of route 3 we find two ex-LCC E class cars, and 1930 series E/1 552 being pursued by an STL on the Sunday extension of route 63. This happy scene was about to be intruded upon by trolleybuses, as both E cars carry notices to that effect on their rocker panels. The Es would leave for scrap after the conversion of route 3.** W. A. Camwell

Above **Not much longer will passengers be able to savour the delights of travelling on a 1906 vintage E class tramcar, doubtlessly the most modern tramcar of the Edwardian era. No. 637 is loading up with people on their way to enjoy the delights of a summers day at Parliament Hill Fields.** H. B. Priestley

Left **New trolleybus overhead is in place in this view of 1930 E/1 581 heading for Hampstead on route 5. The original LCC tram stop on the right was destined to see out the trams on this section of route.** H. B. Priestley

The interior of Hampstead depot with a clutch of 1930 E/1s in company with a solitary E on the far right. The date of the photograph is not recorded, but the absence of route number stencils could indicate the E/1s are being prepared for transfer to other depots following a trolleybus conversion. The E has an ominous cross chalked on its dash panel, a portent of a different fate perhaps?
H. B. Priestley

Above **No it's not the height of the rush hour in Grays Inn Road, it is in fact a Sunday, 3rd July 1938. At the head of this line of trams at the Holborn terminus is ex-MET type H car 306 (LPTB 2238) which, despite its smart appearance, was withdrawn the following October. Is Grays Inn Road blessed with such high density transport on a Sunday today?** W. A. Camwell

Left **The conductor raises the pole of open fronted ex-MET type H car 250 (LPTB 2182) as it arrives at Ponders End after a turn on route 49A. There is a distinct lack of private transportation in this view. This section from Ponders End to Enfield was never converted to trolleybuses.** W. A Camwell

Below Left **Waltham Cross before the trolleybuses came. Two handsome MET cars with open-fronted type H 315 (LPTB 2254) nearest the camera wait at London's most northerly tram terminus. It was withdrawn after the conversion of routes 59 and 79 to trolleybus in October 1938, and broken up during the same month. To many the withdrawal of the former MET bogie trams was both premature and wasteful.** W. A. Camwell

On Sunday 16th October 1938 new trolleybus routes 649, 659 and 679 took over from Edmonton depot routes 59, 79, and the northern half (Stamford Hill to Ponders End) of Stamford Hill's route 49. The rest of the 49 down to Liverpool Street, continued to be worked by trams. Route 49A, worked by Edmonton, was replaced by bus routes 107 and 107A. With the Board's axe falling on trams with relentless regularity during 1938 a growing number of enthusiasts had turned out to savour the final journeys. In the knowledge that many of north London's trams were going for scrap anyway, a hooligan element emerged which endeavoured to beat the scrapmen at their own game. The last car back to Edmonton depot on the night of 15th October 1938 was type H 2231, and such was the rowdyism on its final trip that the police were called and removed all passengers. This conversion brought the end of the open-vestibuled H type trams, the last type F cars, and the non-standard Hs (2248-2253), as well as the last of the former LCC E-class cars, the latter ending a 32-year period of service in London.

Above **It's Saturday 15th October 1938, and the last night of trams at Edmonton depot. Three type H cars are on view, 2235, 2188 and 2249, all forlornly waiting their fate which, needless to say, involved one last trip to the scrapyard.** D. W. K. Jones

Right **Symmetry at Stamford Hill depot, the home of ex-LCC E and E/1 cars as we look along the traverser pit. Before the first route withdrawals from the depot 115 trams were scheduled to operate from there on Monday–Friday. The depot survived as a trolleybus depot until 1961 and as a bus garage until 1995, when its new owners Cowie Group plc mothballed it.** W. A. Camwell

Below Right **Service 27 was the haunt of the ex-Walthamstow cars – nicknamed 'Rockets' by enthusiasts on account of their speedy performance. After trolleybus conversion in north London, these trams were shifted to south London routes.**

The next conversion, that of route 27 which ran for the last time on Saturday 5th November, brought with it the withdrawal of the remaining ex-MET G and H cars, G type 2261 making the last trip back to Edmonton depot which now became an all-trolleybus shed. The Gs and Hs were broken up at Hampstead and Purley depots. The Felthams were now all that remained of the once mighty LUT and MET tramway systems. Trolleybus route 627 began running from Edmonton depot the next morning.

It was to be the last full year of peace. Only recently the nation had held its breath as the Munich crisis had been played out, ending in an unstable and uneasy peace. Before long even the most optimistic would admit that war in Europe was inevitable. The country was buzzing with preparation. London Transport was already busily laying plans for, among other things, mass evacuation of the population, the provision of emergency ambulances and the inevitable blackout. At the end of the year even the production of tram headlamp masks was in full swing.

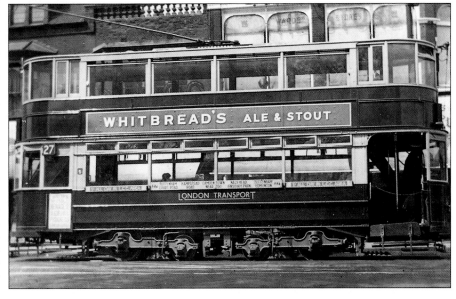

The first conversion of 1939 took place on the night of Saturday 4th February and involved the replacement of routes 43, 47, the southern half of the 49, and the 49EX (all worked from Stamford Hill), 71 (Hackney and Holloway), 75 and 83 (Stamford Hill) by trolleybus routes 643, 647 and 683. The 49, which had been split in half 16 weeks earlier, was now reunited as a 649 through service. Route 71 vanished entirely, being replaced north of Stamford Hill by an extended 643. The southern section was replaced by an augmented route 53 tram service. Extra trams on route 81 replaced much of the former route 71 mileage. It was the end of tramway activity at Stamford Hill depot.

A month later on Sunday 5th March it was the turn of the 11-mile-long horse-shoe shaped 53 route to become trolleybus route 653. This conversion continued the clear-out of trams from the giant Holloway depot and released cars, mostly ex LCC E/1s, which went either for scrap or for further service at other depots. The number of E/1s scrapped after the February and March trolleybus conversions totalled 143. The twenty ex-Walthamstow bogie cars, which had been at Holloway since September 1933, moved down to Bow depot for use on routes 61 and 63.

From Wednesday 10th May, Leyton depot's

Above **Ex-Walthamstow standard bogie car No.40 became 2055 in the LPTB fleet, and is seen here in a traffic jam at Camden Town, along with STL 420. Ahead in the queue is ex-LCC E/1 No.1268 which, although looking almost identical to 2055 is in fact over 20 years older, such was the durability of the E/1 design.**

Right **Nineteen trams, 8 from Hackney and 11 from Holloway, were needed to work the route 71 Monday to Friday schedule. A damp summers day in Bruce Grove finds E/1 967 working a turn on the route. How do we know it's summer? The driver has fixed the white cover on top of his cap, an essential seasonal part of the LT platform staff uniform in summer months, rain or shine.**
H. B. Priestley

allocation on route 61 was transferred to Bow which now assumed responsibility for the whole route. This was to allow trolleybus conversion work to begin at Leyton depot. The work at Leyton was completed by Sunday 11th June when new trolleybus routes 555 (operated by Leyton) together with the 557 (operated by Walthamstow) and the 581 (operated by Hackney and Walthamstow) replaced trams on routes 55, 55EX, 57, 57EX,

81 and 81EX. The conversion allowed more than 70 E/1s to be broken up. Leyton now ceased to operate trams which, as Europe moved closer to war, could now be found north of the river at the following depots only:

    Bow (routes 61,61EX,63,67EX)
    Hackney (routes 31,77)
    Holloway (routes 11,33,35,35EX)
    Poplar (routes 65,65EX,67,77(Sats)
    West Ham (routes 65,65EX,67,67EX)

In the last few tense weeks before the outbreak of the Second World War tram route 14 was withdrawn on 1st August. During this month three HR/2 cars were sold to Leeds; this was part of a proposed transfer of 25 trams, but the war intervened to prevent further trams going north. On the night of 9th/10th August 1939 a full ARP blackout rehearsal was staged throughout the system.

Above **The Tottenham Court Road terminus, seen here with car 1278 and a Feltham, was situated just north of the busy Euston Road. The replacing trolleybuses were extended further towards the West End. ST 34 on route 29 does not suffer any route-bound restrictions as it prepares to cross the road junction in the direction of Victoria.** Capital Transport Collection.

Left **Soon trolleybuses, like the one seen in the distance turning right into Forest Road, will be gliding down Woodford New Road, surrounded for much of its length by the leafy glades of Epping Forest; but for the moment E/1 1205 working from Hackney depot on route 81 has the road to itself.** H. B. Priestley

LONDON TRAMS AT WAR

On Friday 1st September 1939, as the German armies crossed the Polish frontier to make war in Europe a certainty, the Government took control of all Britain's public utilities, including transport. The following Sunday Britain declared war on Germany. One of the first tasks in a war plan formulated over many months was the evacuation of children and the sick away from the danger of aerial bombardment to the relative safety of the countryside. Many trams were commandeered for the job of ferrying the vulnerable to railway stations for the onward journey to safety.

It is interesting to note that of the 1,255 London trams still in service, over half had been around at the start of the Great War 35 years before. Such statistics were, of course, far from the mind as the effects of being at war unfolded. The horrors of sustained aerial bombardment had been ably demonstrated by the Germans during the Spanish Civil War. Also, Alexander Korda's 1936 adaptation of H. G. Wells's 'The Shape Of Things To Come' had graphically created for cinema audiences the devastating effects of an air-raid on London. Few were thus in any doubt of the possible dangers and little was going to be left to chance.

One immediate measure was the imposition, during the hours of darkness, of a blackout and 20 mph speed restriction. The trappings of blackout were applied to London's trams. Fenders and steps were painted white. The headlamp mask units manufactured at the end of 1938 were duly fitted. Interior lighting was reduced by 50%. Later, following numerous complaints, it was enhanced with the aid of light shades. At change pits and terminal points, shrouds with illumination underneath were placed above the overhead to allow conductors to see to place trolley arms.

But the abandonment of London's tramway continued. On Sunday 10th September trolleybuses on new service 677 took over from trams on route 77. The 77 was operated daily by Hackney depot, but with a small Saturday afternoon augmentation from Poplar. The E/1s displaced from Hackney, which ceased to operate trams, transferred to other depots or were scrapped. From 23rd September, in an effort to conserve fuel supplies, the first of many changes were made to bus services, effectively reducing their strength along routes also served by trams and trolleybuses, which used home-produced food.

The next tram/trolleybus conversion took place on Sunday 5th November, when it was the turn of busy routes 61, 61EX and 63 to become 661 and 663. Bow depot ceased to operate trams, and more E/1s went for scrap. The total did not reflect all the trams made redundant from Bow, which included former East Ham and West Ham standard bogie cars. Eighteen of these, (ex-East Ham 81, 83, 91, 92, 100, and ex-West Ham 298-308, 310 and 311) were fitted with canopy screens and made the move south to Abbey Wood, displacing older E/1s, with the remainder going into store at Hampstead. Ex-Walthamstow cars 2042-2047 transferred from Bow to Wandsworth, while 2049-2061 moved to Telford Avenue to join the Felthams and one of their own, number 2048, which had been there since September. Now there were no former LCC cars left at Telford Avenue or Brixton Hill. Forty ex-Leyton E3s went from Bow to pastures new, 171-178 and 195-210 to New Cross, 179-187 to Clapham and 188-194 to Camberwell.

Above **1939 was overshadowed by the threat of war, a threat that became reality in September. Route 77 lost its trams one week after the formal declaration.** H. B. Priestley

While the country had been living under the threat and then the reality of war, the good folk of Highgate village had been agonising over the threatened conversion of their local tram route, the 11, to trolleybus. The 11 had been due for replacement in September 1938, but the lack of a convenient turn for the trolleybuses had delayed matters. All was resolved by Sunday 10th December when route 611's new trolleybuses glided up the Highgate Hill for the first time. From the same date route 31 was withdrawn between Bloomsbury and Hackney and diverted to Islington Green. Its allocations from Hackney, which now severed its link with trams, and Wandsworth, went to Holloway.

Apparently the delay in converting the 11 had caused some problems for the tram cascading programme. The Hackney allocation on route 31, which required 15 trams, had to be retained because there was insufficient room in Holloway to move it there while Holloway still ran the 11 which required 22 cars in rush hours. It was not until the 10th December that Holloway could accommodate the 31 and sufficient spare E3s and HR2s were available to move elsewhere. Twelve E3s moved from Hackney to Thornton Heath, and six to Wandsworth. Of the five E3s released by Holloway three went to Wandsworth and one each to Clapham and Norwood. The operating department wanted rid of all remaining unscreened E/1s, around 100 of which were still in service at the end of 1939, and the Hurst Nelson built batch of 1922 series E/1s (1727-1776), the body trussing of which required strengthening before higher powered motors could be fitted. London Transport was able to place many of these cars into store as a result of the November/December 1939 route changes, with more following in 1940. More alterations in route responsibility took place on 10th December when Clapham took over Camberwell's allocation on route 34, surrendering its daily work on the 26 and 28 to Wandsworth. Camberwell took over the New Cross allocation on route 66. These changes were made to create space at New Cross for the additional cars needed to augment routes serving Woolwich Arsenal. Although trams and trolleybuses ran more frequently in peak hours, services were reduced off-peak, and travel for pleasure was actively discouraged.

Above **A busy late 1930s scene in Romford Road, Manor Park with ex-West Ham bogie car 74 (LPTB 301) heading for Aldgate. Forty-two trams were needed to operate the 63 Monday-Friday schedule, and the observer was always certain of seeing a good variety of tramcar types, both LCC and municipal in origin, working on the route. By this time trams were the butt of criticism from the ever growing fraternity of motorists and few probably mourned the passing of route 63 along this busy road. The Police Box on the left is being used for its intended purpose, and not as transportation for time travellers.** H. B. Priestley

Left **The 'phoney' war has begun and the trolley-bus wires are in place at Highgate Village. All grim stuff for the locals who had fought to prevent this unwanted intrusion into the area. Trolleyless HR2 car 155 draws into the terminus of route 11, just to the north of the trolleybus turning circle which awaits its first occupants.**

The white-painted 'blackout' bumper bars of E/1 car 1066, stopping in East Ham on its journey to Barking, already look worn in this view taken on 8th June 1940, the last day of east London's trams. The rocker panel poster proclaims the imminent introduction of trolleybuses, the last time such a poster would appear on London trams. Only fifty new trolleybuses were still on order and, with it being unlikely any more would be built until hostilities ended, that, for the time being, was the end of the tram replacement programme. J. C. Gillham

The bombing raid on Camberwell depot in September 1940 destroyed the two experimental HR1s, 1852 and 1853. Here is 1852 working on hilly route 60. Visually it resembled the 1930 batch of E/1s with redesigned top deck and thick central lower-deck pillar. No.1853, on the other hand, had window pillars of equal width, and thus resembled the E/3s.

Traditionally the chimes which herald a New Year are a signal for celebration. Not so at the cusp of 1939/1940. London was in darkness, and although there had been some relaxation of restrictions on evening entertainment, there was still a marked difference from years past.

The London of 1st January 1940, a Monday, possessed 934 scheduled trams. North of the Thames the three routes using the Kingsway Subway were joined by the slender threads of Clerkenwell Road and Old Street to the routes still operating from Poplar and West Ham depots, which jointly supplied 131 cars on Mondays to Fridays to the 65, 65EX, 67 and 67EX.

The Commercial Road services were withdrawn on the night of Saturday 8th June. Routes 65 and 67, along with their peak hour augmentations, were replaced directly by routes 665 and 567. New trolleybus route 565 provided a convenient connection around the Holborn loop. The trams released from this conversion went into store as a buffer against possible losses due to enemy action, a wise move as it turned out. Between September 1939 and May 1940 a total of 113 E/1s had been broken up, but now the tramcar scrapping programme, which had continued almost without a break since 1933, was halted. The 65 and 67 proved to be the last routes replaced by trolleybuses, although at the time it was still the Board's intention to convert the south-side tram system to trolleybus as well. Indeed a detailed plan with route numbers had been drawn up and was still scheduled for introduction at the end of the war.

The tram services in wartime proved a mixed blessing to London Transport. They, and the trolleybuses, did not require their own fuel, already being rationed, and so they could be used for appropriate service augmentation. The big minus was their vulnerability to bomb blasts. The 'phoney war', as the relative calm of the first few months of war on the home front came to be called, ended with a jolt during August when the first long-feared air raids took place over London. The first real blitz came on the afternoon and evening of Saturday 7th September when the docklands of east London were the target. During the early hours of Sunday the 8th, the Luftwaffe scored a direct hit on Camberwell depot, destroying 29 trams and damaging in some way all the others in the depot. Among the losses were the two experimental HR1 cars 1852 and 1853. The rest consisted of five E/1s, 15 HR2s and seven E3s. Twelve E/1s were destroyed in a similar attack on Clapham depot on Tuesday 17th September. Two more E/1s were blitzed beyond repair before the month was out. The serious depletion of the HR2 fleet at Camberwell, necessary for the Dog Kennel Hill services, was made good by exchanging 15 of Holloway's HR2s with a similar number of E3s.

The ominous turn in war from the skies resulted in the Board taking the urgent decision to glue blast-protecting wire mesh to the windows of all trams, trolleybuses, buses and Underground trains to prevent injury in the event of the glass shattering. At first the mesh was in one piece. It did the job so effectively that it was difficult for passengers to see out, so a diamond-shaped opening was later cut in it. However the mesh could only prevent minor injury if a bomb exploded some distance away. It could not save the lives of three passengers on the morning 25th October 1940 when a railway bridge across Blackfriars Road received a direct hit and two E/1s passing beneath were blown to pieces, thankfully after many of the passengers had been led to safety.

Above **This wartime view of E/1 No.913 at Greenwich working on route 68, shows an early attempt to provide better visibility through the anti-blast window mesh by cutting small squares in it.** V. E. Burrows

Left **Rehabilitated E/1 No.1893 illustrates how more acceptable visibility was achieved through the mesh after diamond shapes had been cut.** V. E. Burrows

Carnage at Abbey Wood depot following a direct hit during the night of 8th November 1940. The row of cars in the background includes former East Ham and West Ham vehicles. Six trams were completely destroyed in the blast. LT Museum U32223

On the night of 7th/8th November, Abbey Wood depot was hit. Six trams were completely destroyed, including a rehabilitated E/1 and a West Ham standard bogie car. Lastly, on Friday 27th December New Cross suffered the loss of six more E/1s, including three 'rehabs'. More was to come, but the upheaval was enough to bring many of the stored trams languishing in Hampstead depot back into active service. Most were without platform screens but were eventually fitted with them. Some also received more powerful motors salvaged from damaged vehicles. The platform screening programme continued during the war. Between April and December 1941 some 75 cars, mainly E/1s but also fifteen East Ham and five West Ham bogie cars, received screens. The damaged, but seemingly repairable, cars were taken to Purley depot to await attention. Many transfers had to be made to cover shortages.

Some regulations appear to have been relaxed for several standard wooden-framed E/1s appeared on Kingsway Subway route 33, hitherto worked rigidly only by metal-framed vehicles. One regulation which does appear to have been upheld however was the requirement that tram drivers had to have six months practical experience before they could take a tram through the Kingsway Subway. The war had brought problems on the recruitment front. As all Holloway's routes now worked through the subway, difficulties arose when drivers retired. Periodically duties, and even tramcars, had to be temporarily transferred to south London depots until experienced drivers could join Holloway's roster.

Although blackout masks have been applied to the headlamps of both these E/3s, 1999 (left) and 1989 (right), the white paint has yet to be applied to the fenders in this early wartime view at the Embankment end of Kingsway Subway, taken before the completion of the new southern portal which was not finished until 1940. Both the trams would survive until the very end of the London system. The tunnel entrance still exists today. D. W. K. Jones

Left **Even though the war in Europe will be over in just a few weeks, London is still the principal target of the last of the German flying bomb raids. This scene in Jamaica Road, Bermondsey in March 1945 shows repairs under way to the conduit track at one of the very few places on the London system of that time where single track was still necessary. The surrounding area will need some attention too it seems.** LT Museum U36771

Below **Everything possible was done to conserve energy, and tram drivers were reminded of the part they could play by depot posters like this one.** LT Museum

During the first wave of bombing there were countless incidents where tram services had to be curtailed through track being rendered unusable. Bombs, which blasted huge craters in roads, devouring track and overhead wires, paralysed services for many hours, days and sometimes weeks. Trolleybuses could manoeuvre under battery power, and often it was possible to erect overhead wiring at quite short notice. Motor buses of course just found a suitable diversion. Often it took several days, or even weeks, to restore through services, making sectionalised working a feature of many tram routes. Often buses were used as replacements, being able to negotiate the sometimes lengthy resultant diversions with ease. The close network of tram routes in the Lambeth and Southwark areas allowed many useful diversions to be implemented and through services to be maintained.

In 1941, after a year of havoc, things – on the home front at least – quietened down. Just seven trams, six ex-LCC and one ex-Croydon E/1, were damaged beyond repair by incidents during the year. Nevertheless, the war was taking its toll on resources, including fuel for the power stations, and some severe cuts in services were made late in the year. From 29th October, 8% of trams were effectively lopped from the schedules. A new route, the 38EX, operated by Abbey Wood, provided extra journeys between Downham/Catford and Woolwich. Brixton Hill regained its Saturday only allocation on routes 2A/4A and 22/24, albeit briefly, because from 1st April 1942 the 2A and 4A were withdrawn completely and the Saturday allocation on

the 22 and 24 reverted to Clapham operation only. After 28th October 1942, New Cross no longer ran any Saturday journeys on route 46EX. From 21st April 1943 Brixton Hill gained a Saturday allocation on routes 8 and 20 and on 20th October most of the daily service on route 31 terminated south of the Kingsway Subway at Westminster instead of going to Bloomsbury.

SAVE LABOUR AND SPARE PARTS

Labour is short for repairs and Spare parts difficult to obtain

Keep your eyes on the points

Reduce speed at junctions

Shut off power at "DEAD" sections and section insulators

Close poling may mean costly repairs

Try to avoid sudden use of brake

Save current - coast downhill

GOOD DRIVERS TAKE GOOD CARE

In August 1941 a deputation from Sheffield had been round Hampstead Depot. The group had come to inspect surplus ex East Ham and West Ham bogie cars with a view to their purchase. Wartime needs dictated that any spare vehicles would be gratefully received by hard pressed tramways in industrial areas. However, these particular London trams were deemed unsuitable for the Sheffield system, which up to then had persevered with single truck cars. Eventually some old four-wheelers from Newcastle were acquired and the former east London trams rejected by the steel city went on to perform sterling service on routes south of the Thames.

By 1943, shortages of everyday commodities such as paint were causing cosmetic problems to the tram fleet, as well as other LT vehicles. As a stop-gap measure some cars received a coat of a creamy yellow paint and a brown paint called Indian red oxide.

In the spring of 1944 one of the unique ME3 cars, 1441, burnt out while in service and was scrapped. From 19th April 1944 Purley depot gained a daily allocation on busy routes 16 and 18, the depot buzzing once again to the sound of living trams. In mid-year, after close on four years of relative calm, the terror from the skies returned. The Germans had developed the fearsome V1 flying bomb designed to bring mass destruction to urban areas. V1s began falling on London in early summer and on Friday 24th August one landed at Kennington Gate, destroying two Walthamstow E/1s 2044 and 2051 and ex MET Feltham 2109.

RETURN TO PEACE

In May 1945 the war in Europe was over. It had been a long hard battle for London Transport: 48 members of the tram and trolleybus staff had been killed on duty. Seventy-three trams had been completely destroyed by enemy action with most others suffering damage of some kind or other. Only Norwood depot had escaped the bombing; Camberwell and Clapham would need almost complete rebuilding. The war had played havoc with London's roads and public transport, and the capital's tram services had suffered along with the rest, but now things could begin the return to normal as people started to pick up the threads of life at peace once more. Soon all evidence of the blackout would go, all that is except the trams' head-lamp masks which were to remain a feature, albeit modified to emit more light.

In June 1945 Purley depot lost its alloca-tion on routes 16/18 and closed once more as an operational shed, but it was still the home of many trams which had suffered bomb damage. North of the river Hampstead depot resumed its sad role as a tram scrapyard. The tracks linking it to Holloway depot were still in situ and a tram made one return journey between the two depots each Friday to keep them 'open'. On the night of 1st October 1946

there was a serious fire in the depot, and fire safety precautions were tightened. The scrap-ping contractor, George Cohen's 600 Group, vacated Hampstead when the contract to break trams there expired in January 1947, and the depot was eventually handed over to British Road Services. Tram scrapping continued where sufficient room could be found. Clapham was used from 1947, with Brixton Hill and Purley taking over during 1949. New Cross was also used for a time and some cars were even scrapped at Charlton works.

Between December 1945 and December 1949 over 200 trams were disposed of, mostly for scrap. The total consisted mainly of ex-LCC E/1s, but one ex-Croydon car (376), ex-LUT Feltham (2122) and ex-West Ham bogie cars (325, 328 and 329) were in the final total, as were 30 of the 1922 series of ex-LCC E/1s. Not all the doomed cars were scrapped however. A few were sold off for other uses, some even ending up as holiday homes on the south coast.

The serviceable fleet was in a decrepit state, five years of neglect readily apparent, especially in vehicles long past their prime. Some essential track repairs were held up because of a shortage of new rail.

From 19th June 1946 the night services were given route numbers. These were:
1 Embankment – Blackfriars – Elephant – Brixton – Streatham – Tooting – Clapham – Elephant – Blackfriars – Westminster – Elephant (Double circular figure-of-eight and vice versa)
3 Battersea (Princes Head) – Blackfriars
5 Downham – Catford – Lewisham – New Cross Gate – Old Kent Road – Elephant – Blackfriars – Embankment (Savoy Street)
7 New Cross Gate – Camberwell – Elephant – Blackfriars – Embankment (Savoy Street)
26 Clapham Junction – Westminster Station – London Bridge, via daytime route
35 Highgate (Archway) – Bloomsbury

On 16th August Croydon local service 42 was extended over existing tracks to Coombe Road, South Croydon.

It's July 1946, and London slowly gets back to normal. Rehabilitated E/1 1366 is in the company of a 1930-vintage double-decker of the ST/LT family at Loughborough Junction. Soon the LPTB will be announcing plans for the post-war rejuvenation of its road services fleets. Both the trams and the majority of pre-war buses were down for urgent replacement, the latter eventually being viewed by the Board as the priority target. G. F. Ashwell

Later in the year, in an effort to improve conditions for tram pointsmen, canvas huts were provided at many junctions. This all-weather job now offered some protection against the elements.

On 15th November 1946 the Board announced that when the tram replacement programme resumed, diesel buses instead of trolleybuses would be used. Apart from the greater flexibility offered by buses, demonstrated clearly during wartime diversions, other persuasive factors included the steadily lessening value of the power supply infrastructure. This had been an important consideration in the 1934 decision to replace trams with trolleybuses rather than with motor buses. There was a heavy load on power stations after the war, and it was argued that a reduction in the level of electric transport would ease the burden. Also the once cheaper-to-run trolleybus now cost much the same to operate as a bus, and the use of buses would permit a better co-ordination of services. In 1939 the LPTB had unveiled its latest masterpiece, RT 1, a bus with a handsome body designed and built at Chiswick and mounted on an AEC chassis. In the early post-war years, RT family buses were ordered to replace not only London's ageing and dilapidated fleet of pre-war double-deck buses, but also the remaining trams.

The timescale for the post-war tram replacement programme could not at that time be determined because the Board viewed replacement of its worn-out buses a greater priority. So the trams won yet another

reprieve, and an intense programme of heavy overhauls was begun at Charlton works, continuing for the rest of the decade. Before long a considerable difference in the appearance of the fleet could be noticed, with cars looking spic and span once again, albeit with many showing signs of strengthening support in the form of truss bars fitted to the lower side panels of older cars, especially the surviving 1922 batch of E/1s.

A view which typifies for many their memories of south London's trams in the post war era, looking a bit down at heel, but soldiering on in all weathers. An Embankment bound 1922 series E/1 takes up the plough at the Tooting change pit still complete with Edwardian lighting.

Dun roamin'! One of the E/1s sold just after the war as a south coast holiday home finds it hard to melt into its new identity. LCC Tramways Trust

Below **A dramatic end for E/1 car 1780 in Queens (now Queenstown) Road, Battersea after jumping the rails at the junction with Cedars Road on 3rd July 1946. Thirty-three people were injured. It was one of several trams to run away at this junction. The car had survived a couple of minor air raid incidents, but following this accident it was towed back to Clapham depot where it stayed until being broken up in March 1947.**

In the early months of 1947 the country endured the hardest winter for many decades. As if to vindicate the Board's decision to abandon its trams, the surviving 102 miles of London's tramway, 75% of which was still on conduit, and the remaining 733 scheduled tramcars, were severely tested against a litany of broken ploughs, frozen points and iced-up track.

One of the measures in the manifesto of the incoming Labour government in July 1945 had been the nationalisation of Britain's public transport. On 6th August the 1947 Transport Act received Royal Assent and it took effect on Thursday 1st January 1948. On this day the London Transport Executive (LTE) replaced the LPTB which ended a sixteen and a half year existence. The new Executive was an element of the British Transport Commission (BTC), along with British Railways, British Road Services, and British Waterways. Its policy towards its tramway matched that of its predecessor. Lord Ashfield, leading light of the LGOC and the Underground Group, the creator of London Transport and LPTB Chairman until 31st October 1947, when he resigned on being appointed a member of the BTC, died in November 1948. The Chairman of the LPTB for its final two months, and thereafter of the new LTE, was Lord Latham, who had been a member of the LPTB since 1935.

For the trams the new regime meant little visible change. Their livery, and that of all other London Transport vehicles, remained much the same under the new Executive. Indeed some experimentation was still being undertaken with the rolling stock. In March 1948 three ex-Croydon E/1s, 378, 382 and 387 were fitted with carbon trolley heads, and they retained these for about a year. During 1948 Purley depot became a satellite of Charlton Works and began carrying out some tramcar renovation and repair work.

Now that London's tram system had a finite life, the detailed planning of the replacement services began. The planners considered a range of issues from route numbering to terminus points. One suggestion, to use the existing tram route number prefixed by the letter 'T' was not adopted, but passenger surveys were carried out to determine the most favoured routeings. The Executive was anxious to reduce the number of terminal points in the City and central London, a prominent feature of the tramway suffering a virtual exclusion from the Cities of London and Westminster. As 1949 progressed more preparations were made. In March London Transport leased three acres of land adjacent to Penhall Road, Charlton, for use as a scrapyard.

With conversions planned to take place at roughly three-monthly intervals a large area would be needed. The one-site, open-air option was considered the only workable choice because no space would be available in depots to carry out the task, especially as many would be undergoing modification to bus garages. Preparations were soon being made to kit out the new site with a change pit and traverser.

In the early summer London Transport concluded an agreement with Leeds Corporation for the sale of the remaining 92 Felthams. On 20th September ex-MET Feltham 2099 left London for trials.

The task of converting a tram depot to a bus garage was formidable. Traversers had to be removed and diesel fuel storage tanks installed. It had been decided to erase the system in a sweep from west to east, with Clapham and Wandsworth depots being the first to lose their trams. By this calculation New Cross and Abbey Wood would be the last. All depots would need some modification to accommodate diesel buses, except Brixton Hill, Norwood and Purley, which were to be closed. Two brand new bus garages were planned, at Peckham and Stockwell.

And that was how the plan panned out. In June 1949 a start was made on converting Clapham and Wandsworth depots for bus operation which necessitated the running capacity of both being considerably reduced. Thus a massive relocation in depot work and vehicles was made over the night of 7th/8th June. Wandsworth lost half its allocation on route 26, together with 17 1922 E/1s, to Clapham, which in turn lost all its work on route 34 to Camberwell, the latter surrendering its duties on route 66 to New Cross. Clapham's share of routes 8/20 was now vested in Streatham which assumed full control of the two services. Clapham lost part of its 22/24 allocation to Streatham as well. A large number of Clapham's E/1s were transferred to either Camberwell or New Cross. Streatham now shared route 10 with Norwood which received some rehabilitated E/1s to work alongside its E3s. Norwood also took seven E3s from Thornton Heath. For tramcar enthusiasts the changes brought, albeit a little late in the day, some variety to the system. For example the E/1s which had formerly operated on route 12 were now replaced by E3s. The 34 had a mixture of E/1s, E3s and HR2s instead of being wholly E/1 as had been the case before, and the 22/24 routes were now worked by Felthams in addition to the usual E/1s.

More changes came on 30th November when nine workings on routes 8/20 and 22/24 were transferred to Brixton Hill while its

parent depot, Telford Avenue, was being rebuilt for bus operation. Next it was the turn of Thornton Heath which, LT had decided, needed to be completely rebuilt to perform its new role as a bus garage. It closed on New Year's Eve 1949 and from 1st January 1950 its 35 trams and its work on routes 16/18 were transferred to Purley, which once again saw life as a working tram depot.

A feast of Electric traction as two trolleybuses accompany car 2154 on route 20 as it takes the curve outside Tooting Broadway station.
The 20 was one of a number of routes involved in reallocations in June 1949 to enable the start of work on converting Clapham and Wandsworth depots to become bus garages. *W. A. Camwell*

Outside Norwood Depot in July 1949 stands rehabilitated E/1 car 1352. It had recently moved there as part of the 1949 reshuffles *J. H. Meredith*

INTO THE 1950s

In July 1950 London Transport published its detailed plans for the withdrawal of London's remaining trams. The first conversion was earmarked for the night of Saturday 30th September 1950. To coincide with the announcement, London Transport merged the Tram & Trolleybus operating department with Central Buses, sweeping away a generation of written, and unwritten, tramway practices in the process. One measure was the renaming of certain tram and trolleybus depots where they bore the same name as a bus garage nearby. Camberwell depot was renamed Walworth, Holloway became Highgate, Streatham (Telford Avenue) became Brixton. No move was made to rename Brixton Hill or Norwood, which were down for closure when their tram services were due for replacement. For the purpose of this narrative the original depot names will continue to be used. Each tram and trolleybus depot was allocated a running code letter in bus garage style. The trolleybuses

were soon fitted with stencil holders to carry the code plates, but the trams were not. Only two existing motor-bus garages were renamed to avoid duplication with tram or trolleybus depots; Hanwell became Southall, and Hammersmith was renamed Riverside.

In contrast with the preparations for the conversion programme, work started in 1950 on new conduit tracks for a one way layout at County Hall. This formed part of improved traffic arrangements necessary for the Festival of Britain which was held in 1951. Enthusiasts were treated to the heartening spectacle of brand new points and rails which threaded new thoroughfares like Addington Street. The eastbound tracks along Westminster Bridge Road opened on 11th June 1950, to be followed by the westbound route via Stangate and Lambeth Palace Road on 12th October.

By the summer, work on the Penhall Road scrapyard was complete. It had been well under way since January, and in July E/1 car

1322 gained the unwanted distinction of being the first tram to be burned there to test the likelihood of possible nuisance to the nearby residential and industrial areas. To protect nearby property, four trams were permanently parked on a lengthened siding to act as a fire-screen. As completed the Penhall Road yard could accommodate 150 trams. There were 32 tracks situated on the north side of the traverser which were used for scrapping the cars, plus a further seven reception sidings on the south side of the yard. In August, Felthams 2077, 2082, and 2097 were withdrawn in preparation for the move to Leeds.

Above **A summer's day in Clapham and the motorman of car 161 accelerates away on route 34, which was subjected to a cut-back late in life when Battersea Bridge waas closed for repair. The destination display 'Latchmere' indicated the south side of Battersea Bridge.**
Don Thompson

Passengers board 1922 E/1 car 1845 on route 4 at Tooting Broadway on Saturday 13th May 1950. At this time the London tramway mileage was still virtually at its 1940 level, but much had changed in that time, not least the rise of the motor car. As car ownership increased so a walk into the roadway to board a tram became more hazardous, even if, in this case, it's only to avoid a lone Hillman Minx. Pamlin Prints

The first occupants of the Charlton Tramatorium await their fate. Snowbroom 020 (ex-LCC B class 182), was one of the first works cars broken up there during the first week of October 1950. Author's collection

Two rehabilitated 1922 rehabilitated E/1s 1775 and 1744 pass on Lavender Hill by the junction of Cedars Road used by route 34. Both trams were withdrawn and scrapped after Stage 1. The Hemmings bakery on the left was a frequent target of runaway trams which failed to stop at the foot of Cedars Road. W. A. Camwell

Right **Lower deck view of E/3 car 1961 as it rests in its depot on 4th June 1950. Soon it will be out in the sunshine again, carrying Londoners about their business, and will continue to do so until the very last day of London's trams in exactly 25 months time.** H. B. Priestley

On the night of Saturday 30th September 1950 the rather insensitively named 'Operation Tramaway' commenced, bringing the first large scale tram withdrawals for over ten years. Wandsworth depot's routes 12, 26, and 31, together with night route 3, and trolleybus route 612, were withdrawn. The depot also lost its allocations on trolleybus routes 626 and 628 and became in one fell swoop a bus garage. The last car on route 31 was ex-Leyton E/3 195, which happily was destined to enjoy further service, along with Wandsworth's other E/3s which in the cascading process were transferred to other depots. The ex-LCC examples went to New Cross and Norwood, while the ex-Leyton cars went to Telford Avenue to replace the first wave of Felthams destined for Leeds. There were 24 of them and they were taken across to Penhall Road to prepare for their trip north.

Over at Clapham it was the last night of routes 26 and 28, and at Camberwell the last car on route 34 ground back into the depot. The ex-Leyton E/3s released from Camberwell went to Telford Avenue to join their peers newly arrived from Wandsworth. The surplus cars from Holloway depot went to New Cross. Bus routes 44 (Mitcham – London Bridge), 168 (Wandsworth – Farringdon Street), 170 (Wandsworth – Hackney) and two night services, 168 and 288 (both Wandsworth – Farringdon Street) took over from Wandsworth 'garage' the following morning, respectively replacing routes 12/612, 26, 31, and night routes 26 and 3. The section of route 26 from Savoy Street to London Bridge (Hop Exchange) was replaced by an extension of tram route 72.

Despite an imminent end to trams in the area, track repair was still an essential part of the back-up service right up until the last day. Two cars on route 34, rehabilitated E/1 1377 and a 1930 E/1, meet at The Falcon, Clapham Junction during the summer of 1950. W. A. Camwell

Left **Near the same spot in August 1950, trams 1847 and 1764 are seen at the terminus of routes 28 and 26, the greater parts of which had been replaced by trolleybus routes 628 and 626 before the war.** O.J. Morris

At Clapham on 1st October, new bus route 45 (Battersea Bridge – Farringdon Street) made its debut, replacing tram 34. Camberwell bus garage shared the allocation of the 168 with Wandsworth and also ran new route 169 (Clapham Junction – Victoria) to replace tram 28. The capacity reduction at Camberwell tram depot enabled work on converting it to a bus garage to begin.

With newer and better condition rolling-stock installed in their new homes, out of the bottom of the pack dropped 48 elderly E/1s and 37 rehabilitated cars including all "rehabs"

from the "1922" batches. These went to Penhall Road for the commencement of the tram scrapping programme which got into gear the following Monday when rehabilitated E/1 1656 became the first car displaced by the post-war tram replacement programme to be torched. The task at Penhall Road was arranged so that as many as sixteen trams could be broken up each week, although the usual number was around ten and the flow was maintained as evenly as possible. An interesting feature of Penhall Road from the early days was the utilisation of four E/1s as

"administrative buildings". Number 1231 was used as an office, 1727 as a canteen, and 1730 and 1768 as cloakrooms. They survived in their new role until the early days of 1953.

In October two Felthams, 2144 and 2162, caught fire in Brixton Hill depot and were of no further use. As they had been purchased by Leeds Corporation, London Transport offered Bluebird car number 1 to Leeds as a compensatory replacement. This helped secure a happier fate for number 1 for in the more enlightened later 1950s it was preserved and today resides at the Crich Tramway Museum.

Stage Two of the planned nine-stage programme took place on the night of Saturday/Sunday 6th-7th January 1951. Four depots were affected, Clapham being cleared of trams in the process. The routes withdrawn were 2, 4, 6, 22 and 24 (operated by Clapham), 8/20 plus part of 22/24 (operated by Telford Avenue and Brixton Hill), route 10 (operated by Telford Avenue and Norwood) and night route 1 (shared by Clapham and Telford Avenue). Trams cascaded to other depots for further service included Clapham's remaining 1922 series E/1s which went to New Cross. Seventy-one elderly E/1s made their way to the Penhall Road fires. Twenty-nine more Felthams were withdrawn from London service and made ready for their new owners. Norwood transferred the cars from route 10 to its 16/18 allocation. Telford Avenue now had only ten scheduled tram workings on its roster against 40 bus duties. Clapham depot became Clapham bus garage.

Replacing bus routes were as follows: 50 (Telford Avenue – Horse Guards Avenue), 57 (Tooting Broadway – Victoria), 57A (Streatham – Victoria), 95 (Tooting Broadway – Cannon Street), 104 (Tooting Mitre – Horse Guards Avenue), 155B and 155W (Wimbledon – Embankment loop), and 189/189A (Cannon Street – North Cheam/Raynes Park). There was also a night route, the 287 (Tooting – Embankment loop) which replaced the complicated figure-of-eight night tram route 1. Of interest were the 'B' and 'W' suffix letters on route 155 which denoted which direction the bus would proceed around the Embankment loop. 'B' indicated Blackfriars as the first point reached, while 'W' meant that the bus would reach Westminster first.

Above Right **On 6th January 1951 we find second series E/1 1823 on route 6 bound for the City. Despite its rather run down appearance 1823 survived until Stage 5 in October 1951.**
Alan B. Cross

Right **Passing the Locarno in Streatham, one of south London's most famous dance halls, is ex-Walthamstow bogie car 2052 working on route 20 from Telford Avenue depot. A deserted push cart sits forlornly in the middle of the road, and an elderly lady totters along the roadway in front of a 10T10 type Green Line coach. When one thinks of how busy this wide thoroughfare is today such a scene is of a different world.**

E/1 1596's only concession to tramcar design development in its 40 years of service is the vestibule windscreen together with a red and cream livery. Otherwise, externally at least, it is 100% original, even down to the pre-1913 route colour code lights over the destination screen. It survived until **June 1951.** Capital Transport Collection

Below When this view of the Wimbledon terminus was taken in 1950 trams and trolleybuses had shared the road space at this spot for almost twenty years. On the night of 6th January 1951 it all came to an end when routes 2 and 4 were withdrawn. New Q1 class trolleybuses, like the one seen to the right, had only recently replaced the 1931 vintage "Diddler" types on the local Kingston area routes. The wealth of street furniture on show in this view would lend style to any working transport museum today. W. A. Camwell

At Stage Three, which took place thirteen weeks later on the night of Saturday 6th April five routes were withdrawn and two depots closed. The routes were 16/18 (operated by Purley, Brixton Hill and Telford Avenue), peak hour services 16EX/18EX (operated by Purley and Norwood), and Croydon local route 42 (operated by Purley). Brixton Hill and Purley depots were finally closed and sold. Telford Avenue became Brixton bus garage from the morning of 8th April and Thornton Heath, now completely rebuilt, rejoined the fold as a bus garage. Norwood soldiered on with its work on routes 33, 48 and 78.

The 'Bluebird' car was withdrawn from London service with this conversion after undertaking an enthusiasts' tour of some remaining routes, including a trip through the Kingsway Subway, reminding some perhaps of the much longer trip from Waltham Cross to Purley made back in 1938. Later in the day the participants transferred to number 2079, which had been the sole survivor of the ex-MET Felthams since January, for a trip to the City, Victoria and Westminster, returning to Telford Avenue in the early evening.

The South London routes had survived twelve years longer than most of their North London counterparts, long enough to find quite a niche in the hearts of those they served and had transported during the grim years of the war. Thus there was inevitably more emotion and ceremony with each stage of Operation Tramaway, not just from the loyal band of enthusiasts but from local groups like Ratepayers and Chambers of Commerce, conscious of the passing of a local landmark. The Croydon and Streatham conversions were no exception. LT drafted in two rehabilitated E/1s to perform the last

rites. These were 839 and 947, and both were destined to be withdrawn after 7th April. The use of two "doomed" trams was London Transport's insurance against the inevitable plundering of fixtures and fittings, which in the event was a wise move as the souvenir hunters who rode on the cars had a field day. The Croydon and Purley Chamber of Commerce hired 839 while 947 carried boisterous members of the Streatham Ratepayers

Association. The money taken from the premium five shilling (25p) fares went to charity. The two E/1s joined the last service car from the area, ex-Croydon 384, and several hundred people turned out to see them. For the record the new bus routes introduced from 7th April were 109 (Purley – Embankment loop), this time minus the B and W suffix letters, and 190 (South Croydon – Thornton Heath High Street).

Above **Local Croydon route 42 was also a casualty of Stage Three. Bogie car 399 (ex-Croydon 55) crosses from North End into the High Street in the company of a splendid pre-war limousine.**
C. Carter

Left **399 again, and an orderly queue board on route 18 as a Feltham draws up behind. Interestingly, the ultimate destination of 399 is shown in smaller type than its more important via point.**

The casualties of this conversion were 61 E/1s, many based at New Cross, which was becoming the springboard to Penhall Road. The total included 32 'rehabs' and 1444, the last survivor of the hybrid ME3 class. As these filed off on their sorry journey to Penhall Road their places were taken by E/3s, and E/1s in better condition, including the surviving 23 ex-Croydon bogie-cars which had been based at Purley. The last 40 Felthams, all but one of LUT origin, went to

Penhall Road to prepare for life in Leeds. Also withdrawn at this time were three ex-West Ham cars which had been deployed as Charlton Works staff cars. Their places were taken by three E/1s including two 1922 series examples.

The arrival of the slightly longer E3s at New Cross had caused some capacity problems in the depot and this, combined with the need to begin converting New Cross to operate buses, caused a relocation of some trams to

Penhall Road which also served as a running outstation while New Cross (and later Abbey Wood) were adapted for bus operation. Two roads at Penhall containing around 12 trams were earmarked for temporary use by cars operating mainly on route 40. All went well with this situation until staff arrived one morning to discover that all the controller keys had been stolen. A van had to be sent from Charlton Works with replacement keys, delaying the start of service that day.

Above Stage 3 brought the end of London's handsome Feltham cars, at least so far as service in the capital is concerned. No.2157 (ex-LUT 388), complete with badly dented dash plate, seen working on route 16 became 586 in the Leeds fleet. One interesting fact about the Felthams was their corner route number blinds which were wound horizontally rather than vertically.

Left The cascading process following the completion of Stage 3 of the tram/bus conversion programme resulted in three more casualties. They were the three ex-West Ham bogie cars which had been used as Charlton Works staff cars. Number 327 heads the line as they wait in the entrance to the Works to take staff on their homeward journey. G. F. Ashwell

Stage Four was a relatively small conversion involving just two routes, the 68 (Greenwich – Elephant – Waterloo) and 70 (Greenwich – London Bridge). It had been intended to convert the Kingsway Subway routes 33 and 35 at Stage Four, but delays in completing Stockwell bus garage meant the 33 and 35 had to be kept going a bit longer. This, together with the rebuilding of Creek Bridge in Deptford, traversed by routes 68 and 70, made these routes good candidates for replacement instead.

From Wednesday 11th July 1951 new bus routes 70 (Greenwich – London Bridge), peak hour route 70A (Greenwich – Horse Guards Avenue) and 188 (Greenwich – Chalk Farm) took to the road just hours after the last cars on routes 68 and 70 had been given the now customary send off. An additional route alteration with this conversion was the withdrawal of the 72 between Savoy Street and London Bridge, only ten months after this extension had started.

Ex-Leyton E/3 208 was the last 72 away from the Borough, and 1930 E/1 587, hired by the Electric Traction Group for the evening, was the last car to leave the Tooley Street terminus at London Bridge. It was one of twenty 1930 E/1s withdrawn for scrap after this conversion, the first big inroad to be made on this type. The total number of withdrawn trams came to 33. This included six standard E/1s, six '1922' E/1s, and a solitary West Ham example.

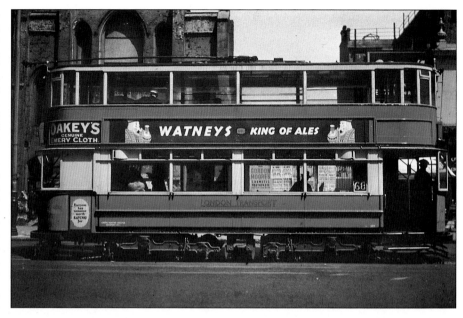

A side view of 1930 built E/1 tram No. 589, showing clearly the thicker central pillar on the lower deck, unique to this batch of E/1s. Also visible is a corner advertisement for Oakeys household abrasives, a feature on LCC trams since their earliest days. Oakeys sandpapers are still sold today, so some things don't change. C. Carter

Route 70, and its sister route the 68, were withdrawn at stage four of Operation Tramaway, which took place on the night of Tuesday 10th July 1951. E/1 car 840, virtually unaltered externally since Edwardian days, takes on passengers on a route 70 journey to London Bridge. No.840 survived until October 1951, making it one of the last of the original E/1s in service. Dave Jones Collection

On Wednesday 3rd October 1951 the last Feltham, ex-LUT car 2158, left Penhall Road for Leeds, six months after its withdrawal from London service. The following Saturday the curtain fell on the network of routes connecting Victoria, the Embankment and the City with Camberwell, Dulwich, Brockley and Forest Hill, along with Greenwich and the Blackwall Tunnel. They were the 56, 58, 60, 62 and 84 (operated by Camberwell), along with the 38EX, 66 and night route 7 (operated by New Cross). Camberwell depot officially became Walworth bus garage from the following morning, its work on the 35 being taken over by New Cross for the duration. Routes 58, 60, 56/84 and 62 climbed and descended the steep and quaintly named Dog Kennel Hill in Dulwich, with its unique four-track layout laid down in 1912 by the LCC as a safety measure, consecutive cars taking it in turns to use alternate tracks to prevent collisions caused by possible runaways. The last tram to descend the hill was HR2 number 1893, which was to see out a few more months of activity.

Not so lucky were the 106 trams rendered surplus after 6th October, including 36 class HR2 cars from the 101-159 batch not fitted with trolleys for working overhead line sections. All remaining services bar route 35 included some stretches of overhead. The displaced HR2s were taken to Penhall Road, four of them, 101-104, serving as fire safety screens until cessation of scrapping. The remaining HR2s went to New Cross where more unlucky E/1s, seven 'originals', six 'rehabs' and the 49 surviving 1922-series versions were released for incineration at Penhall Road. Two, 1798 and 1804, won a brief reprieve as Charlton Works staff cars. Three ex-Croydon bogie-cars, a 1930 E/1, an HR2 and a solitary E/3 were also disposed of in Stage Five. A handful of trolleyless HR2s were apparently recalled for service on route 35 because of a temporary shortage of trams. They survived until January 1952.

New bus routes starting from the following day were 36A (West Kilburn – Brockley Rise), replacing tram 66 from Victoria; 176 (Catford – Horse Guards Avenue) replacing most of the 62; peak hour route 176A (Dulwich Plough – Cannon Street), replacing tram 60; 180 (Woolwich – Catford Garage), replacing the 38EX; 184 (Brockley Station – Embankment loop), replacing routes 56 and 84; 185 (Blackwall Tunnel – Victoria), replacing tram route 58, and new night route 286 (Brockley Rise – Charing Cross), replacing the 7 via Peckham from New Cross Gate.

This was the last tram/bus conversion of 1951. It left the number of trams scheduled for service at 294, and the route allocations looking like this:

    33 (Norwood/Holloway)
    35 (Holloway/New Cross
    36/38 (Abbey Wood/New Cross)
    40 (New Cross)
    44 (Abbey Wood)
    46/46EX (Abbey Wood/New Cross)
    48 (Norwood)
    52/54 (New Cross)
    72/72EX (New Cross)
    74 (New Cross)
    78 (Norwood)

HR2 No. 1879 takes on passengers outside The Railway Tavern in Catford while a motorist can only wait, no doubt impatiently, for the tram to move off and continue its journey to Blackwall Tunnel. C. Carter

The Blackwall Tunnel terminus of route 58, with southern portal in the background. The scene reeks with nostalgia, with trolleyless HR2 car No. 147 joined only by pedestrians, cyclists and a lone Ford delivery van against a backdrop of a cafe and a fishing tackle shop outside which someone has left a cycle. Capital Transport

A trolleyless HR2 on route 84 waiting to depart from Elephant & Castle for Peckham Rye. Anyone tempted to make a visit to the exhibition organised by the London Co-operative Society at the Central Hall, Westminster, could go almost door to door on an 84 (operated jointly with the 56). C. Carter

Left 'Rehabilitated' HR2 car 1885 on the Embankment working route 56. The old Scotland Yard building is in the background. C. Carter

Right A fine group of trams at Camberwell Green on a crisp, sunny day. Of the four tram routes visible only the 48 was to survive into 1952, the rest falling at Stage 5, Number 102, nearest the camera, ended its days at Penhall Road as a protective fire screen. C. Carter

Left The first trolleyless HR2, No.101, seen in Greenwich South Street on 28th September 1951 working on route 58, which like No.101 and the bulk of the trolleyless HR2s, was withdrawn early the following month as part of Stage Five of Operation Tramaway. No.101, which appears to be in excellent condition, externally at least, survived for a further year in the role of fire screen at Penhall scrap yard. The sight of a lone Austin Devon further down the road brings home just how much the private car has increased its presence on London streets in the half century since the view was taken. O. J. Morris

Right This view, showing much of the side elevation of trolleyless HR2 No.137, reveals signs of general wear and tear giving a down-at heel appearance to a tramcar nearing the end of its working life. However this was not the general rule as comparison with the condition of No.101, photographed about the same time, will show. Also visible in this view are the stone sets in the roadway supporting the track and conduit slot, long after the sections either side have had tarmac laid to smooth the ride of other road users. C. Carter

Left Practically every photograph taken of Dog Kennel Hill, Dulwich, in tram days shows a marked absence of other road traffic and, in many cases, people. This one is no exception. Three trolleyless HR2s ascend and descend the hill with only what looks like a Ford V8 Pilot for company.

Right New Cross based E/3 1922, one of sixteen allocated to route 66, passes Camberwell depot, which ceased to operate trams after Stage 5 in October 1951. D. A. Thompson

Above **Now it was the turn of the newer trams to take on a down at heel appearance, and Norwood's E/3 1937 is no exception. Dirty paintwork and a dented dash plate is the order of the day at Norwood High Street on route 78, but it did survive until the final day of London's trams.**

Facing Page Top **Number 161, the very first Leyton E/3, in Milkwood Road, Norwood on route 48. This road was one of the London tramway backwaters and tram track covers two-thirds of the road width in this view.** C. Carter

Facing Page Bottom **All the remaining former Croydon and Walthamstow bogie trams were withdrawn with Stage 6, although a couple of the Walthamstow cars survived until the end of London's trams as they were the very last Charlton Works staff cars. One was 2055 (the other 2056) seen here at Grove Park on the 54, a route withdrawn in January 1952.** C. Carter

Although the number of routes was steadily diminishing there were still some sizeable allocations, New Cross for example was operating almost 200 trams in rush hours. But not for much longer. The New Year was only a few days old when on Saturday 5th January New Cross routes 52, 54, 74 and night route 5, together with Norwood's 48 and 78, carried their last passengers. The conversion took trams away from Victoria, their busiest terminus, and areas south of Lewisham. More significantly it spelt the end for all the remaining original E/1s, 68 in all, including 30 'rehabs'. All that was left of this famous class were those survivors from the 1930 batch. It is worth noting that despite the many changes made to the E/1 fleet since the 1920s, the neater upper-deck panelling, the newer-style destination boxes and of course the 'rehabs', some members of the class ended

their days complete with many original features even down to the quarter end poster panels where advertisements for Oakey's household abrasives could still be seen. Apart from the livery they still appeared very similar to how they had looked when new back in the Edwardian era.

Also en route to Penhall Road after this conversion were the remaining ex-Croydon bogie-cars and all but two of the Walthamstow types; the escapees, 2055 and 2056, being used as Charlton Works staff cars. In all 105 trams were rendered surplus. One happy move on LT's part was the preservation of E/1 car 1025 which had been assembled by the LCC at its Leytonstone works in 1908, from parts supplied by Hurst Nelson. This unrehabilitated car had been in service at New Cross, its only concession to subsequent E/1 developments, apart from 1920s

Pullmanisation, being its repanelled top deck with simplified advertisement mouldings. Today it resides in the London Transport Museum in Covent Garden, just yards away from the Embankment and Savoy Street which it must have visited countless times during its 43 years of active service.

A big switch round of trams took place after this conversion. Twenty-three E/3s left Norwood for New Cross, which in turn sent eight cars (the 1935 built number 2, three ex-Leyton E/3s and four series three E/1s) to Abbey Wood. Six new daytime and one new night bus route joined the growing list, the 48 (West Norwood – Cannon Street), 69 (Grove Park – Victoria), peak hour route 149 (Grove Park – Cannon Street), 178 (West Norwood – Victoria), 179 (Grove Park – Farringdon Street) and nighter 285 (Downham – Blackfriars – Charing Cross Station).

Only two tram routes were withdrawn at Stage Seven which took place on the night of Saturday 5th April, but they focussed the attention of the capital on its rapidly disappearing tram system, because they took with them one of London's most unusual landmarks, the Kingsway Subway. The routes were the 33 and 35, including the latter's night operation, and their withdrawal ended Holloway depot's association with trams and caused the closure of Norwood depot too. Trams were no longer seen in areas like Brixton and Norwood where they had been part of the scenery for so long, and of course they no longer ran north of the Embankment. The subway was not deemed suitable for use by buses and was closed. There was more than the usual level of last day interest, with many special trips being made. Various trams were hired by different groups, but the one people wanted to ride on most was the last service car through the Subway, the honour falling to ex-Leyton E/3 number 185. She was packed to the seams with excited enthusiasts who witnessed a ceremonial closing of the southern portal gates behind her as she made the last run

through the subway and back to Highgate. A few hours later the subway gates were opened again to allow Holloway's E/3s back onto the Embankment and on to south London where many of them, including 185, were destined to eke out a few more weeks of service at New Cross. The replacement bus routes 171 (Bruce Grove – West Norwood) and 172 (Archway Station – Forest Hill) took an overground route from Bloomsbury to the Embankment, and London had lost one of the more fascinating features of its transport system.

Fifty-two trams were withdrawn after Stage Seven, but 74 were released to Penhall Road as London Transport began to whittle the fleet to the bones releasing for scrap many cars which had been held as spares. The batch included 34 E/3s, 31 of which were ex-Leyton in origin, 20 HR2s and thirteen 1930 series E/1s. Also in the bundle were six ex-West Ham and one ex-East Ham bogie cars from Abbey Wood, one E/3 from Norwood and two from Holloway. Later in June two ex-West Ham cars, two 1930 E/1s, six HR2s and twelve E/3s, including two 'Leytons', were scrapped prior to the final stage.

Above **One tramway relic almost intact today is the entrance road at the north end of the Kingsway Subway. Still complete with track, albeit rusting away, it is now a curiosity to generations who never saw it in use. Here it is seen in its latter days of service, still in a fine state of maintenance.** Don Thompson

Upper Right **A splendid study of car 1946 as it negotiates Green Lanes by Clissold Park. The 641 trolleybus will soon have the road to itself. Only in emergencies could a tram driver use the trolleybus overhead.** Don Thompson

Right **In the last few days of operation through the Kingsway Subway, E/3 1912 is seen at Holborn station. A poster to its left announces the Subway's imminent closure**

Far Right **The Angel, Islington in post-war London. Two E/3s, now definitely in the minority in this trolleybus dominated territory, head north. No. 1992, nearest the camera, was withdrawn when the Kingsway Subway closed in April 1952. In front of the trams is one of the trolleybuses which 14 years previously had helped to oust trams from their extensive route network in north London.** C. Carter

Left **An unidentified Kingsway Subway car loads up at Charing Cross on the Embankment. The Bisto kids, with their tatty clothes and floppy hats, were obviously not role models to the smartly dressed little band boarding the tram. In 1996 the makers of Bisto decided that 'the kids' no longer reflected the real world, and took them off the advertising.** C. Carter

Below **Another Subway car, E/3 No.1971 is about to lose its blind, as the glass cover of the K-Ray destination box has come open. Note the variety of slip boards on the side of the tram, together with two good suggestions for teatime.** C. Carter

Left **A group of E/1s pass through New Cross Gate, with a rehabilitated car leading the line-up. The view enables a comparison to be made between the rehabilitation body modifications of the lead car and the other two, which, apart from the addition of driver's vestibule screens, have received only token exterior refurbishment during their 40 years of active life.** C. Carter

Below **Ex-West Ham bogie car No.312 in Eltham in front of an East Ham standard bogie tram. Trams from these two east London council systems were a formidable force in south east London in the closing years of the London system. The narrower advertisement panels on the West Ham trams restricted their use as poster sites, but in this case a suitable size poster is available. Unfortunately this feature meant that the West Ham cars could not carry 'Last Tram Week' publicity.** C. Carter

Above **1930 vintage E/1 tram No. 582 passes beneath the Queens Road railway bridge in Peckham heading for Savoy Street, but displaying a wildly incorrect destination. It still carries its original between decks corner advertisement panels, but has acquired an earlier type of destination box. The view abounds with period items of street furniture, including an early LPTB tram stop.** Don Thompson

Right **A still from the film 'The Elephant Will Never Forget' – the classic documentary film of the last week of London's old trams. An Austin Atlantic convertible leads the way.**

Now all that was left was Stage Eight. It had originally been planned to have nine stages, with routes 36 and 38 lasting out until October, but London Transport decided to amalgamate the last two stages into one and it was duly announced that the last trams would run in on the night of Saturday 5th July 1952. Special commemorative tickets were issued, depicting on the back an E/3 and George Train's original street car from 90 years before. The last routes were (from New Cross) 36, 38, 40, 46, 72 and 72EX, and (from Abbey Wood) 36, 38, 44 and 46. These were to be replaced by bus routes 163 (Plumstead Common – Horse Guards Avenue), 177 (Abbey Wood – Embankment loop), 182 (Cannon Street – Eltham – Woolwich) and 186 (Woolwich – Crystal Palace). Nine other bus routes were altered in the process.

How many of the people in this view taken on Catford Bridge about 1951 owned a motor car? Perhaps a few of them did, but for the moment their transportation is provided by foot and pedal power, new RT-type buses, and ex-Leyton E/3 No.203, working on route 74. By January 1952, when the 74 was withdrawn, post-war petrol rationing had ended and car ownership had begun its steady and relentless rise. C. Carter

The pointsman's canvas hut – an unknown luxury before 1946 – will not enjoy many more weeks of use as a shelter for the pointsman, who can just be seen at its entrance talking to an inspector. A 1930 E/1, followed by an unidentified car, halts at a tram stop in New Cross Gate. The end cannot be far as a new RT on route 69 introduced under Stage Six of Operation Tramaway in January 1952 can be seen approaching on the right. C. Carter

London's Traffic Will Speed Up As The Last Tram Goes Home

By "News of the World" Reporter

IT'S getting near the end of the road for London's trams. The familiar thunder will fade down in the Old Kent Road next Saturday night. There will be one last screech of steel wheels on steel tracks at midnight as the last tram from Central London makes its way to New Cross depot.

And so the final £9,000,000 post-war switch from trams to buses will have taken place. From Peckham garage, at 4.13 a.m., the first bus will take over after 50 years of electric tram services.

To mark the occasion, Lord Latham, chairman of London Transport, has invited the chairman of the L.C.C., Mr. Edwin Bayliss, and the Mayors of nine London boroughs, to be his guests at a midnight reception at New Cross depot. They will witness the passing of an era.

The old familiar vehicle, number 1952—labelled "London's Last Tram"—will travel on route 40 from Woolwich, driven by Mr. John Cliff, deputy-chairman of the London Transport and former tram driver, who started his career 52 years ago in Leeds.

What will be the effect on London's traffic when the trams have gone? My estimate is that there will be a general speed-up of 10 miles an hour.

CONGESTION EASED

Recently I have motored over many of the old tracks and have found the congestion is already eased.

At the old "black spot" crossings at Elephant nad Castle, New Cross Gate, and Kennington Oval, I was delayed a maximum of 90 seconds. In the tram days it could easily have been 10 or 15 minutes.

From Blackfriars Bridge to New Cross I passed 25 tram stopping places, but was only called upon to halt at the three cross roads. Before the trams were taken off—and not all have yet been withdrawn on this road—there would have been 20 stops for tram passengers.

How will the old tram drivers like the change? William Moore, of Downham Estate, Bromley, who has been on the job for 35 years, is glad to change to a bus. "For one thing, I can sit down now," he said, "and there's more comfort in bad weather.

"Certainly there's less traffic congestion. At the Elephant and Castle, it sometimes took me 30 minutes to get across. Breakdowns are a bugbear, too. Often my journey from New Cross to Blackfriars and back has taken 90 minutes instead of the scheduled 50.

"With my bus—which I started driving last January—I've never been more than a couple of minutes late on schedule. A five-mile section of my journey averages 10 to 20 minutes quicker."

A London transport official told me that in recent years the London trams have been losing £1,000.000 a year.

Mr. W. V. Gibson, secretary of the Automobile Association, congratulating London Transport Executive on completing their scheme, said the withdrawal of trams had produced a much-needed speeding up in

—and this is a ticket for the last tram week.

the flow of traffic. Motorists no longer had to keep halting for passengers wishing to board or alight.

There was also greater safety. Tram passengers had to cross part of the carriage-way in the face of oncoming traffic. That difficulty was now removed.

The next step is to remove all the lines, which are often dangerous. Many local authorities had already made progress.

Accident figures given by Scotland Yard show improved safety. In 1950 there were 57 accidents reported concerning boarding or alighting from trams in the whole of London. In the following year, the first of the change-over, the figure fell to 38.

To remove the 202 miles of track remaining will be a costly business. To pull them up and re-lay the roadway costs about £20,000 per double track mile.

Throughout England I find that though the tendency in recent years has been to change to buses there are still 12 towns operating trams.

These are Aberdeen, Belfast. Birmingham, Blackpool, Dundee, Edinburgh, Glasgow, Leeds, Liverpool. Sheffield, Sunderland and Swansea.

Many of these may soon follow London's example.

The tram halts . . . traffic jerks to a standstill as passengers hurry off the pavement. Buses will bring faster and safer transport.

An unidentified E/3 passes along the Embankment opposite the Royal Festival Hall, completed the year before as part of the Festival of Britain. The E/3 will carry passengers just a few days more; modern London had no place for the tram. LT Museum

Below This nearside view of rebuilt E/1 car 1370 crossing Westminster Bridge illustrates well the all-round taper of the top-deck in the style of LCC No.1, which the vehicle acquired in 1933 following an accident. The precise date of the view is unknown, but as the bridge is full of sightseers it may be the opening day of the Festival of Britain celebrations in May 1951. The festival's Skylon is visible in the background. Roy Hubble

On the last morning 160 trams were available for service from New Cross and from Abbey Wood. They consisted of 94 E/3s, including 17 ex-Leyton examples, 17 trolley fitted HR2s, eight 1930 series E/1s, 19 ex-East Ham and 22 ex-West Ham E/1s. In the weeks between stages seven and eight 19 cars and many of the works cars like snow brooms had been withdrawn piecemeal for scrap at Penhall Road, and the storage lines there awaited their last occupants.

The warm sunshine on the last day brought the crowds thronging to all parts south east of Westminster. All the remaining tram routes carried heavier than usual loads. From the Embankment to Eltham, Westminster to Woolwich, to Lewisham and Lee, down through Peckham and across to Abbey Wood the trams were filled to bursting. Although the last routes were all LCC in origin, it was fitting that trams from three London area municipalities were present at

the end as well as a testimony to the fact that London's tramway system had spread across the London county border into what today is Greater London. Young and old took a last ride, and a last look at an institution which for many years had been despised and derided by the press, public safety "experts" and other progressives. No doubt they had a point, but on that sunny July day all thoughts were on the service the trams had given to London in over 90 years. As would be expected there were many special trips organised by tramway supporters and enthusiasts groups, even the Infantile Paralysis Group hired a tram, its occupants appropriately decked out in Edwardian costume. The Embankment was crowded until darkness fell, people taking the last opportunity to place pennies on the tracks for tram wheels to leave a souvenir imprint.

Above **Was this to be London's very last tram? Car 87 of East Ham origin is reputed to have still been in service, carrying passengers, on route 44 some time after 1am on 6th July, at the time when the last New Cross based cars had ended their final journeys. Just hours before, bathed in brilliant sunshine, it loads up at Eltham Church. Bona fide passengers mingle with those hoping to have a last ride.** C. Carter

Left **Ex-LCC E3 car 1908 stands in Addington Street, Waterloo on a 'last day' enthusiasts outing. RT1864 slips past on tram replacement route 109. A few hours hence the diesel bus will sweep the tram from London streets after 91 years.**

LONDON'S LAST TRAM WEEK

On Saturday 5 July London says a final goodbye to its trams. Next day the six remaining tram services will be replaced by buses. Here are the routes on which the last trams are running:—

36 & 38 Victoria Embankment to Abbey Wood (*Over Black-friars and Westminster bridges*)

40 Victoria Embankment to Plumstead (*Over Westminster Bridge*)

44 Woolwich to Eltham Gn.

46 City (Southwark) to Woolwich (*Over Southwark Bridge*)

72 Victoria Embankment to Woolwich (*Over Westminster Bridge*)

You, have a last chance to give yourself and your children a ride on a London tram.

DURING LAST TRAM WEEK SPECIAL SOUVENIR TICKETS WILL BE ISSUED ON LONDON TRANSPORT'S REMAINING TRAMS

History records that, officially, London's last tram was number 1951 of class E/3 working on route 40 from Woolwich to New Cross depot. It was scheduled to leave Woolwich at 11.54pm, arriving back at New Cross at 12.30am on Sunday 6th July. It was carrying London Transport's then Chairman Lord Latham, together with his Deputy, long-time Board member and former tram driver John Cliff, who was invited to drive 1951 back into New Cross depot. Lord Latham then made a speech proclaiming the end of London's trams.

And that should have been that, but it wasn't. Car 187, an ex-Leyton E/3 working on route 72, arrived back at New Cross at 1.20 am on Sunday 6th July, after all the carefully planned ceremony had been acted out. Delayed by eager crowds and leaving Woolwich after the last route 40 car, it took the longer way round via Lee and Lewisham and duly arrived back at New Cross some time after the farewell speeches had been made from the platform of 1951 and the crowds were drifting home. To save embarrassment 187 was not taken into the depot but swiftly despatched to Penhall Road.

Top **A poster produced to proclaim the end of London's trams, and entice anyone fancying a last ride to take advantage of the remaining services before it was too late.**

Centre **Abbey Wood depot on the penultimate night of London's trams, 4th July 1952, with LCC, East Ham and West Ham cars in evidence. Work on adapting the premises to be a bus garage is still under way.** John Gillham

Left **A large crowd surrounds E/3 No. 1951 as it arrives at New Cross at the end of the last journey on route 40. Standing on the steps of the tram is Lord Latham, Chairman of the LTE.**

So was car 187 London's last tram? Maybe not. There was, of course, another depot still operating trams in London that evening, Abbey Wood, six miles east of New Cross. It seems that London Transport had wished to concentrate the last ceremony at New Cross, so Abbey Wood was largely forgotten about. Its last service car on 5th July was ex-East Ham E/1 number 87 working on route 46. In normal circumstances the last 46 would have been due back at Abbey Wood at about 12.42 am, after the last 40 into New Cross, but as Abbey Wood's trams were going straight from service to the Penhall Road yard instead of back to the depot, which was now full of buses anyway, number 87 should have ended its journey at Woolwich earlier. It was, however, running over ninety minutes late when it finally got back to Woolwich and continued straight on to Penhall Road, still apparently with some enthusiastic passengers on board, arriving there before the last cars, E/3s 1909, 1931, 1952, 1988 and 1995, were being brought in from New Cross. These cars had spent the last day on 'special duties' such as enthusiasts' tours. Whether or not this account of number 87's last trip is true the undisputed fact is that by 3am on Sunday 6th July 1952 all London's trams had arrived at their last destination. An era was over.

Many photographs exist of London Transport dignitaries welcoming the last New Cross tram home in the early hours of 6th July 1952, but here we see Charlton Works staff giving their own special farewell to their last staff car, one of two ex-Walthamstow bogie trams allocated there for the purpose since January 1952, It poses by the entrance to the Works with lights, flags and a suitably decorated 'Last Tram Week' commemorative poster between the decks. Fox Photos

The sodium street lighting reflects on the tram tracks in this night view taken at the deathly quiet junction of Westminster Bridge Road and Kennington Road, just as it had done for decades. But this is not just any night. It's the night of 5/6 July 1952, and trams have run over these tracks for the very last time. John Gillham

APPENDIX:
THE SCRAPPING OF LONDON'S TRAMS, 1933–1953

This listing denotes the months that individual London trams were scrapped. It should not always be taken as an indication of withdrawal dates, because there were numerous occasions when trams were stored for weeks, months, or even years, before being broken up.

(† – denotes car rehabilitated by LPTB between 1925 and 1937)
(s – denotes car known to have been sold as a holiday home)

Stock numbers of trams not renumbered by LPTB in 1934 *shown in italics*.

Trams scrapped by LPTB prior to September 1934

Ex-Bexley *1–33*
Ex-Croydon *349–360, 362, 364*
Ex-East Ham *45, 47, 50, 52, 55, 61–67*
Ex-Erith *1, 4, 15–19*
Ex-MET (B) 2499, 2501, 2502, 2505, 2506, 2508, 2509, 2510, 2513, 2514, 2518, 2519
Ex-Walthamstow *2062–2065*

Trams scrapped September 1934 onwards, month by month analysis

September
Ex-Croydon (W/1) 348
Ex-East Ham 51, 54
Ex-Erith 6
Ex-LCC (M) 1452, 1462
Ex-MET (B) 2504, 2512, 2520
Ex-SMET (P) *47*

October
Ex-Erith 9
Ex-LCC (M) 1448, 1453, 1455, 1456, 1458, 1460, 1463, 1467, 1471–1475, 1686
Ex-Walthamstow 2031

November
Ex-Erith *3, 5*
Ex-LCC (M) 1445, 1447, 1450, 1451, 1457, 1461, 1464, 1465, 1466, 1469, 1470, 1476, 1682, 1713, 1716

December
Ex-LCC (M) 1454, 1703, 1712

1935

April
Ex-LUT (U) 2386

June
Ex-Croydon (W/1) 361
Ex-East Ham 58
Ex-LCC (E) 404

August
Ex-East Ham 46, 53
Ex-Erith *2*

September
Ex-MET (B) 2498, 2515, 2517

October
Ex-East Ham 71
Ex-Erith *10*
Ex-LUT (U) 2370; (W) 2523–2528
Ex-MET (B) 2500
Ex-SMET (J) *10, 11, 12, 15*
Ex-West Ham 220

November
Ex-Croydon (W/1) 349
Ex-LUT (Experimental) 2317 'Poppy'; (W) 2522
Ex-MET (A) 2413, 2429, 2430, 2448, 2450, 2460, 2462, 2464; (B/2) 2467, 2469, 2471, 2472, 2478; (B) 2503, 2521

December
Ex-LUT (W) 2529
Ex-MET (A) 2428, 2435, 2461; (B/2) 2468, 2470, 2474–2477, 2479

1936

January
Ex-East Ham 48
Ex-MET (A) 2427, 2440, 2442, 2447, 2449, 2451, 2452, 2457, 2459, 2463, 2465; (B/2) 2473, 2507
Ex-SMET (J) *2, 8*
Ex-West Ham 215

February
Ex-East Ham 49, 56, 57, 59, 69, 73–77, 79, 80
Ex-Erith *7, 8, 11–14*
Ex-MET (A) 2416, 2417, 2455, 2466
Ex-SMET (J) *1, 3–7, 9, 13, 14, 16*; (M) *39, 43, 44, 45*
Ex-West Ham 213, 223, 225, 227, 228, 240, 243, 248

March
Ex-Croydon (W/1) 345, 346, 347
Ex-East Ham 72, 78
Ex-MET (A) 2420, 2421, 2423, 2426, 2453, 2454, 2458; (B/2) 2480; (B) 2511
Ex-West Ham 214, 218, 219, 234, 241, 244
Ex-SMET (M) *36, 37, 38, 40, 41, 42, 46, 48–51*

April
Ex-East Ham 60, 68, 70
Ex-MET (A) 2456; (B) 2516

June
Ex-LUT (T) 2318, 2332, 2338; (U) 2359, 2401

July
Ex-LCC (M) 1449, 1459
Ex-LUT (T) 2339, 2342; (U) 2360, 2361, 2362, 2364, 2366–2369, 2371–2380, 2383, 2384, 2385, 2388–2392, 2394, 2395, 2397, 2399, 2400; (WT) 2410
Ex-MET (C/2) 2490

August
Ex-LUT (T) 2322, 2340, 2341, 2343, 2354; (U) 2358, 2363, 2365, 2381, 2382, 2387, 2393, 2402; (WT) 2406; (XU) 2411
Ex-MET (H) 2195, 2213; (C/2) 2283, 2285, 2293, 2295, 2298, 2299, 2481–2489, 2491–2496; (A) 2414, 2415, 2419, 2422, 2424, 2432, 2433, 2434, 2436, 2438, 2439, 2443–2446

September
Ex-LUT (T) 2319, 2320, 2321, 2323, 2336, 2337, 2344, 2345–2348, 2356; (U) 2396, 2398; (U2) 2403, 2404, 2405; (WT) 2407, 2408, 2409
Ex-MET (A) 2412, 2418, 2425, 2437, 2441; (C/2) 2497

October
Ex-LCC (M) 1718
Ex-LUT (T) 2334
Ex-MET (C/2) 2282, 2287
Ex-Walthamstow 2004–2008, 2010, 2011, 2012, 2015, 2016, 2017, 2021, 2023, 2024, 2025, 2028, 2032, 2035, 2040
Ex-West Ham 221, 230, 245, 249, 250, 252, 255, 257

November
Ex-Croydon (B/2) 366–369, 372
Ex-LCC (E) 410, 448, 449, 453, 472, 500
Ex-LUT (T) 2331, 2333

December
Ex-Croydon (B/2) 370, 373, 374
Ex-LCC (E) 468, 474, 481, 505, 508
Ex-LUT (T) 2324–2330, 2335, 2349–2353, 2355, 2357

1937

January
Ex-Croydon (B/2) 365, 371
Ex-LCC (E) 408, 416, 425 ,431, 437, 442
Ex-Walthamstow 2013, 2019, 2020, 2026, 2030, 2037

February
Ex-LCC (E) 424, 426, 435, 440, 443, 444 ,445, 459, 484, 506, 519;
    (M) 1690, 1695, 1722, 1726
Ex-MET 2168 (Experimental Feltham) – (*Sold to Sunderland*)
Ex-Walthamstow 2022, 2027, 2033, 2041

March
Ex-Croydon 363
Ex-LCC (E) 403, 405, 411, 418, 421, 436, 457, 496, 497

April
Ex-LCC (E) 420 (*lower deck of 420 fitted with new top deck and renumbered* 1597), 462, 490

May
Ex-West Ham 222, 229
Ex-LCC (M) 1683, 1688, 1720
Ex-Walthamstow 2009, 2039

June
Ex-Ilford 30, 41, 44
Ex-LCC (M) 1430, 1443, 1468, 1679, 1680, 1701, 1714, 1719, 1724
Ex-West Ham 211, 231, 232, 236, 237, 242, 253, 264, 274, 276, 278, 286
Ex-Walthamstow 2034

July
Ex-Ilford 42, 43
Ex-LCC (M) 1429, 1431–1434, 1437 –1440, 1442, 1693, 1694, 1699, 1702, 1706, 1707, 1708, 1710, 1725.
Ex-West Ham 216, 224, 235, 251, 254, 256, 270, 271, 277, 280, 287, 288, 289, 292
Ex-Walthamstow 2014, 2018, 2029, 2036, 2038

August
Ex-LCC (M) 1427, 1428, 1435, 1436, 1677, 1684, 1685, 1687, 1689, 1692, 1696, 1705, 1709, 1715, 1717, 1721, 1723
Ex-MET (E) 2307, 2310
Ex-West Ham 238, 239, 262, 263, 266, 285

September
Ex-Ilford 38 (*Sold to Sunderland*)
Ex-LCC (M) 1678, 1681, 1697, 1711
Ex-MET (Experimental Feltham) 2166
Ex-West Ham 233, 246, 247, 267, 284, 293

October
Ex-LCC (E) 402, 407, 413, 417, 422, 439, 455, 458, 465, 470, 471, 473, 476, 479, 480, 494; (M) 1700
Ex-MET (Experimental) 2255 'Bluebell'
Ex-West Ham 212, 217, 226, 258, 259, 268, 283

November
Ex-LCC (E) 412, 429, 446, 487, 491, 493, 501

December
Ex-LCC (E) 450, 451, 456, 461, 466, 467†, 477, 482, 495, 503, 507;
    (M) 1698, 1704
Ex-West Ham 275

1938

January
Ex-Ilford 5
Ex-LCC (E) 406, 414, 415, 419, 423, 427, 428, 430, 432, 433, 434, 438, 447, 452, 454, 460, 463, 464, 469, 475, 483, 485, 486, 488, 489, 492, 498, 499, 502, 504, 509–514, 516, 517, 518

February
Ex-Ilford 6–29, 31, 32, (33–37, 39, 40 *Sold to Sunderland*)
Ex-LCC (E) 409, 441, 478, 515, 631; (E/1) 763, 786
Ex-MET (H) 2199, 2206; (C/2) 2290;
    (E) 2302, 2303, 2304, 2306, 2308, 2309, 2311–2315

March
Ex-LCC (E) 545–551, 610–618, 620–629, 632, 633, 638, 640–644, 646, 647, 648, 651–656, 660, 661, 665, 666, 671.
Ex-LCC (M) 1691
Ex-MET (H) 2244; (C/2) 2284, 2286, 2288, 2289, 2291, 2292;
    (E) 2305, 2316
Ex-West Ham 260, 261, 269, 279, 282

April
Ex-LCC (E) 602, 619, 645, 649, 650, 657, 658, 659, 662, 663, 664, 667–670, 672–680
Ex-MET (C/2) 2300; (H) 2239
Ex-West Ham 265, 272, 273, 281, 290*, 291, 294 (* *preserved by LPTB*)

May
Ex-LCC (E) 603–607, 681–686, 689, 691, 692, 694–697, 698, 701, 704, 705, 708, 709, 711, 712, 713, 718, 719, 720, 725, 727, 740, 741, 748
Ex-MET (H) 2180, 2183–2185, 2187, 2190, 2194, 2204, 2205, 2210, 2212, 2215, 2218, 2221, 2227, 2232, 2241; (F) 2257, 2259; (C/2) 2294, 2296

June
Ex-LCC (E) 687, 688, 690, 693, 702, 703, 710, 714, 733, 747, 749
Ex-MET (H) 2191, 2208, 2209; (G) 2272; (C/2) 2297
Ex-West Ham 313–317, 319, 322, 324

July
Ex-LCC (E) 520, 521 523–532, 534, 535, 536
Ex-MET (H) 2181, 2186, 2193, 2197, 2202, 2207, 2211, 2219, 2222, 2228, 2234; (F) 2256; (C/2) 2301
Ex-West Ham 318, 320, 321, 323

August
Ex-LCC (E) 537–544, 608, 609, 634–637, 639, 699, 716, 721, 729, 731, 732, 736, 743, 744, 745, 750 ; (E/1) 755, 758, 764, 765, 767

September
Ex-LCC (E) 522, 533; (E/1) 752, 754, 761, 769, 773, 776, 778, 795, 803, 809, 850, 910, 941, 945
Ex-MET (G) 2274

October
Ex-MET (H) 2188, 2196, 2198, 2201, 2203, 2229, 2242, 2249, 2250, 2252, 2253, 2254

November
Ex-LCC (E) 706, 707, 715, 717, 722, 723, 724, 726, 732, 734, 735
Ex-MET (H) 2176, 2182, 2189, 2214, 2220, 2223, 2224, 2225, 2230, 2231, 2237, 2240, 2245, 2246, 2248, 2251, 2258, 2260 ; (G) 2276

December
Ex-LCC (E) 700, 728, 730, 737, 738, 739, 742, 746, 751; (E/1) 756
Ex-MET (H) 2170, 2171, 2172, 2174, 2175, 2178, 2192, 2200, 2226, 2236, 2247; (G) 2261, 2265, 2266, 2269, 2270, 2271, 2275, 2280

1939

January
Ex-LCC (E/1) 753, 864, 880, 911, 915, 1126, 1130, 1133, 1148, 1151, 1153, 1155, 1156, 1158, 1159, 1161, 1287, 1347, 1348,
Ex-MET (H) 2169, 2173, 2177 , 2179, 2216, 2217, 2226, 2233, 2238, 2243; (G) 2262, 2263, 2264, 2267, 2268, 2273, 2277, 2278, 2279, 2281

February
Ex-LCC (E) 630; (E/1) 757, 759, 760, 762, 766, 768, 770, 771, 772, 782, 785, 787, 789, 806, 856, 858, 869, 875, 895, 926, 928, 1051, 1060, 1074, 1105, 1122, 1276, 1280, 1323

March
Ex-LCC (E/1) 777, 779, 780, 783, 784, 790, 791, 792, 796, 798, 801, 804, 807, 808, 811, 812, 813, 817, 822, 828, 829, 832, 835, 851, 859, 866, 878, 879, 886, 889, 903, 908, 909, 922, 929, 938, 999, 1102, 1113, 1164, 1168, 1197, 1257, 1261, 1274, 1279, 1285, 1290, 1296, 1298, 1299, 1331, 1333, 1345

April
Ex-LCC (E/1) 774, 775, 781, 788, 810, 814, 816, 830, 833, 841, 849, 852, 853, 855, 919, 920, 921, 925, 930, 934, 935, 939, 997, 998, 1052, 1125, 1129, 1132, 1135, 1136, 1210, 1253, 1256, 1271, 1289, 1300, 1301, 1303, 1311, 1319, 1325, 1334, 1341, 1346

May
Ex-LCC (E/1) 793, 860, 861, 912, 917, 918, 1104, 1127, 1131, 1134, 1169, 1307, 1314, 1321, 1324

June
Ex-LCC (E/1) 799, 857, 883, 885, 891, 899, 1047, 1065, 1111, 1114, 1120, 1121, 1154, 1157, 1167, 1192, 1221, 1258, 1269, 1272, 1283

July
Ex-LCC (E/1) 794, 831, 846, 862, 863, 865, 873, 884, 888, 897, 1001†, 1043, 1045, 1046, 1048, 1064, 1071, 1106, 1110, 1162, 1185, 1193, 1194, 1196, 1198, 1199, 1202, 1207, 1278, 1297, 1335, 1337

August
Ex-LCC (E/1) 805, 824, 837, 847, 872, 874, 876, 877, 882, 887, 893, 898, 900, 901, 902, 907, 967, 983, 1183, 1200, 1203, 1281, 1295, 1327, 1330, 1340, 1342, 1344
Ex-LCC (HR2) 1881 (*Sold to Leeds Corporation*)

September
Ex-LCC (E/1) 819, 890, 894, 904, 1044, 1055, 1063, 1150, 1206, 1268

October
Ex-LCC (HR2) 1883 (*Sold to Leeds Corporation*)

November
Ex-LCC (HR2) 1886 (*Sold to Leeds Corporation*)

1940

January
Ex-LCC (E/1) 820, 834, 881, 896, 905, 950, 954, 956, 957, 970, 971, 974, 975, 976, 987, 988, 990, 991, 1006, 1008, 1010, 1031, 1039, 1069, 1098, 1160, 1188, 1189, 1205, 1224, 1235, 1239, 1242, 1332, 1336, 1339, 1356

February
Ex-LCC (E/1) 823, 868, 870, 892, 937, 946, 963, 964, 965, 968, 969, 980, 1004, 1015, 1040, 1080, 1082, 1097, 1100, 1101, 1112, 1138, 1186, 1232, 1237, 1240, 1254, 1328, 1360, 1376

March
Ex-LCC (E/1) 821, 845, 906, 927, 942, 943, 944, 949, 951, 958, 959, 973, 1013, 1014, 1020, 1021, 1026, 1029, 1058, 1084, 1085, 1093, 1095, 1179, 1184, 1201, 1209, 1222, 1228, 1265, 1309, 1318, 1349

April
Ex-LCC (E/1) 952, 1034, 1035, 1037, 1086, 1141, 1214

May
Ex-LCC (E/1) 842, 854, 989, 1036, 1041, 1091, 1181, 1245, 1264

Tram scrapping programme temporarily suspended due to war.

Trams destroyed by enemy action or other causes September 1940–December 1944

8 September 1940 (At Camberwell depot)
Ex-LCC (E/1) 1515, 1523, 1524, 1526, 1536;
   (HR1) 1852, 1853;
   (HR2) 112, 123, 124, 125, 129, 130, 131, 1865, 1889, 1898, 1899, 1900, 1901, 1902, 1903; (E/3) 1967, 1972, 1973, 1976, 1978, 1983, 1985

17 September 1940 (At Clapham depot)
Ex-LCC (E/1) 1023, 1543, 1575, 1578, 1580;
   (E/1-1922) 1736, 1799, 1807, 1821; (E/1-1930) 597

September 1940 (Others)
Ex-LCC (E/1) 1403, 1649

October 1940
Ex-LCC (E/1) 1600; (E/1-1922) 1825
Ex-MET (Feltham) 2113

8 November 1940 (At Abbey Wood depot)
Ex-West Ham 331
Ex-LCC (E/1) 826†, 1028, 1241, 1371, 1373

November 1940 (Others)
Ex-LCC (E/1) 1173, 1379

27 December 1940 (At New Cross Depot)
Ex-LCC (E/1) 962†, 972†, 1421†, 1490; (E/1-1930) 583

December 1940 (Others)
Ex-LCC (HR2) 148; (E/3) 1982

April 1941
Ex-LCC (E/1) 1351†, 1394, 1586, 1591; (E/1-1922) 1808

May 1941
Ex-Croydon 396

July 1941
Ex-LCC (E/1-1922) 1831

February 1942
Ex-LCC (E/1) 1234, 1305

March 1942
Ex-LCC (E/1) 1517†

February 1943
Ex-LCC (E/1) 1556, 1625

July 1943
Ex-LCC (E/1) 1078†, 1173, 1367

May 1944
Ex-LCC (ME3) 1441

August 1944
Ex-MET (Feltham) 2109

October 1944
Ex-Walthamstow 2044, 2051

December 1944
Ex-LCC (E/1) 1425

Scrapping programme resumes – November 1945

November 1945
Ex-Croydon 376
Ex-LCC (E/1) 966, 979, 1016, 1018, 1027, 1056, 1061, 1075, 1115, 1176, 1178, 1180, 1243, 1282, 1329, 1354, 1379, 1411, 1426, 1482, 1509–1513, 1518, 1539, 1551, 1554, 1559, 1605, 1637;
   (E/1-1922) 1735, 1746, 1748, 1751, 1757

December 1945
Ex-LCC (E/1) 1146; (E/1-1922) 1731, 1742, 1752.

1946

February 1946
Ex-LCC (E/1) 1558

March
Ex-LCC (E/1) 992, 1002, 1081, 1099, 1412, 1483, 1521†

April
Ex-LCC (E/1) 923, 986, 1505, 1552

May
Ex-LCC (E/1) 1000, 1313

June
Ex-LCC (E/1) 797, 818, 825, 838, 848, 914, 931s, 977, 1053, 1054, 1057s, 1070, 1072, 1107, 1118, 1123, 1147, 1236, 1262, 1263, 1266, 1292, 1294, 1315, 1326, 1416, 1477, 1479, 1497, 1560, 1584, 1616s, 1634;
   (E/1-1922) 1741, 1745, 1792

August
Ex-LCC (E/I) 1259s, 1284, 1622s, 1635

September
Ex-LCC (E/I) 815, 843, 1067, 1119, 1124, 1308, 1320, 1607, 1609

October
Ex-LCC (E/I) 844, 924, 1066, 1304, 1583, 1615, 1633;
    (E/1-1922) 1747

November
Ex-LCC (E/I) 932, 1062, 1108, 1117, 1217, 1484, 1639

December
Ex-LCC (E/I) 800, 933, 1068, 1073, 1116, 1152, 1166, 1286, 1405, 1417,
    1418, 1516, 1519, 1632;
    (E/1-1922) 1749

1947

January
Ex-West Ham 325
Ex-LCC (E/I) 867, 913, 1011, 1012, 1059, 1139, 1238, 1302, 1306, 1389,
    1522, 1528, 1535, 1550, 1585, 1641;
    (E/1-1922) 1737

February
Ex-LCC (E/I) 1165, 1374; (E/1-1922) 1729, 1734, 1753, 1760

March
Ex-LCC (E/I) 871, 1293; (E/1-1922) 1780, 1816

April
Ex-LCC (E/I) 955, 1149, 1187, 1338, 1424

May
Ex-LCC (E/I) 1050, 1076, 1077, 1288, 1420, 1620
Ex-LUT (Feltham) 2122

June
Ex-LCC (E/I) 1277

July
Ex-LCC (E/I) 1343

1948

May
Ex-LCC (E/I) 827†, 1404

June
Ex-LCC (E/I) 1079

July
Ex-LCC (E/I) 1666

1949

May
Ex-West Ham 328, 329
Ex-LCC (E/I) 1109, 1668†;
    (E/1-1922) 1728, 1732, 1733, 1738, 1754, 1755, 1756, 1765, 1767, 1774

June
Ex-LCC (E/I) 1229, 1249, 1572, 1611;
    (E/1-1922) 1739, 1740, 1750, 1776, 1800

September
Ex-MET (Feltham) 2099

December
Ex-LCC (E/I) 1364†; (E/1-1930) 569
Ex-MET (Feltham) 2067, 2091
Ex-LUT (Feltham) 2130, 2163, 2165, 2167

1950

July
Ex-LCC (E/I) 1322 *(First tram scrapped at Penhall Road)*

August
Ex-LCC (E/1-1930) 576
Ex-MET (Feltham) 2077, 2082, 2097 *(Sold to Leeds Corporation)*

September
Ex-LUT (Feltham) 2139 *(Sold to Leeds Corporation)*
Ex-MET (Feltham) 2066, 2069–2076, 2078, 2080, 2081,
    2083–2088, 2093, 2096, 2100, 2105, 2108, 2115, 2116, 2118
    (Sold to Leeds Corporation)

October (Start of 'Operation Tramaway')
Ex-LCC (E/I) 953†, 1022†, 1024†, 1033†, 1049, 1089†, 1096, 1140, 1143,
    1145, 1170, 1172, 1190†, 1191†, 1219, 1220, 1270, 1317, 1383, 1385†,
    1395, 1396†, 1407, 1527, 1529, 1531, 1562, 1613, 1617, 1645†, 1647†,
    1652†, 1654†, 1656†; (E/1-1922) 1762†

November
Ex-LCC (E/I) 1142, 1204, 1208, 1213, 1227†, 1260, 1355, 1358, 1372,
    1397†, 1422†, 1480, 1485, 1499, 1623, 1646, 1665; (E/1-1922) 1744†,
    1758†, 1761†, 1763†, 1766†, 1769†, 1772†, 1773, 1775†

December
Ex-LCC (E/I) 1174, 1399†, 1413, 1540;
    (E/1-1922) 1743†, 1764, 1770†, 1771†, 1805, 1835

1951

January
Ex-LCC (E/I) 948†, 960†, 978†, 981†, 984†, 993†, 1007, 1030, 1088†,
    1163, 1171, 1195†, 1247†, 1267, 1291, 1350, 1384†, 1402†, 1496,
    1500†, 1530, 1570, 1577†, 1590, 1592, 1597, 1662, 1667;
    (E/1-1922) 1777, 1786, 1832
Ex-MET (Feltham) 2068, 2089, 2090, 2092, 2094, 2095, 2098, 2101–2104,
    2106, 2107, 2110–2112, 2114, 2117, 2119 *(Sold to Leeds Corporation)*

February
Ex-LCC (E/I) 802, 1090†, 1092, 1182, 1216†, 1218, 1273, 1312, 1357†,
    1488, 1489, 1566†, 1587†, 1589, 1606†, 1608†, 1621, 1636†, 1640,
    1659, 1674

March
Ex-LCC (E/I) 1032, 1094, 1137, 1175, 1211, 1225, 1233, 1244, 1246†,
    1251, 1359†, 1362, 1363, 1381†, 1393†, 1401†, 1415, 1486, 1491†,
    1501, 1503, 1504, 1506†, 1588, 1671

April
Ex-LCC (Experimental 'Bluebird') 1 *(Sold to Leeds Corporation)*
Ex-LCC (E/I) 836†, 839†, 940†, 947†, 961, 1019, 1042†, 1083, 1128,
    1215†, 1223†, 1275†, 1365†, 1375†, 1398†, 1492†, 1533, 1595, 1626,
    1629, 1642†, 1644; (ME3) 1444; (E/1-1930) 553
Ex-West Ham 326
Ex-LUT (Feltham) 2120, 2121, 2123–2129, 2131–2138, 2140–2143,
    2145–2161, 2164 *(Sold to Leeds Corporation)*
Ex-MET (Feltham) 2079 *(Sold to Leeds Corporation)*

May
Ex-LCC (E/I) 1003†, 1009†, 1017†, 1087†, 1230, 1248†, 1310†, 1352†,
    1369†, 1377†, 1382†, 1408†, 1498, 1525, 1544, 1545†, 1564†, 1573,
    1579†, 1582, 1599†, 1603, 1627, 1630, 1638, 1643†, 1651, 1657, 1661†,
    1673.
Ex-LUT (Feltham) 2144, 2162

June
Ex-LCC (E/I) 996†, 1361, 1388†, 1409, 1419, 1478, 1481†, 1538†, 1549,
    1568, 1569†, 1596, 1604
Ex-West Ham 327, 330

August
Ex-LCC (E/I) 1380†, 1598, 1624, 1650†, 1669;
    (E/1-1922) 1784, 1785, 1795, 1796, 1797, 1836, 1850;
    (E/1-1930) 552, 558, 561, 573, 590, 595
Ex-West Ham 331

September
Ex-LCC (HR2) 155; (E/1-1920) 1848;
    (E/1-1930) 554, 555, 556, 566, 572, 584–587, 589, 591, 594, 599

October
Ex-Croydon 384, 387, 397
Ex-LCC (E/I) 840, 916, 936†, 1226†, 1250, 1252, 1400†, 1502†, 1508†,
    1537, 1542, 1565; (E/1-1922) 1809–1815, 1817, 1818, 1819, 1822, 1826,
    1829, 1833, 1837, 1838, 1840, 1844, 1847, 1851;
    (E/1-1930) 600; (E/3) 1957

November

Ex-LCC (E/1) 1392†; (E/1-1922) 1778, 1781, 1790, 1802, 1803, 1806, 1823, 1824, 1827, 1828, 1830, 1834, 1839, 1841, 1843, 1845, 1846; (E/1-1930) 582; (HR2) 1895; (E/3) 1975

December

Ex-LCC (E/1) 1316, 1493, 1507†; (E/1-1922) 1779, 1782, 1783, 1787, 1791, 1793, 1794, 1799, 1801, 1820, 1849; (HR2) 105–111, 113–117, 119, 120, 126, 127, 128, 136, 137, 141–144, 147, 149–153, 156, 158.

1952

January

Ex-LCC (E/1) 982, 985, 994†, 1025*, 1103†, 1144†, 1177†, 1212†, 1255, 1353†, 1366†, 1368†, 1370†, 1378, 1386†, 1387†, 1390, 1391†, 1406, 1410, 1414, 1423, 1487, 1494, 1495, 1514†, 1520†, 1532, 1534†, 1546, 1555, 1557, 1571, 1581, 1610†, 1612, 1614†, 1618, 1619†, 1660, 1664, 1676†; (E/1-1922) 1798 (* – *preserved by London Transport*)

Ex-Walthamstow 2053, 2054, 2057– 2061

February

Ex-Croydon 375, 377, 378, 380–383, 385, 388

Ex-LCC (E/1) 995†, 1005, 1038†, 1541†, 1547†, 1548, 1553†, 1561, 1563†, 1567, 1574†, 1576†, 1593, 1594, 1601, 1602, 1628, 1631, 1648†, 1653, 1655†, 1663, 1670, 1672, 1675; (E/1-1922) 1804

Ex-Walthamstow 2042, 2043, 2045–2050, 2052

March

Ex-Croydon 379, 386, 389, 390–395, 398, 399

Ex-LCC (E/1) 1658; (E/1-1930) 574, (HR2) 133, 134, 139, 140, 145, 146, 154, 157, 159, 1879

April

Ex-East Ham 81

Ex-Leyton (E/3) 164, 182, 191, 195

Ex-LCC (E/1-1930) 562, 563, 570, 571, 596, (HR2) 118, 122, 135, 1888, 1890, 1894; (E/3) 160, 1959

Ex-Walthamstow 2056

Ex-West Ham 296, 301, 306, 308, 310

Works 02, 018, 021, 035, 037

May

Ex-Leyton (E/3) 161, 163, 167, 178, 197, 198, 199, 202, 203, 205, 206, 207, 209, 210

Ex-LCC (E/1-1930) 564, 567, 568, 579, 581; (HR2) 121, 132, 138, 1878, 1880, 1882, 1884, 1885, 1887, 1891, 1892, 1896, 1897, (E/3) 1924, 1997

Ex-West Ham 333

June

Ex-Leyton (E/3) 162, 170–172, 174, 177, 188–190, 192–194, 201, 204, 208

Ex-LCC (E/1-1930) 557, 575, 580, 588, 601; (HR2) 1860, 1866, 1868, 1870, 1874, 1876, 1893; (E/3) 1919, 1944, 1949, 1958, 1960, 1963, 1968, 1986, 1990, 1992

Ex-West Ham 300, 338

Works 03, 016, 026, 028, 036

July

Ex-East Ham 88, 89, 90, 93, 97, 98

Ex-Leyton (E/3) 166, 187, 200

Ex-LCC (E/1-1930) 559, (HR2) 1858 (*preserved*), 1862, 1864, 1872; (E/3) 1912, 1937, 1941, 1951, 1970, 1971, 1994

Ex-Walthamstow 2055

Ex-West Ham 302, 304, 307, 334, 343

August

Ex-East Ham 82, 86, 87, 99

Ex-Leyton (E/3) 168, 169, 173

Ex-LCC (E/1-1930) 560, 577, 592, 598; (HR2) 1863, 1867; (E/3) 1904, 1917, 1926, 1939, 1940, 1946, 1947, 1965, 1977, 1998, 2001

Ex-West Ham 295, 332, 344

September

Ex-East Ham 84, 85, 96

Ex-Leyton (E/3) 165, 176, 196

Ex-LCC (E/1-1930) 565, 578; (HR2) 1854, 1869, 1871, 1877; (E/3) 1906, 1909, 1910, 1911, 1920, 1938, 1942, 1945, 1950, 1954, 1969, 1988, 1989, 1991, 1995, 2003

Ex-West Ham 305, 311, 337, 339

October

Ex-Leyton (E/3) 181, 184

Ex-LCC (HR2) 1855, 1856, 1875; (E/3) 1908, 1916, 1922, 1923, 1927, 1929, 1932, 1933, 1935, 1936, 1943, 1948, 1955, 1962, 1964, 1966, 1980, 1984, 1993, 1996, 2002

Ex-West Ham 340

November

Ex-East Ham 83, 91, 92, 94, 95, 100

Ex-LCC (HR2) 101f, 102f, 103f, 104f, 1857, 1859, 1861, 1873; (E/3) 1905, 1907, 1913, 1914, 1915, 1918, 1921, 1925, 1928, 1930, 1931, 1934, 1952, 1953, 1956, 1961, 1974, 1979, 1981, 1987, 1999, 2000

Ex-LPTB 2

Ex-West Ham 297, 298, 299, 309, 312, 335, 336, 341

(f – *Used as fire screens October 1951 – November 1952*)

December

Ex-Leyton (E/3) 175, 180, 183, 185, 186

Ex-LCC (E/1-1930) 593

Ex-West Ham 342

1953

January

Ex-LCC (E/1) 1231; (E/1-1922) 1727†, 1730†, 1768 (*used as scrapyard premises since October 1950*)

Ex-Leyton (E/3) 179 (**Last London tram to be scrapped — 29th January 1953**)